A-Z NOTTING

Key to Maps

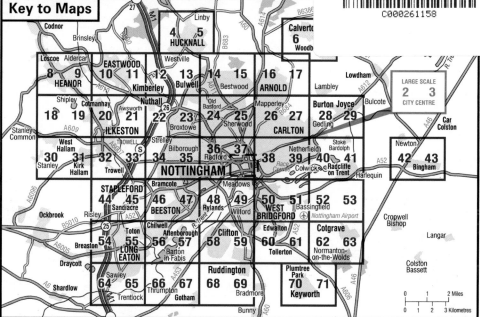

Reference

Motorway	M1
A Road	A52
Under Construction	
Proposed	
B Road	B6004
Dual Carriageway	
One Way A Roads Traffic flow is indicated by a heavy line on the Driver's left.	
Pedestrianized Road	
Restricted Access	
Track	
Footpath	

Residential Walkway	
Railway	Level Crossing Station
Built Up Area	MILL ST.
Local Authority Boundary	
Posttown Boundary By arrangement with the Post Office	
Postcode Boundary Within Posttown	
Map Continuation	10 Large Scale City Centre 3

Ambulance Station	✚
Car Park	P
Church or Chapel	†
Fire Station	■
Hospital	H
House Numbers A & B Roads only	83 96
Information Centre	i
National Grid Reference	³40
Police Station	▲
Post Office	★
Toilet with facilities for the Disabled	▽ ♿

Scale

1:15,840
4 inches to 1 mile

Copyright of the Publishers Geographers' A-Z Map Co. Ltd.

Head Office : Fairfield Road, Borough Green, Sevenoaks, Kent TN15 8PP Telephone 01732 781000
Showrooms : 44 Gray's Inn Road, Holborn, London WC1X 8HX Telephone 0171 242 9246

The Maps in this Atlas are based upon the Ordnance Survey 1 :10,560 Maps with the permission of the Controller of Her Majesty's Stationery Office. © Crown Copyright

© 1996 EDITION 4

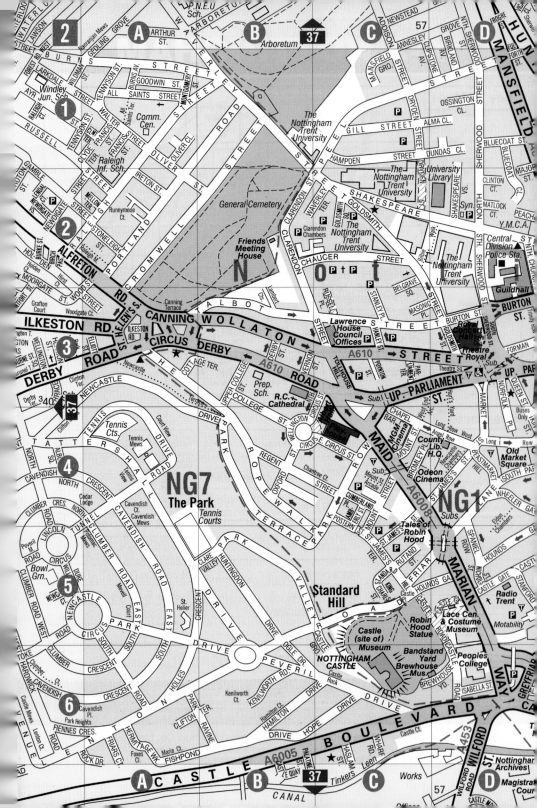

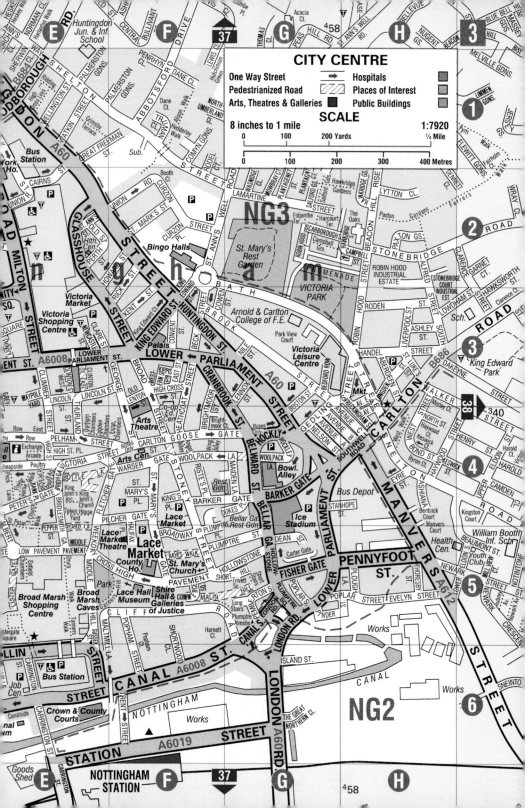

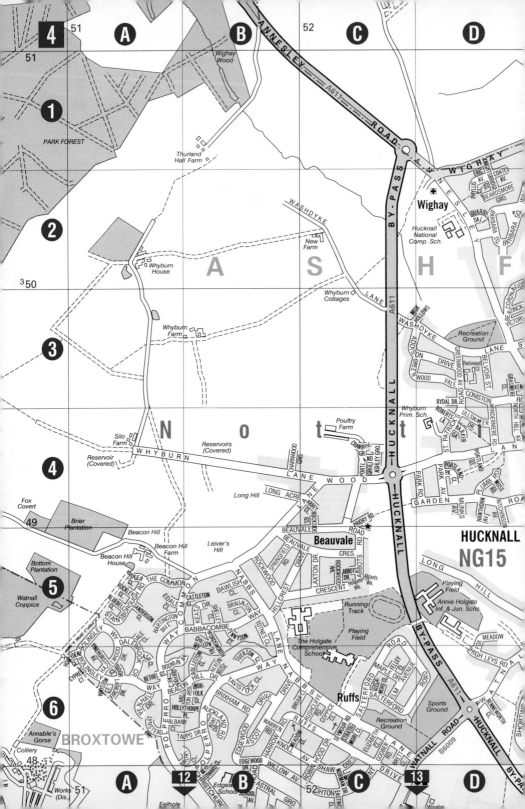

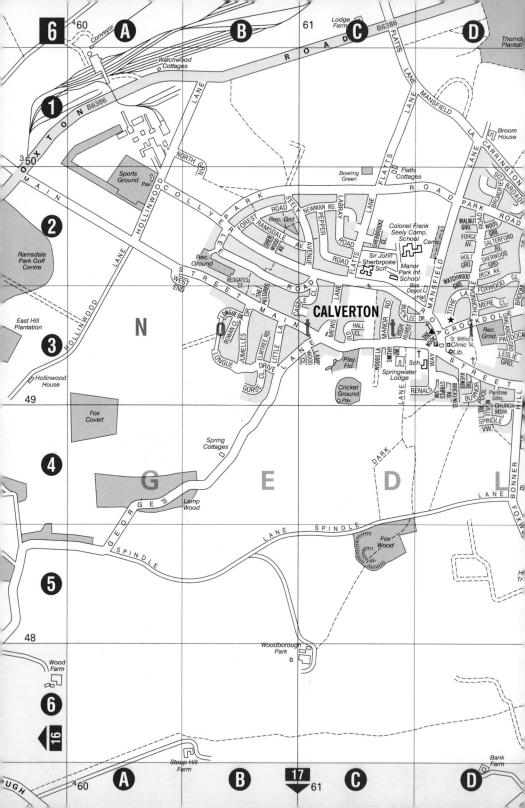

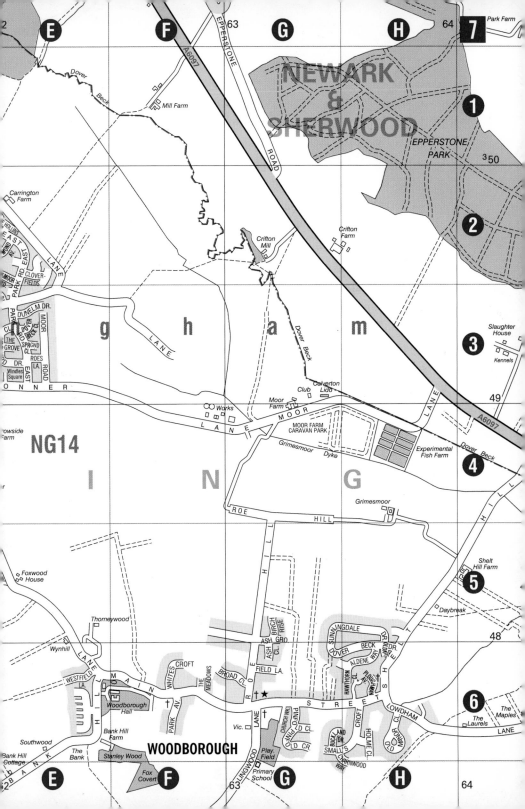

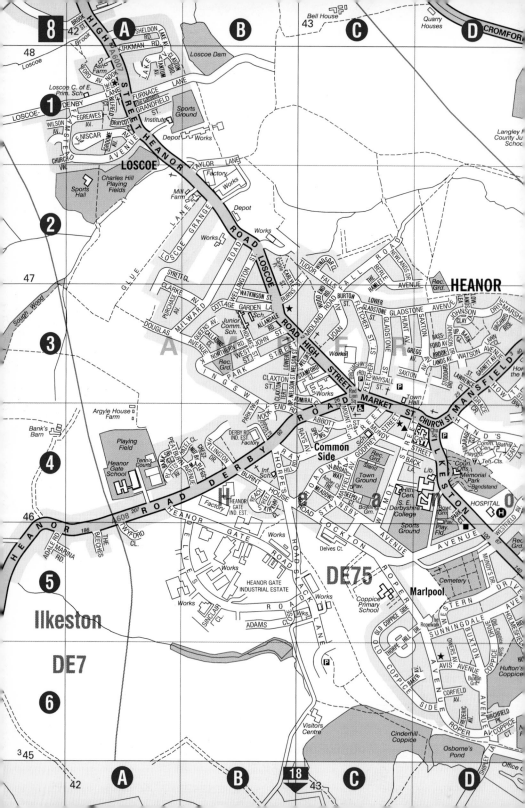

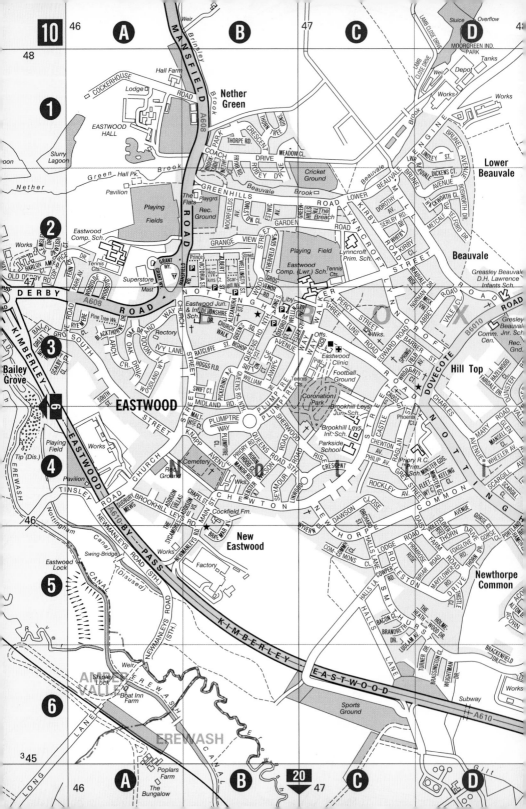

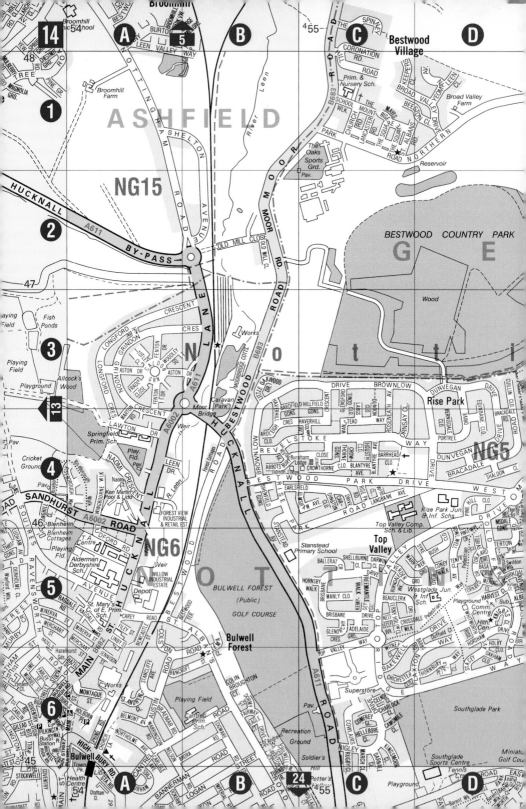

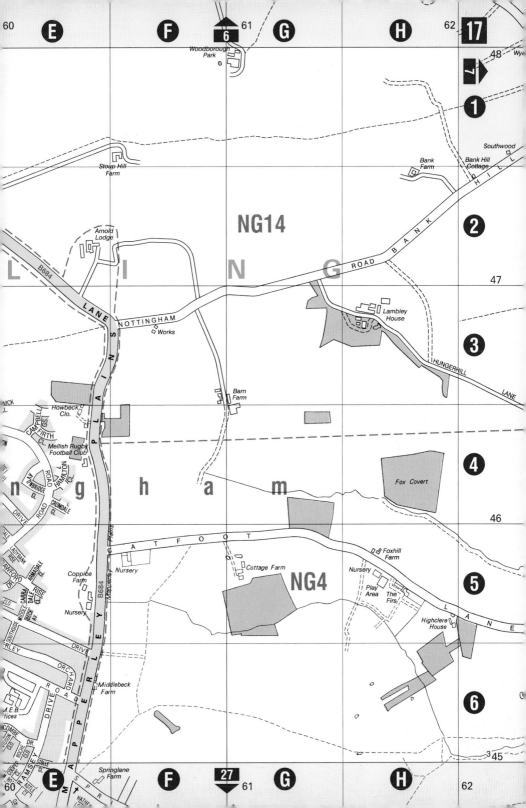

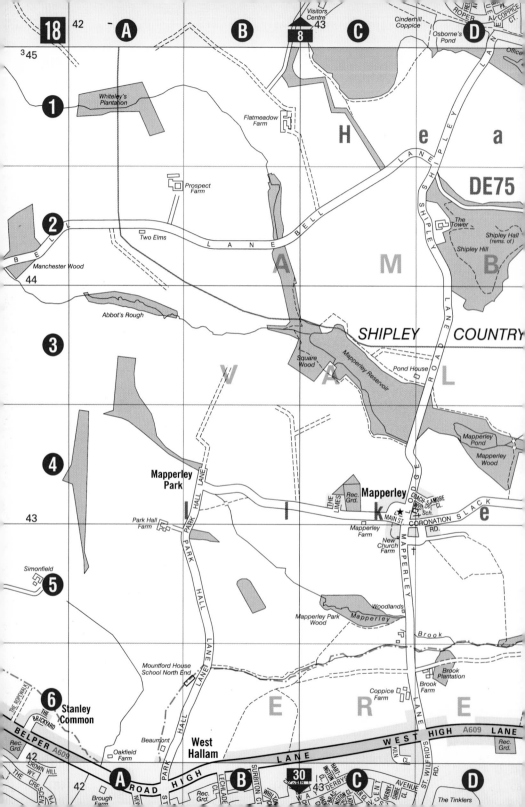

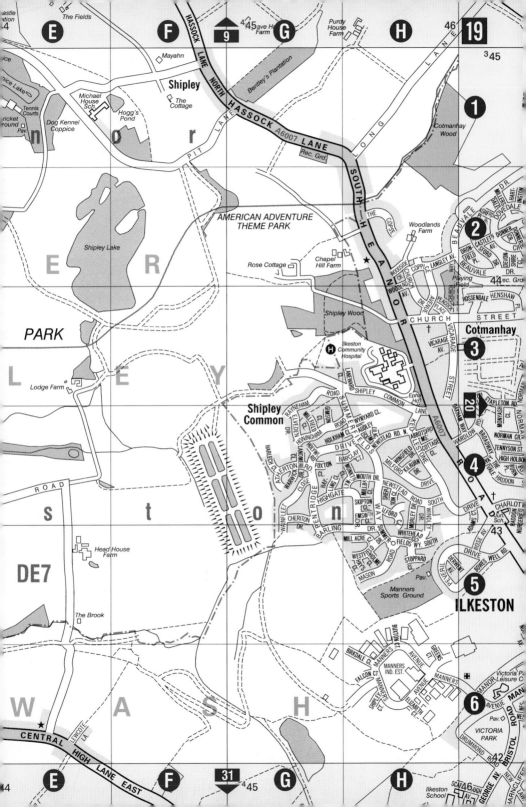

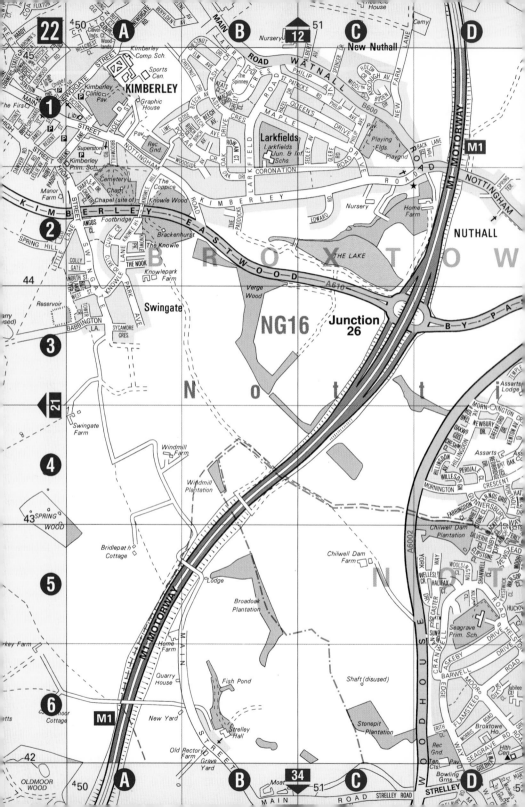

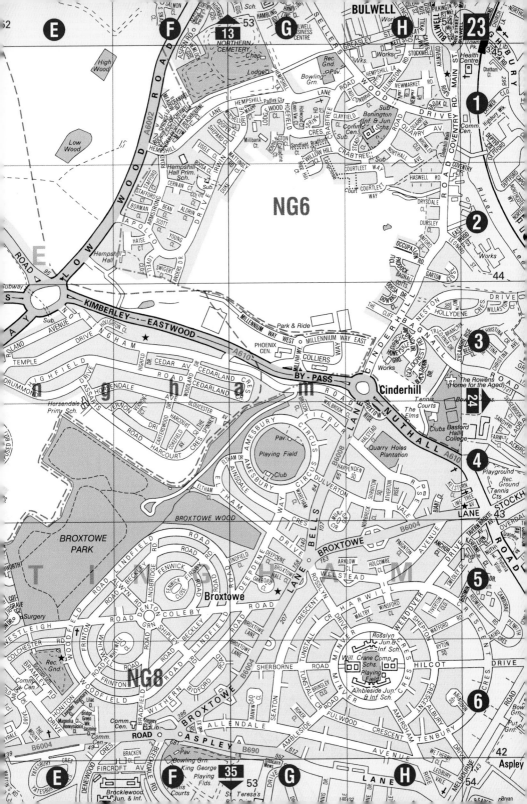

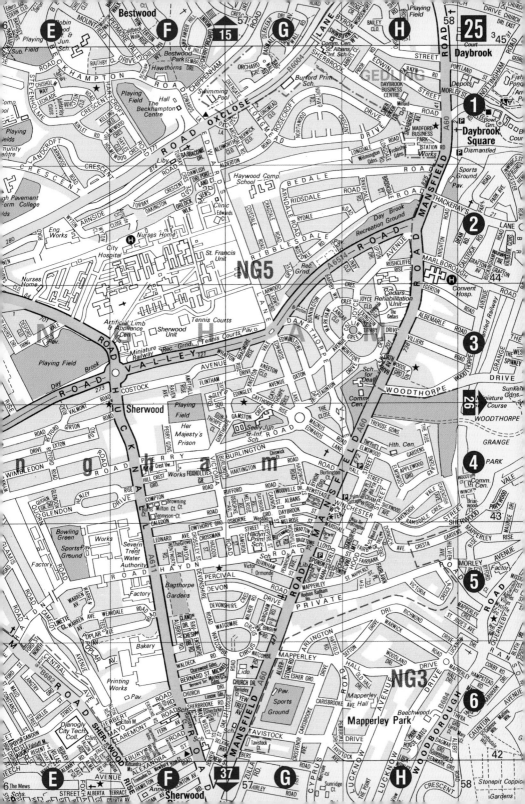

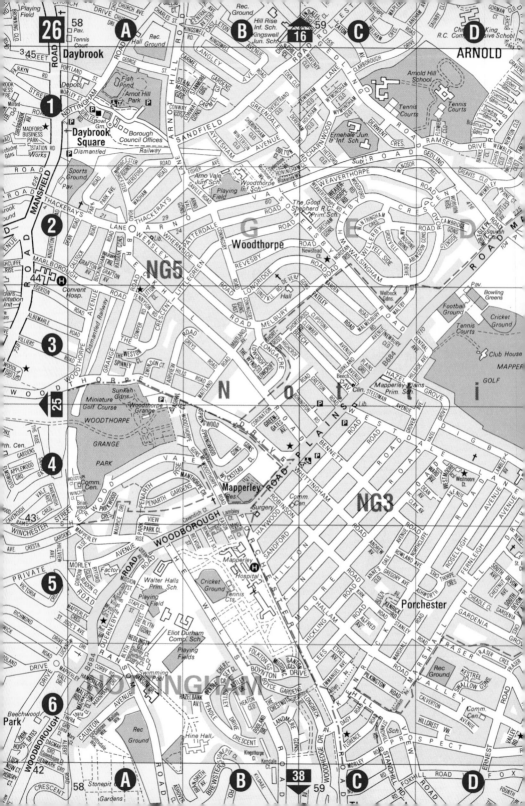

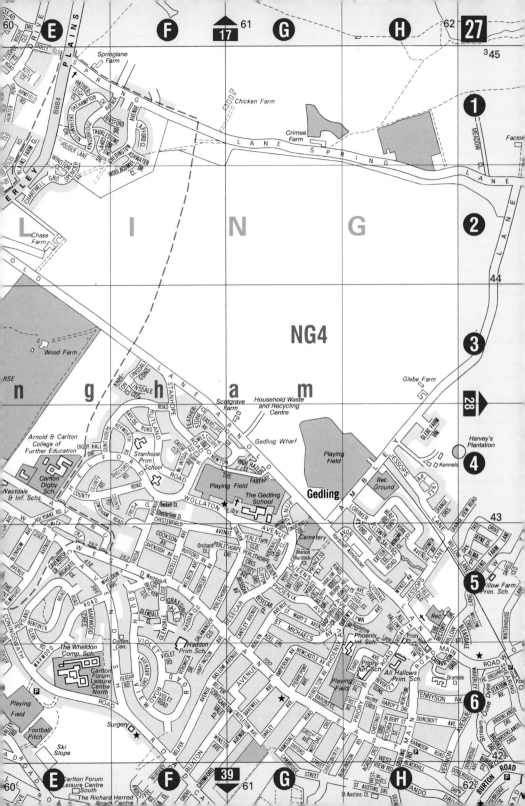

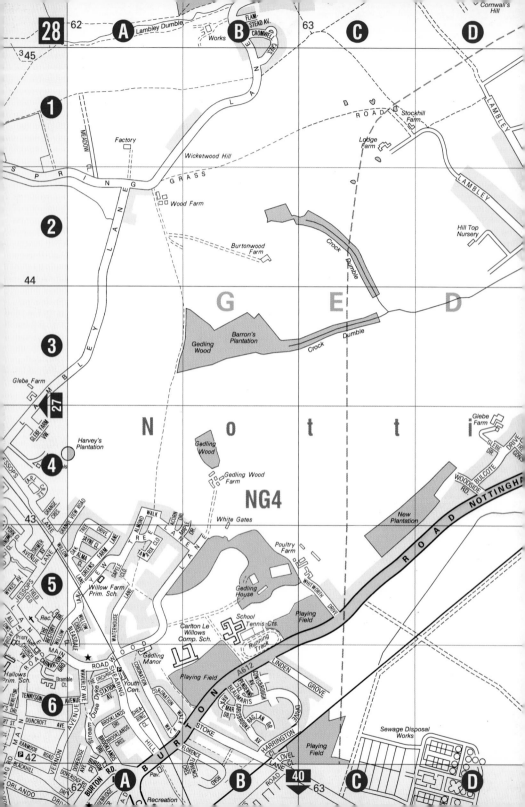

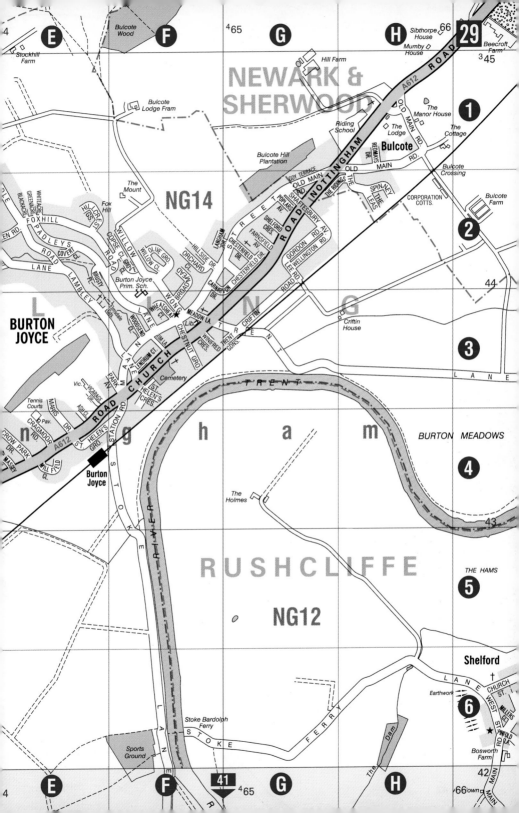

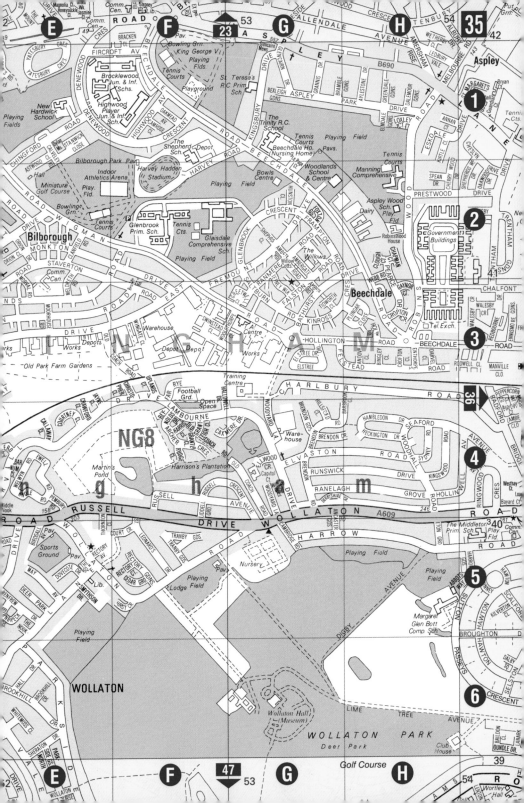

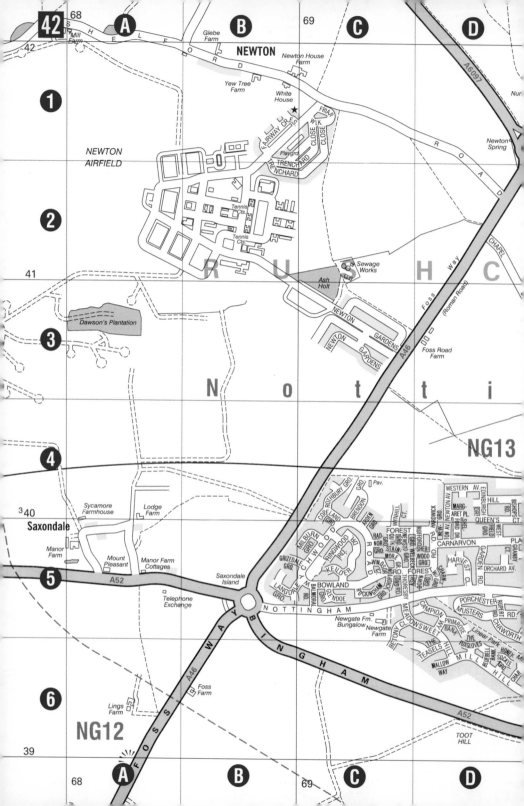

E
F
G
H
70
71
72
42
41
40
39
1
2
3
4
5
6
A46
Woodside Farm
Bulwell House
Parrots Nest
Burrowsmoor Holt
Thoroughfare Holt
MICKLEMOOR
MICKLEMOOR
LANE
LA.
Margidvnvm Roman Town
High Westing Farm
Bottom Plantation
Car Dyke
Car Dyke
L I F F E
Holme Farm
n g h a m
Moor Bridge
Parson's Hill
MOORBRIDGE
MOORBRIDGE
RD. E.
RD.
Moorbridge Ct.
BINGHAM INDUSTRIAL PARK
Tennis Ct.
Playing Field
Bingham
Pav.
CARNARVON CL.
PLACE
KIRKHILL
GILLOTTS CL.
MOOR LA.
Old Mill Ct.
LANGTREE GDS.
STATION ST.
Robert Miles Jun. Sch.
Offs.
CHURCH LA.
ST. MARYS
CHURCH CL.
RUTLAND RD.
GROVE RD.
ROAD
LANE
PRIORS CL.
BROWNES RD.
VICTORIA RD.
NURSERY RD.
CARR RD.
DOUGLAS RD.
BANES RD.
ABBEY ROAD
BUTT RD.
Playgrd.
Sch.
NEWGATE ST.
MARKET PL.
Lib.
Health Cen.
NEEDHAM ST.
UNION S.
MARKET S.
CHURCH ST.
CHERRY ST.
Longacre Prep. Sch.
Ct.
Bowl. Gn.
EAST ACRE
EAST GRO.
HOLME
MANOR RD.
ST.
FOSTERS LA.
CROW CT.
COGLEY
Carnarvon Primary School
FAIRFIELD ST.
CHESTNUT AV.
CARNARVON
LONG
ROAD
WALKERS CL.
The Crofts
THE PADDOCK
MELVYN DR.
BANKS CRES.
FISHER LA.
BANKS PADDOCK
JEBB'S LA.
ACRE
LONG ACRE EAST
PINFOLD
PERRY GRO.
DARK LA.
RAYMOND DR.
ROWAN CL.
LARCH CL.
POPLAR CL.
WILLOW
Oak Lodge
Beech Lodge
ASPEN CL.
OAK AV.
HOLLY CL.
JUNIPER
BLACKTHORN CL.
GDS.
Nursery
ASH CL.
WILLOW RD.
MAPLE CL.
BEECH AV.
CEDAR CL.
SYCMORE CL.
ELM A.
HAZEL CL.
ROAD
DERRY LA.
THE BANKS
GRANTHAM
ROAD
Sports Centre
Cemy.
Belvoir Vale Centre
Toot Hill Comp. Sch.
Playing Field
Tennis Courts
BINGHAM
Playing Fld.
Sports Arena
BY-PASS
GRANTHAM
A52
ROAD
Mill Mound
TITHBY ROAD
LANGAR RD.
LANGAR RD.
Sub.
TITHBY ROAD

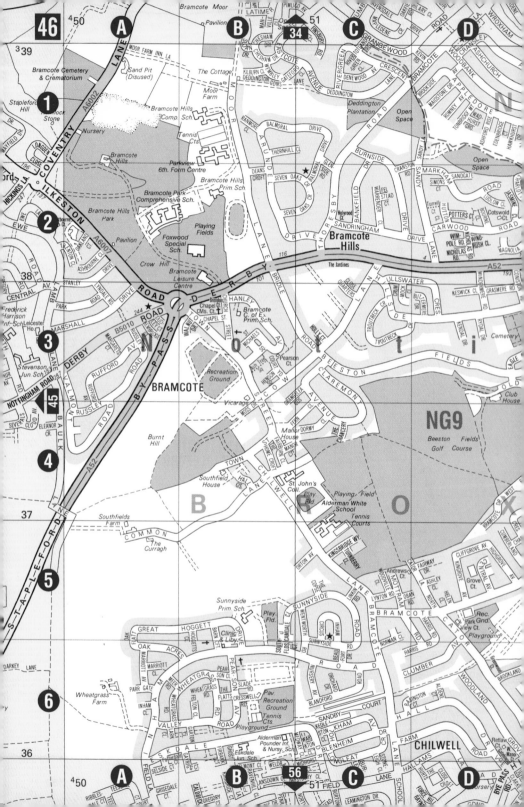

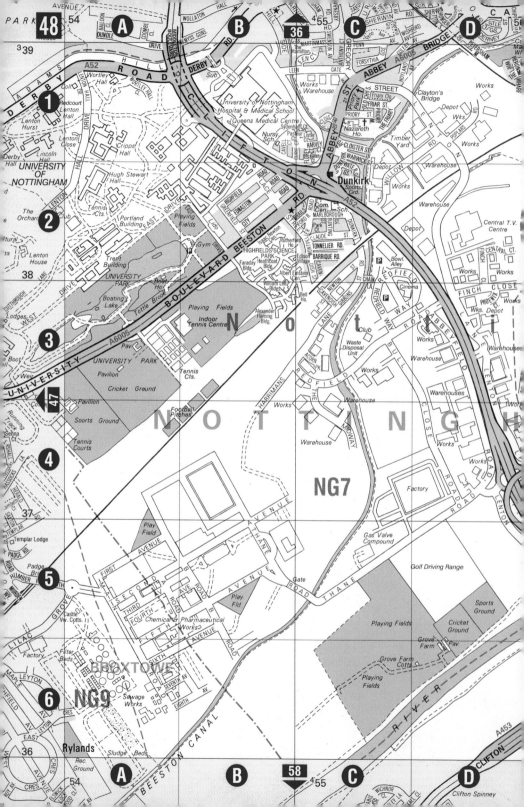

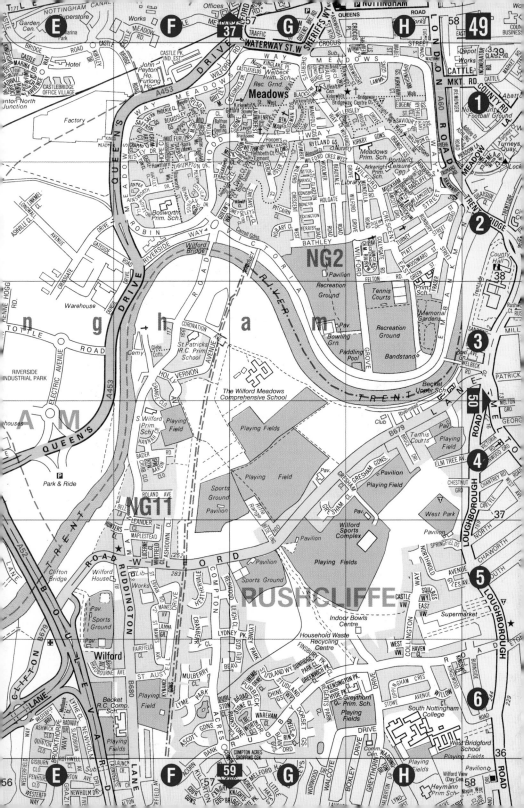

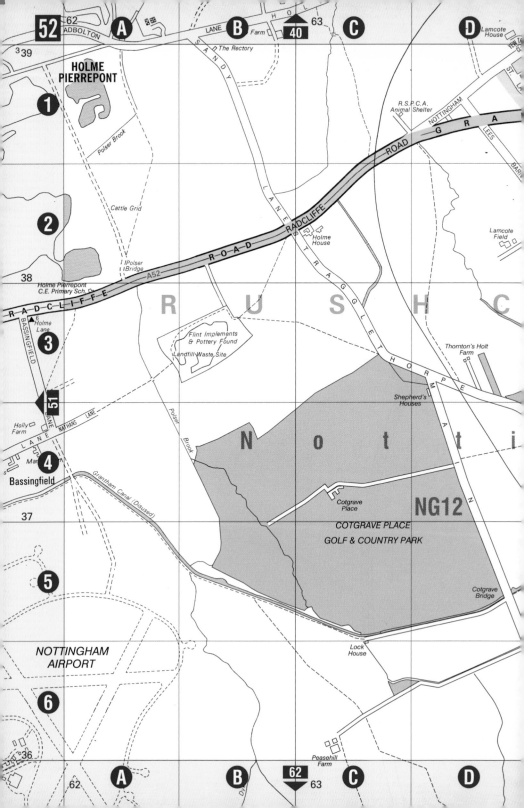

E **F** **G** **H** 66 **53**

41

³39

Comp. Sch.

Dewberry Hill

Club House

1

RADCLIFFE ON TRENT GOLF COURSE

Radcliffe on Trent Junior School

Cemetery

DEWBERRY LA.

RADCLIFFE ON TRENT

ees Barn

Sunpit Plantation

2

Radcliffe Barn Farm

38

Hall Farm

Works

L I F F E

F F E

3

Cockedhat Plantation

North Farm

n g h a m

Stragglethorpe

4

Paddock Cottages

37

Brown's Cotts.

5

Lock

Sports Ground

Pav.

Hollygate Farm

Brown's Bridge

Lock

Weirs

COTGRAVE COLLIERY

6

HOLLYGATE

Homefields

36

Gozen Lodge

E Windmill Hill

F 63 ⁴65 **G** HOLLYGATE (Disused) Canal **H** 66

Grantham

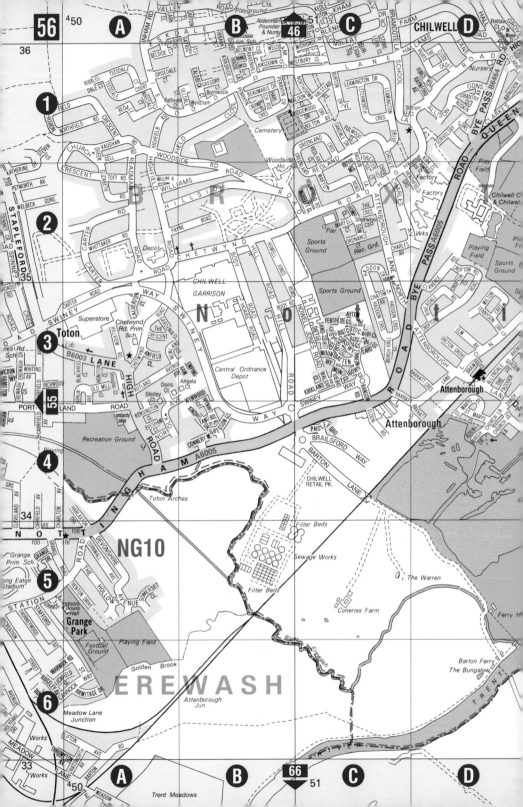

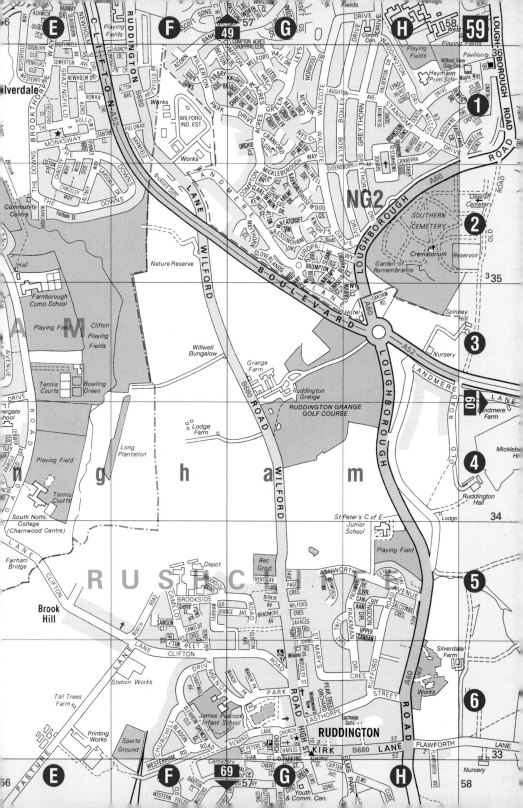

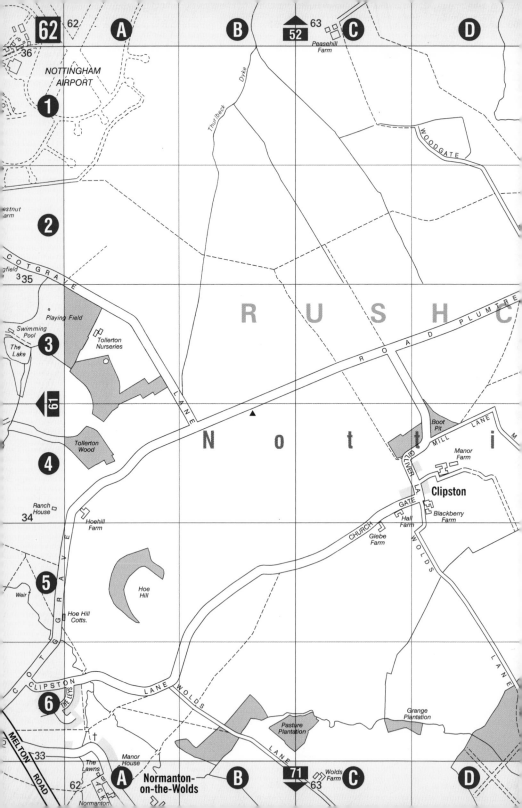

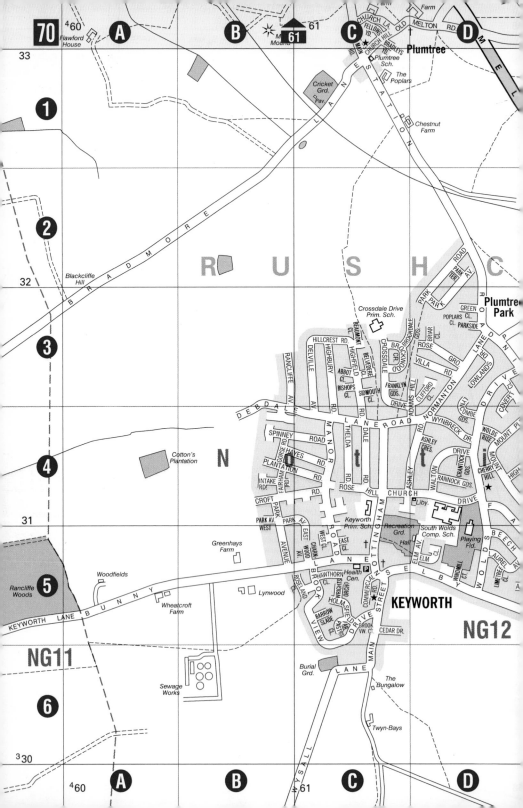

INDEX TO STREETS

HOW TO USE THIS INDEX

1. Each street name is followed by its Posttown or Postal Locality and then by its map reference; e.g. Abbeyfield Rd. Nott —3D **48** is in the Nottingham Posttown and is to be found in square 3D on page **48**. The page number being shown in bold type.
   A strict alphabetical order is followed in which Av., Rd., St., etc. (though abbreviated) are read in full and as part of the street name; e.g. Ashley Clo. appears after Ash Lea Clo. but before Ashley Dri.

2. Streets and a selection of Subsidiary names not shown on the Maps, appear in the index in *Italics* with the thoroughfare to which it is connected shown in brackets; e.g. *Breaston Ct. Nott —5E 15 (off Erewash Gdns.)*

3. The page references shown in brackets indicate those streets that appear on the large scale map pages 2 & 3; e.g. Abbotsford Dri. Nott —3H **37** (1F **3**) appears in square 3H on page **37** and also appears in the enlarged section in square 1F on page **3**.

GENERAL ABBREVIATIONS

All : Alley	Chyd : Churchyard	Gdns : Gardens	Mans : Mansions	Sq : Square
App : Approach	Circ : Circle	Ga : Gate	Mkt : Market	Sta : Station
Arc : Arcade	Cir : Circus	Gt : Great	M : Mews	St : Street
Av : Avenue	Clo : Close	Grn : Green	Mt : Mount	Ter : Terrace
Bk : Back	Comn : Common	Gro : Grove	N : North	Up : Upper
Boulevd : Boulevard	Cotts : Cottages	Ho : House	Pal : Palace	Vs : Villas
Bri : Bridge	Ct : Court	Ind : Industrial	Pde : Parade	Wlk : Walk
B'way : Broadway	Cres : Crescent	Junct : Junction	Pk : Park	W : West
Bldgs : Buildings	Dri : Drive	La : Lane	Pas : Passage	Yd : Yard
Bus : Business	E : East	Lit : Little	Pl : Place	
Cen : Centre	Embkmt : Embankment	Lwr : Lower	Rd : Road	
Chu : Church	Est : Estate	Mnr : Manor	S : South	

POSTTOWN AND POSTAL LOCALITIES ABBREVIATIONS

Arn : Arnold	Clip : Clipston	Ilk : Ilkeston	Old B : Old Basford	Stan W : Stanton-on-the-Wolds
Att : Attenborough	Colw : Colwick	Keyw : Keyworth	Pap : Papplewick	
Aws : Awsworth	Coss : Cossall	Kimb : Kimberley	Park : The Park	Sto B : Stoke Bardolph
B Vil : Bestwood Village	Cotg : Cotgrave	Lamb : Lambley	Plum : Plumtree	Stock : Stockhill
Bart : Barton-in-Fabis	D Abb : Dale Abbey	Lan M : Langley Mill	Rad T : Radcliffe on Trent	Strel : Strelley
Bees : Beeston	Day : Daybrook	Lent : Lenton	Red : Redhill	Thorn : Thorneywood
Bilb : Bilborough	E'wd : Eastwood	Lent A : Lenton Abbey	Ris : Risley	Thrum : Thrumpton
Bing : Bingham	Edw : Edwalton	Lin : Linby	Rud : Ruddington	Toll : Tollerton
Bradm : Bradmore	Epp : Epperstone	Long E : Long Eaton	S'fd : Stapleford	Tot : Toton
Bram : Bramcote	For F : Forest Fields	Los : Loscoe	Sand : Sandiacre	Trow : Trowell
Breas : Breaston	Gam : Gamston	M'ley : Mapperley (Ilkeston)	Shard : Shardlow	W Bri : West Bridgford
Bul : Bulcote	Ged : Gedling	Map : Mapperley (Nottingham)	Shelf : Shelford	W Hal : West Hallam
Bulw : Bulwell	Gilt : Giltbrook	N'fld : Netherfield	Sher : Sherwood	Wat : Watnall
Bun : Bunny	Got : Gotham	New B : New Basford	Sher R : Sherwood Rise	Wd'p : Woodthorpe
Bur J : Burton Joyce	Greas : Greasley	Newt : Newthorpe	Ship : Shipley	Wdbgh : Woodborough
Calv : Calverton	Hean : Heanor	Nor W : Normanton-on-the-Wolds	Smal : Smalley	Wilf : Wilford
Carl : Carlton	High S : Highfields Science Park	Nott : Nottingham	Snei : Sneinton	Woll : Wollaton
Carr : Carrington		Nut : Nuthall	Stan : Stanley	
Chil : Chilwell	Hol P : Holme Pierrepont	Nwtn : Newton	Stan C : Stanley Common	
Clif : Clifton	Huck : Hucknall		Stan D : Stanton-by-Dale	

INDEX TO STREETS

Aaron Clo. Nott —4F **49**
Abba Clo. Kimb —6H **11**
Abbey Bri. Nott —1C **48**
Abbey Cir. W Bri —4C **50**
Abbey Clo. Huck —4C **4**
Abbey Ct. Bees —3F **47**
Abbey Ct. Nott —5D **36**
Abbey Dri. Bees —4F **47**
Abbeyfield Rd. Nott —3D **48**
Abbey Gro. Nott —2B **38**
Abbey Rd. Bees —4F **47**
Abbey Rd. Bing —4G **43**
Abbey Rd. E'wd —3D **10**
Abbey Rd. W Bri —4C **50**
Abbey St. Ilk —5B **20**
Abbey St. Nott —1C **48**
Abbot Clo. Keyw —3C **70**
Abbot Rd. Ilk —3G **31**
Abbotsbury Clo. Nott —4B **14**
Abbots Clo. Day —1H **25**
Abbots Dri. Huck —5C **4**
Abbotsford Dri. Nott
　—3H **37** (1F **3**)
Abbotsford M. Ilk —4H **19**
Abbots Rd. Huck —5C **4**
Abbot St. Aws —3E **21**
Abbots Wlk. Huck —4C **8**
Abbots Way. Nott —5H **35**
Abbott St. Hean —4C **8**
Abbott St. Long E —1F **65**
Abercarn Clo. Nott —6H **13**
Aberdeen St. Nott
　—4A **38** (3H **3**)
Aberford Av. Nott —1B **36**
Abingdon Dri. Rud —5H **59**
Abingdon Gdns. Bees
　—1D **56**

Abingdon Gdns. Wd'p
　—2C **26**
Abingdon Rd. W Bri —4C **50**
Abingdon Sq. Nott —6H **23**
Ablard Gdns. Bees —3C **56**
Acacia Clo. Huck —6F **5**
Acacia Ct. Nott —3H **37**
Acacia Cres. Carl —1H **39**
Acacia Gdns. Wat —6A **12**
Acacia Wlk. Bees —5F **47**
Acadamy Clo. Nott —4C **24**
Acaster Clo. Bees —1H **57**
Acle Gdns. Nott —4H **13**
Acorn Av. Gilt —5D **12**
Acorn Bank. W Bri —1F **59**
Acorn Dri. Ged —4A **28**
Acorn Pk. Lent —3C **48**
Acourt St. Nott —3D **36**
Acton Av. Long E —1G **65**
Acton Av. Nott —3B **24**
Acton Clo. Long E —1G **65**
Acton Gro. Long E —1G **65**
Acton Rd. Arn —5H **15**
Acton Rd. Long E —6G **55**
Acton St. Long E —1G **65**
Adale Rd. Smal —5A **8**
Adams Clo. Hean —5B **8**
Adams St. Ilk —4A **20**
Adams Hill. Keyw —4D **70**
Adams Hill. Nott —1H **47**
Adam St. Ilk —3C **32**
Adbolton Av. Ged —6G **27**
Adbolton Gro. W Bri —1D **50**
Adbolton La. W Bri & Hol P
　—2D **50**
Adbolton Lodge. Carl —3G **39**
Adderley Clo. Nott —1E **25**

Addington Ct. Rad T —5G **41**
Addington Rd. Nott —3D **36**
Addison Dri. Huck —3C **4**
Addison Rd. Carl —1D **38**
Addison St. Nott
　—2F **37** (1C **2**)
Addison Vs. E'wd —4A **10**
Adelaide Clo. S'fd —2H **45**
Adelaide Gro. Nott —5C **14**
Adel Dri. Ged —5G **27**
Adenburgh Dri. Att —4D **56**
Admiral Clo. Hean —3C **8**
Adrian Clo. Bees —4H **55**
Aeneas Ct. Nott —1F **37**
Agnes Vs. Nott —5A **26**
Aidan Gdns. Nott —3E **15**
Ainsdale Cres. Nott —4G **23**
Ainsley Rd. Nott —3B **36**
Ainsworth Dri. Nott —2F **49**
Aintree Clo. Kimb —6G **11**
Aira Clo. Gam —5F **51**
Airedale Clo. Long E —1C **64**
Airedale Ct. Bees —1A **56**
Airedale Wlk. Nott —6C **34**
Aitchison Av. Huck —4D **4**
Alandene Av. Wat —6A **12**
Albany Clo. Arn —6A **16**
Albany Clo. Huck —6A **4**
Albany Ct. S'fd —2G **45**
Albany Rd. Nott —1E **37**
Albany St. Ilk —3C **32**
Albemarle Rd. Wd'p —5H **25**
Alberta Ter. Nott —1E **37**
Albert Av. Carl —2D **38**
Albert Av. Nott —1B **36**
Albert Av. Nut —6C **12**
Albert Av. S'fd —4F **45**

Albert Ball Clo. Nott —5D **14**
Albert Einstein Cen. High S
　—2B **48**
Albert Gro. Nott —4D **36**
Albert Rd. Bees —4H **47**
Albert Rd. Lent —6D **36**
Albert Rd. Long E —5F **55**
Albert Rd. Nott —6H **25**
Albert Rd. Sand —5D **44**
Albert Rd. W Bri —3B **50**
Albert St. E'wd —2B **10**
Albert St. Ged —6H **27**
Albert St. Huck —4F **5**
Albert St. Ilk —1A **32**
Albert St. Nott —5G **37** (5E **3**)
Albert St. Rad T —6F **41**
Albert St. S'fd —4F **45**
Albion Cen., The. Ilk —6B **20**
Albion Rise. Arn —4B **16**
Albion Rd. Long E —5H **55**
Albion St. Bees —4F **47**
Albion St. Ilk —6B **20**
Albion St. Nott
　—6G **37** (6D **2**)
Albury Dri. Nott —6H **23**
Albury Sq. Nott —5E **37**
Aldene Ct. Bees —6D **46**
Aldene Way. Wdbgh —6H **7**
Aldercar La. Lan M —1F **9**
Alder Gdns. Nott —6G **13**
Aldermans Clo. Nott —1G **49**
Alderney St. Nott —6D **36**
Alderton Rd. Nott —1G **25**
Alder Way. Keyw —5C **71**
Aldgate Clo. Nott —5G **13**
Aldred's La. Hean & Lan M
　—4E **9**

Aldridge Clo. Bees —3G **55**
Aldrin Clo. Nott —2F **23**
Aldworth Clo. Nott —1F **25**
Aldwych Clo. Arn —4E **15**
Aldwych Clo. Nut —5D **22**
Alexander Clo. Huck —2F **5**
Alexander Fleming Building.
　High S —3B **48**
Alexander Rd. Nott —5E **37**
Alexandra Cres. Bees —5G **47**
Alexandra Gdns. Nott —6F **25**
Alexandra M. Nott —1F **37**
Alexandra Rd. Long E
　—5F **55**
Alexandra St. E'wd —3B **10**
Alexandra St. Nott —1F **37**
Alexandra St. S'fd —5F **45**
Alford Clo. Bees —6G **47**
　(in two parts)
Alford Rd. W Bri & Edw
　—5D **50**
Alfred Av. Nott —5C **26**
Alfred Clo. Nott —3G **37**
Alfred St. Central. Nott
　—3G **37**
Alfred St. N. Nott —3G **37**
Alfred St. S. Nott
　—4A **38** (2H **3**)
Alfreton Rd. Nott
　—2C **36** (2A **2**)
Alison Av. Huck —2G **5**
Alison Wlk. Nott
　—3H **37** (1F **3**)
Allandale Rd. Hean —3B **8**
Allen Av. Nott —6C **26**
　(in two parts)
Allendale. Ilk —2A **32**

Allendale Av. Att —3D **56**
Allendale Av. Nott —6F **23**
Allen Field Ct. Nott —6D **36**
Allen St. Huck —3E **5**
Allen's Wlk. Arn —4B **16**
Allington Av. Nott —6D **36**
Allison Gdns. Bees —1D **56**
All Saints St. Nott
—3E **37** (1A **2**)
All Saints Ter. Nott
—3E **37** (1A **2**)
Allwood Dri. Carl —1G **39**
Allwood Gdns. Huck —5F **5**
Alma Clo. Ged —5A **28**
Alma Clo. Nott
—3G **37** (1D **2**)
Alma Hill. Kimb —6G **11**
Alma Rd. Nott —3B **38**
Alma St. Nott —1E **37**
Almond Clo. Huck —6F **5**
Almond Clo. Kimb —6G **11**
Almond Ct. Nott —4F **35**
Almond Wlk. Ged —4A **28**
Alnwick Clo. Nott —1A **24**
Alpha Ter. Nott —3F **37**
Alpine Cres. Carl —1G **39**
Alpine St. Nott —4C **24**
Althorpe St. Nott —4E **37**
Alton Av. Nott —1F **59**
Alton Clo. W Bri —2G **59**
Alton Dri. Gilt —5D **10**
Alum Ct. Nott —5D **14**
Alvenor St. Ilk —6B **20**
Alverstone Rd. Nott —6G **25**
Alvey Ter. Nott —4C **36**
Alwood Gro. Nott —2B **58**
Alwyn Ct. Bees —6F **47**
Alwyn Rd. Nott —5F **23**
Alyth Ct. Nott —4D **24**
Amber Ct. Hean —4C **8**
Amber Dri. Lan M —3F **9**
Ambergate Rd. Nott —2G **35**
Amber Hill. Nott —6F **15**
Amberley St. Nott
—5F **37** (4C **2**)
Amber Trading Cen. Kimb
—6F **11**
Ambleside. Gam —4E **51**
Ambleside Dri. E'wd —2H **9**
Ambleside Rd. Nott —6G **23**
Ambleside Way. Ged —1B **40**
Amersham Rise. Nott
—6H **23**
Amesbury Cir. Nott —4G **23**
Amilda Av. Ilk —1B **32**
Ampthill Rise. Nott —3F **25**
Ancaster Gdns. Nott —4G **35**
Anchor Clo. Nott —5H **23**
Anchor Ct. Nott —6F **15**
Anchor Rd. E'wd —2G **9**
Anchor Row. Ilk —1B **32**
Anders Dri. Nott —2F **23**
Anderson Ct. Nott —5E **15**
Anderson Cres. Bees —3E **47**
Andover Clo. Nott —3H **35**
Andover Rd. Nott —1C **24**
Andrew Av. Ilk —2D **32**
Andrew Av. Nott —5C **26**
Andrews Ct. Bees —5C **46**
Andrews Dri. Lan M —1E **9**
Andrews Rd. Nott —2F **37**
Anfield Clo. Bees —3A **56**
Anford Clo. Nott —2H **23**
Angela Clo. Arn —3A **16**
Angela Ct. Bees —3B **56**
Angel All. Nott —5H **37** (4F **3**)
Angel Row. Nott
—5G **37** (4D **2**)
Angrave Clo. Nott —2A **38**
Angus Clo. Arn —4D **16**
Angus Clo. Kimb —2A **22**
Anmer Clo. Nott —2F **49**
Annan Ct. Nott —1H **35**
Anne's Clo. Nott —5C **26**
Annesley Gro. Nott —4F **37**
Annesley Rd. Huck —1B **4**
Annesley Rd. W Bri —4B **50**
Anslow Av. Bees —3G **47**

Anson Ter. Nott —2D **36**
Anson Wlk. Ilk —4B **20**
Anstee Rd. Long E —2E **65**
Anstey Rise. Nott —4B **38**
Anthony Wharton Ct. Nott
—2C **58**
Antill St. S'fd —5F **45**
Apollo Dri. Nott —2F **23**
Appleby Clo. Ilk —3B **32**
Appledore Av. Nott —1D **46**
Appledorne Way. Arn —4D **16**
Appleton Clo. Nott —5A **58**
Appleton Rd. Bees —1H **57**
Appletree La. Ged —5H **27**
Apple Wlk. Nott —1C **38**
Applewood Gro. Nott —4H **25**
Arboretum St. Nott —3F **37**
Arbour Hill. D Abb —6C **30**
Arbrook Dri. Nott —3B **36**
Arbutus Clo. Nott —4A **58**
Archdale Rd. Nott —1G **25**
Archer Cres. Nott —4F **35**
Archer Rd. S'fd —6G **45**
Archer St. Ilk —4A **20**
Arch Hill. Red —2A **16**
Arden Clo. Bees —3G **47**
Arden Clo. Huck —6G **5**
Arden Gro. Bing —4C **42**
Ardleigh Clo. Nott —3E **14**
Ardsley Clo. Hean —3E **9**
Argyle Ct. Nott —4D **36**
Argyle St. Lan M —1F **9**
Argyle St. Nott —4D **36**
Ariel Clo. Nott —3D **24**
Arkers Clo. Nott —4B **24**
Arklow Clo. Nott —3D **36**
Arkwright St. N. Nott —6G **37**
Arkwright St. S. Nott —2H **49**
(in two parts)
Arkwright Wlk. Nott —1G **49**
(in two parts)
Arleston Dri. Nott —6D **34**
Arlington Av. Huck —5D **4**
Arlington Dri. Nott —6G **25**
Armadale Clo. Arn —5E **17**
Armfield Rd. Arn —1E **27**
Armitage Dri. Long E —6A **56**
Armstrong Rd. Nott —2F **23**
Arncliffe Clo. Nott —3C **24**
Arndale Rd. Nott —2G **25**
Arne Ct. Nott —2E **49**
Arnesby Rd. Nott —6C **36**
Arno Av. Nott —1F **37**
Arnold Av. Long E —3C **64**
Arnold Cres. Long E —3C **64**
Arnold La. Nott & Ged
—2D **26**
Arnold Rd. Nott —3C **24**
Arnos Gro. Nott —4D **22**
Arnot Hill Rd. Arn —6A **16**
Arnot Houses. Carl —1G **39**
Arno Vale Gdns. Wd'p
—2A **26**
Arno Vale Rd. Wd'p —2B **26**
Arnside. S'fd —1G **45**
Arnside Clo. Nott —2F **25**
Arnside Rd. Nott —2E **25**
A Rd. Lent —5A **48**
Arran Clo. S'fd —1G **45**
Arthur Av. Nott —5D **36**
Arthur Av. S'fd —3H **45**
Arthur Cres. Carl —2C **39**
Arthur Mee Rd. S'fd —6G **45**
Arthur St. N'fld —3A **40**
Arthur St. Nott —3F **37**
Artic Way. Kimb —6F **11**
Arundel Clo. Sand —1D **54**
Arundel Dri. Bees —1B **46**
Arundel St. Nott —4E **37**
Ascot Av. Kimb —6G **11**
Ascot Clo. Huck —6A **4**
Ascot Dri. Red —5H **15**
Ascot Ind. Est. Sand —4E **45**
Ascot Pl. Ilk —4G **31**
Ascot Rd. Nott —2B **36**
Ascott Gdns. W Bri —6F **49**

Ashbourne Clo. Bees —2A **46**
Ashbourne Ct. Nott —1F **23**
Ashbourne St. Nott —4E **37**
Ashburnham Av. Nott
—5D **36**
Ashchurch Dri. Nott —1D **46**
Ash Clo. Bing —5G **43**
Ash Clo. Bur J —4E **29**
Ash Clo. Huck —6A **4**
Ash Clo. Wdbgh —6G **7**
Ash Ct. Carl —2F **39**
Ash Cres. Nut —1B **22**
Ashdale Av. Huck —6E **5**
Ashdale Rd. Arn —5C **16**
Ashdale Rd. Ilk —3C **32**
Ashdown Clo. Wilf —5F **49**
Ashdown Gro. Bing —5D **42**
Ashe Clo. Arn —6D **16**
Asher La. Rud —2F **69**
Ashfield Av. Bees —6H **47**
Ashfield Rd. Nott —5B **38**
Ashford St. W Hal —1B **30**
Ashford Pl. Ilk —2A **20**
Ashford Rise. Nott —1D **46**
Ashforth St. Nott —3H **37**
Ashgate Rd. Huck —5F **5**
Ash Gro. Keyw —5D **70**
Ash Gro. Long E —1E **65**
Ash Gro. Sand —4C **44**
Ash Gro. S'fd —6F **45**
Ash Gro. Wdbgh —5G **7**
Ashiana. Nott —5A **38**
Ashington Dri. Arn —3C **16**
Ash Lea Clo. Cotg —3F **63**
Ashley Clo. Bees —5D **46**
Ashley Ct. Bees —5E **47**
Ashley Cres. Keyw —4D **70**
Ashley Gro. Huck —4C **4**
Ashley Rd. Keyw —4C **70**
Ashley St. Nott
—4A **38** (3H **3**)
Ashling Ct. Nott —1A **50**
Ashling St. Nott —1H **49**
Ash Mt. Rd. Lan M —2F **9**
Ashness Clo. Gam —5E **51**
Ashover Clo. Nott —1A **38**
Ashridge Way. Edw —1E **61**
Ash St. Ilk —2B **20**
Ashton Av. Arn —3C **16**
Ash Tree Sq. Bees —3B **46**
Ashview Clo. Long E —5C **54**
Ash Vs. Nott —6F **25**
Ashville Clo. Nott —2E **49**
Ashwater Dri. Nott —1F **27**
Ashwell Gdns. Nott —1C **36**
Ashwell St. N'fld —3H **39**
Ashwick Clo. Nott —6E **49**
Ashworth Av. Hean —4E **9**
Ashworth Av. Rud —5G **59**
Ashworth Clo. Nott —4E **39**
Ashworth Cres. Nott —5D **26**
Askeby Rd. Nott —5D **22**
Aslockton Dri. Nott —5B **24**
Aspen Clo. Bing —5G **43**
Aspen Rd. Nott —6F **13**
Asper St. N'fld —2A **40**
Aspinall Ct. Nott —4A **36**
Aspley La. Nott —6F **23**
Aspley Pk. Dri. Nott —1G **35**
Aspley Pl. Nott —3D **36**
Assarts Rd. Nut —3E **23**
Astcote Clo. Hean —4E **9**
Aster Rd. Nott —2H **37**
Astle Ct. Arn —1E **27**
Astley Dri. Nott —6B **26**
Aston Av. Bees —3G **47**
Aston Dri. Nott —3A **14**
Aston Grn. Bees —2G **55**
Astral Dri. Huck —1E **13**
Astral Gro. Huck —1D **12**
Astrid Gdns. Nott —1D **24**
Astwood Clo. Nott —1H **35**
Atherfield Gdns. E'wd
—2B **10**
Atherton Rise. Nott —4H **23**
Atherton Rd. Ilk —4G **19**
Athorpe Gro. Nott —4D **24**

Attenborough La. Att —3D **56**
Attenborough La. N. Bees
—2C **56**
Attercliffe Ter. Nott —2G **49**
Attewell Rd. Aws —2D **20**
Aubrey Av. Nott —5A **38**
Aubrey Rd. Nott —5F **25**
Aubyn Clo. Stan C —1A **30**
Auckland Clo. Nott —4C **36**
Auckland Rd. Huck —6B **4**
Audley Clo. Ilk —4H **19**
Audley Dri. Bees —2F **47**
Audon Av. Bees —6E **47**
Augustine Gdns. Nott —4E **15**
Austen Av. Long E —2E **65**
Austen Av. Nott —2E **37**
Austins Dri. Sand —1D **54**
Austin St. Nott —6A **14**
Austrey Av. Bees —3G **47**
Avalon Clo. Nott —5B **58**
Avebury Clo. Nott —5B **58**
Aveline Clo. Nott —5D **14**
Avenue A. Nott
—5H **37** (4G **3**)
Avenue B. Nott
—5H **37** (4G **3**)
Avenue C. Nott
—5A **38** (4H **3**)
Avenue D. Nott
—5A **38** (4H **3**)
Avenue E. Nott —3H **3**
Avenue, The. Calv —3D **6**
Avenue, The. Rad T —5F **41**
Avenue, The. Rud —2H **69**
Averton Sq. Nott —6B **36**
Aviemore Clo. Arn —4D **16**
Avis Av. Hean —6D **8**
Avocet Wharf. Nott —1E **49**
Avon Av. Huck —1E **13**
Avonbridge Clo. Arn —4E **17**
Avondale. Cotg —2F **63**
Avondale Clo. Long E
—1C **64**
Avondale Rd. Carl —3F **39**
Avondale Rd. Ilk —4G **31**
Avon Gdns. W Bri —4B **50**
Avonlea Clo. Ilk —3D **32**
Avon Pl. Bees —4G **47**
Avon Rd. Ged —5H **27**
Avon Rd. Nott —4D **38**
Awsworth & Cossall By-Pass.
Aws —3D **20**
Awsworth La. Coss —6E **21**
Awsworth La. Kimb —1F **21**
Awsworth Rd. Ilk & Aws
—5B **20**
Axford Clo. Ged —5H **27**
Aylesham Av. Arn —1B **26**
Aylestone Dri. Nott —1H **35**
Ayr St. Nott —3E **37**
Ayscough Av. Nut —1C **22**
Ayton Clo. Nott —1F **49**
Ayton Gdns. Bees —3C **56**
Azalea Ct. Gilt —5E **11**

Babbacombe Dri. Nott
—1F **25**
Babbacombe Way. Huck
—5B **4**
Babbington Cres. Ged
—5G **27**
Babbington La. Kimb —3H **21**
Babbington Ct. Bees —6D **46**
Back La. Hean —4C **8**
Back La. Ilk —5A **20**
Back La. Nor W —1E **71**
Back La. Nut —1D **22**
Bacon Clo. Gilt —5C **10**
Bacton Av. Nott —5H **13**
Bacton Gdns. Nott —5H **13**
Baden Powell Rd. Nott
—5C **38**
Bader Rd. Nott —4F **49**
Badger Clo. Huck —5A **4**
Bagnall Av. Arn —1G **25**
Bagnall Cotts. Nott —2H **23**
Bagnall Rd. Nott —3H **23**
Bagot St. W Hal —1A **30**

Baildon Clo. Nott —6A **36**
Bailey Brook Cres. Lan M
—1E **9**
Bailey Brook Dri. Lan M
—2E **9**
Bailey Brook Ind. Est. Lan M
—3F **9**
Bailey Brook Wlk. Lan M
—2E **9**
Bailey Clo. Day —6H **15**
Bailey Ct. N'fld —2A **40**
Bailey Ct. Rad T —1E **53**
Bailey Gro. Rd. E'wd —3H **9**
Bailey La. Rad T —1E **53**
Bailey St. N'fld —2A **40**
Bailey St. Nott —5C **24**
Bailey St. S'fd —5E **45**
Bainbridge, The. Calv —3E **7**
Bainton Gro. Nott —4D **58**
Baker Av. Arn —4C **16**
Baker Av. Hean —6D **8**
Bakerdale Rd. Nott —3D **38**
Baker Rd. Newt & Gilt
—5E **11**
Bakers Clo. Nott —3C **36**
Baker's Hollow. Cotg —2E **63**
Baker St. Huck —4E **5**
Baker St. Ilk —6B **20**
Baker St. Nott —2F **37**
Bakewell Av. Carl —6G **27**
Bakewell Dri. Nott —6C **14**
Bakewell Rd. Long E —2G **65**
Bala Dri. Nott —6E **15**
Baldwin Ct. Nott —4D **36**
Baldwin St. Newt —4E **11**
Baldwin St. Nott —4D **36**
Balfour Rd. Nott —4D **36**
Balfour Rd. S'fd —5F **45**
Balfron Gdns. Nott —1F **49**
Ballantrae Clo. Arn —5D **16**
Ballerat Cres. Nott —5C **14**
Ballon Wood N. Nott —5C **34**
Ball St. Nott —2B **38**
Balmoral Av. W Bri —3A **50**
Balmoral Clo. Sand —2D **54**
Balmoral Cres. Nott —4C **34**
Balmoral Dri. Bees —1B **46**
Balmoral Gro. Colw —3H **39**
Balmoral Gro. Huck —3F **5**
Balmoral Rd. Bing —5G **42**
Balmoral Rd. Colw —3H **39**
Balmoral Rd. Ilk —4H **31**
Balmoral Rd. Nott —3F **37**
Bamkin Clo. Huck —5F **5**
Bampton Ct. Gam —4F **51**
Bampton Ct. Nott —3D **36**
Banbury Av. Bees —2H **55**
Bancroft St. Nott —6A **14**
Banes Rd. Bing —5H **43**
Bangor Wlk. Nott —3G **37**
Bankfield Dri. Bees —2C **46**
Bankfield Dri. Ilk —3F **31**
Bank Hill. Wdbgh —2H **17**
Bank Pl. Nott —5G **37** (4E **3**)
Banksburn Clo. Hean —4A **8**
Banks Clo. Arn —1D **26**
Banks Cres. Bing —5E **43**
Banks Paddock. Bing —5F **43**
Banks Rd. Bees —2G **55**
Banks, The. Bing —5E **43**
Bank St. Lan M —1G **9**
Bank St. Long E —6G **55**
Bankwood Clo. Nott —6G **23**
Bannerman Rd. Nott —1A **24**
Barbara Sq. Huck —2D **4**
Barber Clo. Ilk —4A **20**
Barber St. E'wd —3C **10**
Barbrook Clo. Nott —4G **35**
Barbury Dri. Nott —6B **58**
Barclay Ct. Ilk —4H **19**
Barden Rd. Nott —3C **26**
Bardfield Gdns. Nott —3B **14**
Bardsey Gdns. Nott —6E **15**
Barent Clo. Nott —1D **24**
Barent Wlk. Nott —1C **24**
Barker Av. E. Sand —5D **44**
Barker Av. N. Sand —5C **44**
Barker Ga. Huck —4D **4**

Barker Ga. Ilk —5B 20
Barker Ga. Nott
—5H 37 (4F 3)
Barkla Clo. Nott —5A 58
Bar La. Nott —5A 24
Bar La. Ind. Pk. Nott —5B 24
Barley Croft. W Bri —1G 59
Barleydale Dri. Trow —1F 45
Barleylands. Rud —1G 69
Barling Dri. Ilk —5G 19
Barlock Rd. Nott —3C 24
Barlow Dri. N. Aws —3D 20
Barlow Dri. S. Aws —3D 20
Barnby Wlk. Nott —2G 25
Barn Clo. Cotg —3E 63
Barn Croft. Bees —5B 46
Barndale Clo. W Bri —2G 59
Barnes Rd. Nott —5D 14
Barnet Rd. Nott —2D 38
Barnfield. Nott —1F 59
Barnsley Ter. Nott —2G 49
Barnston Rd. Nott —4B 38
Barnum Clo. Nott —4E 35
Barons Clo. Ged —6G 27
Barrack La. Nott —5D 36
Barra M. Nott —1F 49
Barratt Clo. Att —4D 56
Barratt Cres. Att —3D 56
Barratt La. Att —3C 56
Barrhead Clo. Nott —4C 14
Barrington Clo. Rad T
—1E 53
Barrique Rd. Nott —2C 48
Barrow Slade. Keyw —5C 70
Barrydale Av. Bees —6F 47
Barry St. Nott —6H 13
Bartlow Rd. Nott —2D 34
Barton Clo. Rud —1F 69
Barton La. Att —4C 56
Barton La. Bart —1G 67
Barton La. Nott —5A 58
Barton La. Thrum —6C 66
Barton Rd. Long E —1A 66
Bartons Clo. Newt —3E 11
Barton St. Bees —6G 47
Barwell Dri. Nott —6D 22
Basa Cres. Nott —5D 14
Basford Rd. Nott —6B 24
Baskin La. Bees —1C 56
Baslow Av. Carl —6F 27
Baslow Clo. Long E —2C 64
Baslow Dri. Bees —2G 47
Bassett Clo. Kimb —6G 11
Bassford Av. Hean —3D 8
Bassingfield La. Gam & Rad T
—5F 51
Bastion St. Nott —4C 36
Bateman Gdns. Nott —2D 36
Bathley St. Nott —2G 49
Bath Rd. Ilk —6A 20
Baths La. Huck —4F 5
Bath St. Nott —4H 37 (3G 3)
Bathurst Dri. Nott —3G 35
Baulk La. S'fd —3H 45
Bawtry Wlk. Nott —3B 38
Bayard Ct. Nott —4A 36
Bayliss Rd. Ged —4F 27
Bayswater Rd. Kimb —6H 11
Baythorn Rd. Nott —3D 34
Beacon Flatts. Bees —5H 47
Beacon Hill Dri. Huck —6A 4
Beacon Hill Rise. Nott
—4A 38 (2H 3)
Beacon Rd. Bees —5H 47
Beaconsfield St. Long E
—5G 55
Beaconsfield St. Nott —1D 36
Bean Clo. Nott —2F 23
Beardall St. Huck —4F 5
Beardsley Gdns. Nott —1F 49
Beardsmore Gro. Huck
—2D 4
Beastmarket Hill. Nott
—5G 37 (4D 2)
Beatty Wlk. Ilk —4B 28
Beauclerk Dri. Nott —5C 14
Beaufort Ct. W Bri —2G 59
Beaufort Dri. Bees —6C 46

Beaulieu Gdns. W Bri
—6G 49
Beaumaris Dri. Bees —1B 56
Beaumaris Dri. Ged —6B 28
Beaumont Clo. Keyw —3C 70
Beaumont Clo. S'fd —2G 45
Beaumont Gdns. W Bri
—1H 59
Beaumont St. Nott —5A 38
Beauvale. Newt —3E 11
Beauvale Cres. Huck —5B 4
Beauvale Dri. Ilk —2H 19
Beauvale Rise. E'wd —2D 10
Beauvale Rd. Huck —5B 4
Beauvale Rd. Nott —2G 49
Beck Av. Calv —2D 6
Beckenham Rd. Nott —3C 36
Beckett Ct. Ged —4F 27
Beckford Rd. Nott —6B 38
Beckhampton Rd. Nott
—5F 15
Beckley Rd. Nott —5F 23
Beckside. W Bri & Gam
—1E 61
Beck St. Carl —1F 39
Beck St. Nott —4H 37 (3F 3)
Bedale Ct. Bees —1A 56
Bedale Rd. Nott —2G 25
Bede Clo. Nott —4E 15
Bede Ling. W Bri —5G 49
Bedford Ct. Nott —1D 36
Bedford Ct. S'fd —2G 45
Bedford Row. Nott
—4H 37 (3G 3)
Bedlington Gdns. Nott
—6A 26
Beecham Av. Nott —3B 38
Beech Av. Bees —6H 47
Beech Av. Bing —5G 43
Beech Av. Breas —5B 54
Beech Av. Huck —4F 5
Beech Av. Keyw —5D 70
Beech Av. Long E —4G 55
Beech Av. Map —3C 26
Beech Av. N'fld —3H 39
Beech Av. New B —1E 37
Beech Av. Nut —1B 22
Beech Av. Sand —4D 44
Beech Clo. Nott —3D 4
Beech Clo. Rad T —1F 53
Beech Ct. Map —3C 26
Beechcroft. W Hal —2C 30
Beechdale Rd. Nott —1F 35
Beeches, The. Long E
—5G 55
Beeches, The. Nott —1C 38
Beeches, The. Smal —5A 8
Beech La. W Hal —2B 30
Beechwood Rd. Arn —5C 16
Beeston Clo. B Vil —1C 18
Beeston Ct. Nott —6B 14
Beeston Fields Dri. Bees
—3C 46
Beeston La. Nott —3H 47
Beeston Rd. Nott —2B 48
Belconnen Rd. Nott —2E 25
Belfield Ct. Los —1A 8
Belfield St. Ilk —5B 20
Belford Clo. Nott —5F 13
Belfry Way. Edw —1E 61
Belgrave M. W Bri —2G 59
Belgrave Rd. Nott —6G 13
Belgrave Sq. Nott
—4F 37 (2C 2)
Bellar Ga. Nott
—5H 37 (4G 3)
Belle-Isle Rd. Huck —5B 5
Belleville Dri. Nott —5E 15
Bell Ho. High S —3B 48
Bell La. Smal & Ship —2A 18
Bellevue Ct. Nott —3A 38
Bellmore Gdns. Nott —4D 34
Bells La. Nott —5G 23
Bell St. Carl —1F 39
Bell Ter. Nott —3C 24

Belmont Av. Breas —5A 54
Belmont Av. Nott —6A 14
Belmont Clo. Bees —1B 56
Belmont Clo. Huck —1G 13
Belper Av. Carl —6F 27
Belper Cres. Carl —6F 27
Belper Rd. Ilk —6A 18
Belper Rd. Nott —2D 36
Belper St. Ilk —2B 32
Belsay Rd. Nott —6E 15
Belsford Ct. Wat —5A 12
Belton Clo. Sand —1D 54
Belton Dri. W Bri —1F 59
Belton St. Nott —1D 36
Belvedere Av. Nott —1D 36
Belvedere Clo. Keyw —3C 70
Belvoir Clo. Ilk —3H 31
Belvoir Clo. Long E —2G 65
Belvoir Hill. Nott —5B 38
Belvoir Lodge. Carl —3G 39
Belvoir Rd. N'fld —2A 40
Belvoir Rd. W Bri —2C 50
Belvoir St. Huck —3D 4
Belvoir St. Nott —5B 26
Belvoir Ter. Nott —5B 38
Belward St. Nott
—5H 37 (4G 3)
Belwood Clo. Nott —3D 58
Bembridge Ct. Bees —3A 46
Bembridge Dri. Nott —1F 25
Bendigo La. Nott —6C 38
Benedict Ct. Nott —4E 15
Ben Mayo Ct. Nott —2B 24
Benner Av. Ilk —4C 32
Bennerley Av. Ilk —3B 20
Bennerley Ct. Nott —5F 13
Bennerley Rd. Bulw —5F 13
Bennett Rd. Nott —4C 26
Bennett St. Long E —2E 55
Bennett St. Nott —5B 26
Bennett St. Sand —6D 44
Benneworth Clo. Huck —6D 4
Bennington Dri. Nott —6C 34
Ben St. Nott —3D 36
Bentinck Av. Toll —5F 61
Bentinck Ct. Nott
—5A 38 (4H 3)
Bentinck Rd. Carl —5E 27
Bentinck Rd. Nott —3D 36
Bentinck St. Huck —3D 4
Bentley Av. Nott —3C 38
Bentwell Av. Arn —6C 16
Beresford Dri. Ilk —2A 20
Beresford Ho. Long E
—2B 64
Beresford Rd. Long E
—2C 64
Beresford St. Nott —4C 36
Berkeley Av. Long E —1E 65
Berkeley Av. Nott —1G 37
Berle Av. Hean —2C 8
Bernard Av. Huck —2F 5
Bernard St. Nott —6F 25
Bernard Ter. Carr —6F 25
Bernisdale Clo. Nott —4D 14
Berridge Rd. Central. Nott
—1D 36
Berridge Rd. E. Nott —1E 37
Berridge Rd. W. Nott —2C 36
Berriedale Clo. Arn —5E 17
Berry Hill Gro. Ged —6E 27
Berwick Clo. Nott —1G 25
Berwin Clo. Long E —4C 54
Beryldene Av. Wat —6A 12
Besecar Av. Ged —5G 27
Besecar Clo. Ged —5G 27
Bessell La. S'fd —6E 45
Bestwick Av. Hean —4F 9
Bestwood Av. Arn —5A 16
Bestwood Clo. Arn —5A 16
Bestwood Footpath. Huck &
B Vil —6H 5
Bestwood Lodge Dri. Arn
—4G 15
Bestwood Pk. Dri. Nott
—4F 15
Bestwood Pk. Dri. W. Nott
—4B 14

Bestwood Pk. View. Arn
—4A 16
Bestwood Rd. Huck —6G 5
Bestwood Rd. Nott —5A 14
Bestwood Ter. Nott —5B 14
Bethel Gdns. Huck —6A 4
Bethnal Wlk. Nott —6H 13
Betony Clo. Bing —5C 42
Betula Clo. Nott —4A 58
Bevel St. Nott —2D 36
Beverley Clo. Nott —5B 34
Beverley Dri. Kimb —6G 11
Beverley Gdns. Ged —6H 27
Beverley Sq. Nott —3A 38
Bewcastle Rd. Nott —4E 15
Bewick Dri. Nott —4E 39
Bexhill Ct. Bees —2E 47
Bexleigh Gdns. Nott —1G 35
Bexwell Clo. Nott —5C 58
Biant Clo. Nott —4H 23
Bidford Rd. Nott —4E 35
Bidwell Cres. Got —5H 67
Biggart Clo. Bees —3C 56
Biko Sq. Nott —1D 36
Bilberry Wlk. Nott —3A 38
Bilbie Wlk. Nott
—4F 37 (2C 2)
Bilborough Rd. Nott —4B 34
Bilby Gdns. Nott —4B 38
Billesdon Dri. Nott —3D 24
Bingham By-Pass. Bing
—5B 42
Bingham Ind. Pk. Bing
—4E 43
Bingham Rd. Nott —5G 25
Bingham Rd. Rad T —6F 41
Bingley Clo. Nott —3A 35
Birch Av. Bees —1H 57
Birch Av. Carl —2F 39
Birch Av. Nott —2D 36
Birch Av. Nut —1B 22
Birch Clo. Nut —1B 22
Birchdale Av. Huck —6E 5
Birchfield Pk. Hean —6D 8
Birchfield Rd. Arn —5C 16
Birch Lea. Red —5H 15
Birchover Pl. Ilk —2A 20
Birchover Rd. Nott —4C 34
Birch Pas. Nott —4F 37
Birch Rise. Wdbgh —5G 7
Birchwood Av. Breas —6B 54
Birchwood Av. Long E
—1E 65
Birchwood Rd. Nott —5C 34
Bircumshaw's Rd. Hean
—3C 8
Birdcroft La. Ilk —4B 32
Birkdale Clo. Edw —2C 60
Birkdale Clo. Ilk —6H 19
Birkdale Way. Nott —5D 14
Birkin Av. Bees —4A 56
Birkin Av. Nott —2D 36
Birkin Av. Rad T —5G 41
Birkin Av. Rud —5G 59
Birkland Av. Map —3C 26
Birkland Av. Nott
—3G 37 (1D 2)
Birley St. S'fd —6F 45
Birling Clo. Nott —6F 13
Birrell Rd. Nott —1E 37
Bisham Dri. W Bri —4D 50
Bishopdale Clo. Long E
—1C 64
Bishops Clo. Keyw —3C 70
Bishops Rd. Bing —4D 42
Bishop St. E'wd —3B 10
Bishops Way. Huck —2F 5
Bispham Dri. Bees —3C 56
Blackacre. Bur J —2E 29
Blackburn Pl. Ilk —4A 20
Blackett's Wlk. Nott —5A 58
Blackfriars Clo. Nut —5D 22
Blackhill Dri. Carl —1H 39
Black Hills Dri. Ilk —3B 32
Blackrod Clo. Bees —3A 56
Blacksmith Ct. Cotg —2E 63
Blackstone Wlk. Nott —1G 49
Blackthorn Clo. Bing —5G 43

Blackthorn Dri. Nott —3H 23
Blackthorne Dri. E'wd —3A 10
Bladon Clo. Nott —5A 26
Bladon Ct. Nott —3D 36
Bladon Rd. Rud —6F 59
Blair Ct. Nott —2G 49
Blair Gro. Sand —1C 54
Blaise Clo. Nott —5C 58
Blake Clo. Arn —6C 16
Blake Ct. Long E —2D 64
Blakeney Rd. Rad T —6H 41
Blakeney Wlk. Arn —2B 26
Blake Rd. S'fd —5G 45
Blake Rd. W Bri —4B 50
Blake St. Ilk —6B 20
Blandford Av. Long E
—1D 64
Blandford Rd. Bees —6C 46
Blanford Gdns. W Bri —6G 49
Blankney St. Nott —3C 24
Blantyre Av. Nott —4C 14
Blatherwick's Yd. Arn —5B 16
Bleachers Yd. Nott —6D 24
Bleasby St. Nott —5B 38
Bleasdale Clo. Ged —5A 28
Blencathra Clo. W Bri —6E 51
Blenheim Av. Nott —5E 27
Blenheim Clo. Rud —6F 59
Blenheim Cotts. Nott —5H 13
Blenheim Ct. Sand —1D 54
Blenheim Dri. Bees —6C 46
Blenheim Ind. Est. Nott
—5F 13
Blenheim La. Nott —4E 13
Blenheim Vs. Nott —5F 13
Blidworth Clo. Strel —5E 23
Blind La. Breas —5A 54
Bloomsgrove Ind. Est. Nott
—4D 36
Bloomsgrove Rd. Ilk —5B 20
Bloomsgrove St. Nott
—4E 36
Bluebell Bank. Bing —6D 42
Bluebell Clo. Huck —5A 4
Blue Bell Hill Rd. Nott
—3A 38
Bluecoat Clo. Nott
—3G 37 (1D 2)
Bluecoat St. Nott
—3G 37 (1D 2)
Blundell Clo. Nott —1B 38
Blyth Gdns. Nott —5A 26
Blyth St. Nott —6A 26
Blyton Wlk. Nott —6F 15
Boatmans Clo. Ilk —5B 20
Bobbers Mill Bri. Nott
—1B 36
Bobbers Mill Rd. Nott
—2C 36
Boden Dri. Nut —1C 22
Boden St. Nott —4D 36
Bodmin Av. Huck —6A 4
Bodmin Dri. Nott —5A 24
Body Rd. Bees —2B 56
Bohem Rd. Long E —2E 55
Bold Clo. Nott —5H 13
Bolero Clo. Nott —4E 35
Bolingley Way. Huck —5A 4
Bolsover St. Huck —4F 5
Bolton Av. Bees —1C 56
Bolton Clo. W Bri —5C 50
Bolton Ter. Rad T —6F 41
Bond St. Arn —5A 16
Bond St. Nott —5A 38 (4H 3)
Bonetti Clo. Arn —2D 26
Boniface Gdns. Nott —4E 15
Bonington Dri. Arn —6D 16
Bonington Rd. Nott —3B 26
Bonner Hill. Calv —4D 6
Bonner La. Calv —3E 7
Bonner's Rd. Aws —3E 21
Bonnington Clo. Nott —1G 23
(in three parts)
Bonnington Cres. Nott
—3G 37
Bonny Mead. Cotg —3E 63
Bonsall Ct. Long E —5G 55
Bonsall St. Long E —5G 55
Bonser Clo. Carl —2G 39

Booth Clo. Nott
—4H 37 (2F 3)
Borlace Cres. S'fd —5G 45
Borman Clo. Nott —2F 23
Borrowdale Clo. Gam —5F 51
Borrowdale Ct. Bees —1B 56
Borrowdale Dri. Long E
—1C 64
Boscawen Ct. Ilk —4B 20
Bosden Clo. Nott —3D 34
Bosley Sq. Bees —3G 47
Bostock's La. Ris —1B 54
Bostock's La. Sand —2C 54
Boston M. Nott —4D 24
Boston St. Nott
—4H 37 (3G 3)
Bosworth Dri. Newt —2D 10
Bosworth Wlk. Nott —2F 49
Bosworth Way. Long E
—2F 65
Botany Av. Nott —2B 38
Botany Clo. W Bri —2G 59
Botany Dri. Ilk —2D 20
Bothe Clo. Long E —1E 65
Bottle La. Nott —5G 37 (4E 3)
Boundary Cres. Bees —2F 47
Boundary La. Lan M —2G 9
Boundary Rd. Bees —2F 47
Boundary Rd. W Bri —1A 60
Bourne Clo. Bees —2D 46
Bourne M. N'fld —3A 40
Bourne St. N'fld —3A 40
Bournmoor Av. Nott —4C 58
Bovill St. Nott —3D 36
Bowers Av. Nott —2H 37
Bowes Well Rd. Ilk —5A 20
Bowland Clo. Nott —2C 38
Bowland Rd. Bing —5C 42
Bowlwell Av. Nott —5D 14
Bowness Av. Nott —5A 24
Bowness Clo. Gam —4E 51
Boxley Dri. W Bri —1G 59
Boyce Gdns. Nott —6B 26
Boycroft Av. Nott —1B 38
Boyd Clo. Arn —4D 16
Boynton Dri. Nott —6B 26
Bracadale Rd. Nott —4D 14
Bracebridge Dri. Nott —3D 34
Bracey Rise. W Bri —2A 60
Bracken Clo. Carl —5F 27
Bracken Clo. Long E —4D 54
Bracken Clo. Nott —6F 23
Brackendale Av. Arn —5B 16
Brackenfield Dri. Gilt —6D 10
Bracknell Cres. Nott —6B 24
Bracton Ct. Nott —3B 38
Bradbourne Av. Nott —6E 49
Bradbury St. Nott —5C 38
Braddock Clo. Lent —5C 36
Braddon Av. S'fd —2G 45
Bradfield Rd. Nott —6F 23
Bradford Ct. Nott —1G 23
Bradgate Clo. Sand —1D 54
Bradgate Rd. Nott —1E 37
Bradley Ct. Bees —5G 47
Bradley St. Sand —6E 45
Bradleys Yd. Plum —6G 61
Bradley Wlk. Nott —5D 58
Bradman Gdns. Arn —1D 26
Bradmore Av. Rud —5G 59
Bradmore La. Keyw —2A 76
Bradshaw St. Long E —2D 64
Bradwell Clo. Gilt —5E 11
Bradwell Dri. Nott —5D 14
Braefield Clo. Ilk —4G 31
Braemar Av. E'wd —5B 10
Braemar Dri. Ged —6B 28
Braemar Rd. Arn —6A 14
Braidwood Ct. Nott —2D 36
Brailsford Rd. Nott —2C 48
Brailsford Way. Chil —4C 56
Bramber Gro. Nott —6C 58
Bramble Clo. Bees —3D 56
Bramble Clo. Long E —3D 54
Bramble Clo. Nott —4B 24
Bramble Ct. Ged —6H 27
Bramble Dri. Nott —2C 38

Bramble Gdns. Nott —1G 35
Brambleway. Cotg —3G 63
Bramcote Av. Bees —5C 46
Bramcote Dri. Bees —4E 47
Bramcote Dri. Nott —6D 34
Bramcote Dri. W. Bees
—4D 46
Bramcote La. Bees —5C 46
Bramcote La. Nott —1D 46
Bramcote Rd. Bees —4E 47
Bramcote St. Nott —4C 36
Bramcote Wlk. Nott —4C 36
Bramerton Rd. Nott —3C 34
Bramhall Rd. Nott —3C 34
Bramley Ct. Kimb —1H 21
Bramley Grn. Nott —6E 23
Bramley Rd. Nott —6E 23
Brampton Av. Hean —3E 9
Brampton Dri. S'fd —6H 45
Brancaster Clo. Nott —3H 23
Brandish Cres. Nott —4B 58
Brandreth Av. Nott —1B 38
Brandreth Dri. Gilt —6G 11
Brand St. Nott —1B 50
Branklene Clo. Kimb —6G 11
Branksome Wlk. Nott
—1G 49
Bransdale Clo. Long E
—1D 64
Bransdale Rd. Nott —4B 58
Branston Gdns. W Bri
—1H 59
Branston Wlk. Nott —3G 25
Brantford Av. Nott —4D 58
Brassington Clo. Gilt —6D 10
Brassington Clo. W Hal
—1C 30
Braunton Clo. Huck —5B 4
Brayton Cres. Nott —2E 24
Breach Rd. Hean —5E 9
Breadsall Ct. Ilk —4B 20
Breaston Dri. Nott —5E 15
(off Erewash Gdns.)
Breaston La. Ris —2A 54
Brechin Clo. Arn —3D 16
Breckhill Rd. Wd'p & Mapp
—2A 26
Breckswood Dri. Nott —6C 58
Brecon Clo. Long E —5C 54
Brecon Clo. Nott —3G 23
Bredon Clo. Long E —5C 54
Breedon St. Long E —2D 54
Brendon Ct. Bees —3B 46
Brendon Dri. Kimb —6H 11
Brendon Dri. Nott —4G 35
Brendon Gdns. Nott —4G 35
Brendon Gro. Bing —4C 42
Brendon Rd. Nott —4G 35
Brendon Way. Long E
—3C 54
Brentcliffe Av. Nott —2C 38
Brentnall Ct. Bees —1D 56
Bressingham Dri. W Bri
—2G 59
Brett Clo. Huck —6C 4
Brewery St. Kimb —1H 21
Brewhouse Yd. Nott
—6F 37 (6D 2)
Brewsters Clo. Bing —5E 43
Brewsters Rd. Nott —1B 38
Breydon Ind. Cen. Long E
—6H 55
Briar Av. Sand —2D 54
Briarbank Av. Nott —1C 38
Briarbank Wlk. Nott —2C 38
Briar Clo. Bees —2E 47
Briar Clo. Keyw —3D 70
Briar Clo. Huck —6B 4
Briar Ga. Cotg —3G 63
Briar Ga. Long E —3C 54
Briar Rd. Newt —5D 10
Briarwood Av. Nott —2C 38
Briarwood Ct. Sher —4A 26
Brickenell Rd. Calv —3D 6
Brickyard. Huck —5G 5
Brickyard Cotts. Nott —2F 59
Brickyard Dri. Huck —6G 5
Brickyard La. Rad T —6H 41

Brickyard, The. Stan C
—6A 18
Bridge Av. Bees —6E 47
Bridge Ct. Bees —4H 47
Bridge Farm La. Nott —3C 58
Bridge Grn. Wlk. Nott —6E 23
Bridge Gro. W Bri —3A 50
Bridgend Clo. S'fd —6F 45
Bridge Rd. Nott —4D 34
Bridge St. Ilk —3B 20
Bridge St. Lan M —2G 9
Bridge St. Long E —4F 55
Bridge St. Sand —6E 45
Bridgeway Cen. Nott —1G 49
Bridgeway Ct. Nott —1H 49
Bridgford Rd. W Bri —2A 50
Bridgnorth Dri. Nott —3C 58
Bridgnorth Way. Bees
—2G 55
Bridle Rd. Bees —2B 46
Bridlesmith Ga. Nott
—5G 37 (4E 3)
Bridlington St. Nott —2C 36
Bridport Av. Nott —4B 36
Brielen Rd. Rad T —6G 41
Brierfield Av. Nott —1F 59
Brierley Grn. N'fld —2A 40
Brightmoor Ct. Nott —4F 3
Brightmoor St. Nott
—5H 37 (4F 3)
Brights Ter. Ilk —1B 32
Bright St. Ilk —4A 20
Bright St. Nott —4C 36
Brindley Rd. Nott —4C 34
Brinkhill Cres. Nott —2D 58
Brinsley Clo. Nott —6G 23
Brisbane Dri. Nott —5C 14
Brisbane Dri. S'fd —2H 45
Bristol Rd. Ilk —6A 20
Britannia Av. Nott —2C 24
Britannia Rd. Long E —4F 55
Brittania Ct. N'fld —3A 40
Britten Gdns. Nott —3B 38
Brixham Rd. Huck —6B 4
Brixton Rd. Nott —4C 36
Bk. Rd. Lent —5B 48
Broad Clo. Wdbgh —6G 7
Broad Eadow Rd. Nott
—6F 13
Broadfields. Calv —2D 6
Broadgate. Bees —4G 47
Broadgate Av. Bees —4G 47
Broadgate Pk. Bees —3G 47
Broadholme St. Nott —6D 36
Broadhurst Av. Nott —5B 24
Broadlands. Sand —2D 54
Broadleigh Clo. W Bri
—2G 59
Broad Marsh Shopping Cen.
Nott —5G 37 (5E 3)
Broadmead. Bur J —2F 29
Broad Meer. Cotg —2E 63
Broadmere Ct. Arn —4D 16
Broad Oak Clo. Nott —2A 38
Broad Oak Dri. S'fd —4F 55
Broadstairs Rd. Tot —3H 55
Broadstone Clo. W Bri
—6G 49
Broad St. Long E —6F 55
Broad St. Nott —4H 37 (3F 3)
Broad Valley Dri. B Vil
—1D 8
Broad Wlk. Nott —4A 24
Broadway. Hean —4C 8
Broadway. Ilk —4A 20
Broadway. Nott
—5H 37 (5F 3)
Broadway E. Carl —3F 39
Broadwood Ct. Bees —3G 47
Broadwood Rd. Nott —5F 15
Brockdale Gdns. Keyw
—3C 70
Brockenhurst Gdns. Nott
—3B 38
Brockhall Rise. Hean —4E 9
Brockhole Clo. W Bri —6F 51
Brockley Rd. W Bri —4D 50
Brockwood Cres. Keyw
—3C 70

Bromfield Clo. Nott —2E 39
Bromley Clo. Nott —1H 23
Bromley Pl. Nott
—5F 37 (4C 2)
Brompton Clo. Arn —3E 15
Brompton Way. W Bri
—2G 59
Bronte Ct. Nott —3E 37
Brook Av. Arn —5D 16
Brook Clo. Long E —2G 65
Brook Clo. Newt —4D 10
Brook Clo. Nott —1H 23
Brook Ct. Lan M —3F 9
Brook St. Ilk —3D 32
Brooke St. Sand —6D 44
Brookfield Av. Huck —6E 5
Brookfield Ct. Arn —6C 16
Brookfield Rd. Arn —6B 16
Brook Gdns. Arn —6C 16
Brookhill Cres. Nott —6E 35
Brookhill Dri. Nott —6E 35
Brookhill Leys Rd. E'wd
—4A 10
Brookhill St. S'fd —6F 45
Brooklands Av. Hean —3D 8
Brooklands Cres. Ged —6A 28
Brooklands Dri. Ged —6A 28
Brooklands Rd. Nott —2D 38
Brooklyn Clo. Nott —2B 24
Brooklyn Rd. Nott —1B 24
Brook Rd. Bees —3F 47
Brooksby La. Nott —4D 14
Brookside. E'wd —1B 10
Brookside. Huck —6F 5
Brookside Av. Nott —1D 46
Brookside Clo. Long E
—5D 54
Brookside Gdns. Rud —5F 59
Brookside Rd. Rud —5F 59
Brook St. Huck —3E 5
Brook St. Los —1A 8
Brook St. Nott —4H 37 (3F 3)
Brookthorpe Way. Nott
—1E 59
Brook Vale Rd. Lan M —3G 9
Brook View Ct. Keyw —5C 70
Brook View Dri. Keyw
—5C 70
Brookwood Cres. Carl
—2E 39
Broomfield Clo. Sand —6C 44
Broomhill Av. Ilk —3B 32
(in two parts)
Broomhill Pk. View. Huck
—6G 5
Broomhill Rd. Huck —6E 5
Broomhill Rd. Kimb —1A 22
Broomhill Rd. Nott —1A 24
Broom Rd. Calv —3D 6
Broom Wlk. Nott —1D 38
Brora Rd. Nott —6B 14
Broughton Dri. Nott —5A 36
Broughton St. Bees —4F 47
Brownes Rd. Bing —4G 43
Browning Clo. Day —6H 11
Browning Ct. Nott —4F 25
Brown La. Bart —1E 67
Brownlow Rd. Nott —4B 14
Browns Croft. Nott —4B 24
Brown's Flat. Kimb —1H 21
Browns La. Keyw —6G 71
Brown's Rd. Long E —5G 55
Brown St. Nott —2D 36
Broxtowe Av. Kimb —1F 21
Broxtowe Av. Nott —4A 24
Broxtowe Dri. Huck —2E 5
Broxtowe Hall Clo. Nott
—5G 23
Broxtowe Ho. Nott —6D 22
Broxtowe La. Nott —6E 23
Broxtowe Rise. Nott —3H 23
Broxtowe St. Nott —5G 25
Bruce Clo. Nott —1H 49
Bruce Dri. W Bri —4H 49

Brunel Av. Newt —1D 10
Brunel Ter. Nott —4E 37
Brunswick Dri. S'fd —6H 45
Brushfield St. Nott —2C 36
Brussells Ter. Ilk —6B 20
(off Bath St.)
Brusty Pl. Bur J —2E 29
Bryan Ct. Nott —1A 36
Buckfast Way. W Bri —4C 50
Buckingham Av. Huck —3F 5
Buckingham Rd. Sand
—1C 54
Buckingham Rd. Wd'p
—2A 26
Buckland Ct. Nott —3D 36
Buckland Dri. Wdbgh —6G 7
Bucklee Dri. Calv —3C 6
Bucklow Clo. Nott —6B 24
Buckminster Rd. Ilk —5G 31
Bulcote Dri. Bur J —4D 28
Bulcote Rd. Nott —2D 58
Bullace Rd. Nott —2B 38
Bull Clo. Rd. Nott —3C 48
Buller St. Ilk —3C 32
Buller Ter. Nott —4H 25
Bullins Clo. Nott —4G 15
Bullivant St. Nott —3H 37
Bulwell Bus. Cen. Nott
—6G 13
Bulwell High Rd. Nott
—6H 13
Bulwell La. Nott —3B 24
Bulwer Rd. Nott —4D 36
Bunbury St. Nott —2H 49
Bunny La. Keyw —5A 70
Bunting Clo. Ilk —3G 31
Buntings La. Carl —2E 39
Bunting St. Nott —2C 48
Burcot Clo. W Hal —1C 30
Burford Rd. Nott —1D 36
Burford St. Arn —5A 16
Burgass Rd. Nott —2C 38
Burge Clo. Nott —1G 49
Burgh Hall Clo. Bees —3C 56
Burhill. Cotg —3G 63
Burke St. Nott —4E 37
Burleigh Clo. Carl —2H 39
Burleigh Rd. W Bri —5B 50
Burleigh Sq. Bees —1C 56
Burleigh St. Ilk —6B 20
(off Stamford St.)
Burlington Av. Nott —4F 25
Burlington Ct. Nott —4G 25
Burlington Rd. Carl —1H 39
Burlington Rd. Nott —4G 25
Burnaby St. Nott —3B 24
Burnbreck Gdns. Nott
—5E 35
Burndale Wlk. Nott —5C 14
Burnham Av. Bees —1F 57
Burnham Clo. W Hal —1B 30
Burnham Lodge. Nott
—4C 14
Burnham St. Nott —5G 25
Burnham Way. Nott —6G 37
Burnor Pool. Calv —3D 6
Burns Av. Nott
—3E 37 (1A 2)
Burns Ct. Nott —4F 25
Burnside Dri. Bees —1C 46
Burnside Grn. Nott —3D 14
Burnside Gro. Toll —4E 61
Burnside Rd. Nott —3D 34
Burnside Rd. W Bri —6A 50
Burns St. Hean —3B 8
Burns St. Ilk —1A 32
Burns St. Nott —3E 37 (1A 2)
Burnt Ho. Rd. Hean —4B 8
Burnt Oak Clo. Nott —4D 22
Burnwood Dri. Nott —4D 34
Burr La. Ilk —6B 20
Burrows Av. Bees —2F 47
Burrows Ct. Nott —4B 38
Burrows Cres. Bees —2F 47
Burtness Rd. Nott —4C 58
Burton Av. Carl —1D 38
Burton Clo. Carl —1A 40
Burton Dri. Bees —1C 56

Burton Manderfield Ct. Nott
—1G 49
Burton Rd. Carl —1H 39
Burton St. Hean —3C 8
Burton St. Nott
—4G 37 (3D 2)
Burwell St. Nott —3D 36
Bush Clo. Nott —5D 14
Bushy Clo. Long E —1D 64
Bute Av. Nott —5D 36
Butler Av. Rad T —5G 41
Butlers Clo. Huck —6G 5
Butler St. Nott —5C 36
Butterfield Ct. Wat —6A 12
Buttermead Clo. Trow —1F 45
Buttermere Clo. Gam —4E 51
Buttermere Ct. Nott —5G 25
Buttermere Dri. Bees —3D 46
Butterton Clo. Ilk —2C 32
Butt Houses. Nott —5C 36
Butt Rd. Bing —5G 43
Butt St. Sand —6D 44
Buxton Av. Carl —6F 27
Buxton Av. Hean —5D 8
Buxton Ct. Ilk —5H 19
Buxton Grn. Hean —6D 8
Byard La. Nott —5G 37 (5E 3)
Bye Pass Rd. Bees —3G 56
Byfield Clo. Nott —3D 36
Byford Clo. Nott —5A 26
Byley Rd. Nott —4C 34
Byrne Ct. Arn —2D 26
Byron Av. Long E —2D 54
Byron Ct. Nott —5A 38 (4H 3)
Byron Ct. S'fd —2G 45
Byron Cres. Aws —3E 21
Byron Gro. Nott —4G 25
Byron Rd. W Bri —4B 50
Byron St. Day —6H 15
Byron St. Huck —5E 5
Byron St. Ilk —6B 20

Caddaw Av. Huck —5E 5
Cadlan Clo. Nott —6E 15
Cadlan Ct. Nott —6E 15
Caernarvon Pl. Bees —1B 56
Caincross Rd. Nott —2D 34
Cairngorm Dri. Arn —3F 15
Cairns Clo. Nott —2E 25
Cairnsmore Clo. Long E
—4C 54
Cairns St. Nott
—4G 37 (2E 3)
Cairo St. Nott —6D 24
Caister Rd. Nott —5C 58
Caithness Ct. Nott —6F 25
Calcroft Clo. Nott —5A 24
Caldbeck Clo. Gam —4E 51
Caldbeck Ct. Bees —1B 56
Caldbeck Wlk. Nott —6F 15
Calderdale. Nott —6B 34
Calderdale Dri. Long E
—1C 64
Calderhall Gdns. Nott —5G 15
Calder Wlk. Nott —6H 13
Caldon Grn. Nott —3A 14
Caledon Rd. Nott —5F 25
Calladine Clo. Hean —3B 8
Calladine Ct. Nott —1G 23
Callaway Clo. Nott —4E 35
Calstock Rd. Wd'p —2A 26
Calveley Rd. Nott —1E 35
Calver Clo. Nott —5A 36
Calverton Av. Carl —6D 26
Calverton Clo. Bees —3A 56
Calverton Dri. Nott —5D 22
Calverton Rd. Arn —4B 16
Camberley Rd. Nott —5G 13
Camborne Dri. Nott —5A 24
Cambria M. Nott —2G 37
Cambridge Ct. Nott —3D 36
Cambridge Cres. S'fd —1F 45
Cambridge Gdns. Wd'p
—2D 26
Cambridge Rd. Nott —3C 36
Cambridge Rd. W Bri —4C 50
Cambridge St. Carl —6G 27
Camdale Clo. Bees —5B 46

Camden Clo. Nott —5A 38
Camelia Av. Nott —4A 58
Camelot Av. Nott —5E 25
Camelot Cres. Rud —5F 59
Cameron St. Nott —5G 25
Camomile Clo. Nott —6C 14
Camomile Gdns. Nott
—2C 36
Campbell Dri. Carl —1E 39
Campbell Gdns. Arn —4E 17
Campbell Gro. Nott
—4H 37 (2G 3)
Campbell St. Lan M —1G 9
Campbell St. Nott
—4A 38 (2H 3)
Campden Grn. Nott —3C 58
Campion St. Arn —5A 16
Campion Way. Bing —5D 42
Camrose Clo. Nott —1F 35
Canal Side. Bees —2H 57
Canalside. Nott
—6G 37 (6E 3)
(in three parts)
Canal St. Ilk —6C 20
Canal St. Long E —4D 54
Canal St. Nott —6G 37 (6D 2)
Canal St. Sand —6D 44
Canberra Clo. S'fd —2G 45
Canberra Cres. W Bri —1H 59
Canberra Gdns. W Bri
—2H 59
Candleby Clo. Cotg —2F 63
Candleby Ct. Cotg —2F 63
Candleby La. Cotg —2F 63
Candle Meadow. Nott —4F 39
Canning Cir. Nott
—4E 37 (3A 2)
Canning Ter. Nott
—4E 37 (3A 2)
—6A 56
Cannock Way. Long E
Cannon St. Nott —4G 25
Canonbie Clo. Arn —4E 17
Canon Clo. Ilk —2B 20
Cantabury Av. Nott —1D 36
Cantelupe Rd. Ilk —1B 32
Cantley Av. Ged —5G 27
Cantrell Rd. Nott —1A 24
Canver Clo. Nott —3C 34
Canwick Clo. Nott —4C 34
Capenwray Gdns. Nott
—5G 15
Capitol Ct. Nott —4G 35
Caporn Clo. Nott —2A 24
Cardale Rd. Nott —3C 38
Cardiff St. Nott —4B 38
Cardinal Clo. Nott —3A 38
Cardington Clo. Nott —4C 14
Cardwell St. Nott —1D 36
Carew Rd. Nott —3C 58
Carey Rd. Nott —5A 14
Carisbrooke Av. Bees —3G 47
Carisbrooke Av. Ged —6B 28
Carisbrooke Av. Nott —6A 26
Carisbrooke Dri. Nott —6G 25
Carlight Caravan Site. W Bri
—2D 50
Carlingford Rd. Huck —5H 5
Carlisle Av. Nott —6A 14
Carlisle Rd. Carl —1G 39
Carlswark Gdns. Nott
—4D 14
Carlton Bus. & Technology
Cen. Carl —2H 39
Carlton Clo. Hean —2E 9
Carlton Fold. Nott —6B 38
Carlton Grange. Carl —2E 39
Carlton Hill. Carl —2D 38
Carlton M. Carl —2E 39
Carlton Rd. Long E —2D 64
Carlton Rd. Nott
—4A 38 (4H 3)
Carlton Sq. Carl —2G 39
Carlton St. Nott
—5H 37 (4F 3)
Carlton Vale Clo. Carl —6F 27
Carlyle Pl. Hean —2B 8

Carlyle Rd. W Bri —4A 50
Carlyle St. Hean —2B 8
Carman Clo. Wat —5A 12
Carmel Gdns. Arn —1B 26
Carnarvon Clo. Bing —4E 43
Carnarvon Dri. Bur J —2F 29
Carnarvon Gro. Carl —1F 39
Carnarvon Gro. Ged —6H 27
Carnarvon Pl. Bing —5D 42
Carnarvon Rd. W Bri —5B 50
Carnarvon St. N'fld —3A 40
Carnforth Clo. S'fd —6F 45
Carnforth Ct. Nott —5G 15
Carnwood Rd. Nott —1E 25
Caroline Ct. Ilk —3C 32
Caroline Wlk. Nott —2H 37
Carradale Clo. Arn —5E 17
Carrfield Av. Bees —3H 55
Carrington La. Calv —1D 6
Carrington St. Nott
—6G 37 (6E 3)
Carroll Gdns. Nott —2G 49
Carr Rd. Bing —4H 43
Cartbridge. Cotg —3F 63
Carter Av. Rad T —6H 41
Carter Av. Rud —1G 69
Carter Ga. Nott
—5H 37 (5G 3)
Carter Rd. Bees —2A 56
Carterswood Dri. Nut —4F 23
Carver St. Nott —1D 36
Carwood Rd. Bees —2D 46
Casper Ct. Nott —5E 15
(off Kedleston Wlk.)
Castellan Rise. Nott —5G 15
Casterton Rd. Nott —5F 15
Castle Boulevd. Nott
—6D 36 (6B 2)
Castlebridge Office Village.
Nott —1E 49
Castle Bri. Rd. Nott —6E 37
Castle Clo. Calv —3B 6
Castle Ct. Nott —6F 37 (6C 2)
Castlefields. Nott —1G 49
Castle Gdns. Nott —6D 36
Castle Ga. Nott
—5G 37 (5D 2)
(in three parts)
Castle Gro. Nott
—5F 37 (5C 2)
Castle Marina Pk. Nott
—6E 37
Castle Marina Rd. Nott
—1E 49
Castle Meadow Rd. Nott
—6F 37
Castle M. Nott —6E 37
Castle Pk. Ind. Est. Nott
—1F 49
Castle Pl. Nott —5F 37 (5C 2)
Castle Quay. Nott —6F 37
Castle Retail Pk. Nott —3C 36
Castlerigg Clo. W Bri —6E 51
Castle Rd. Nott
—5G 37 (5C 2)
Castle Rock. Nott
—6F 37 (6C 2)
Castle St. E'wd —4C 10
Castle St. Nott —5B 38
Castleton Av. Arn —6B 16
Castleton Av. Carl —6G 27
Castleton Clo. Ilk —2A 20
Castleton Clo. Huck —5B 4
Castleton Clo. Nott —1F 49
Castleton Ct. Nott —1F 23
Castle View. Lan M —1F 9
Castle View. W Bri —5H 49
Castle View Cotts. Bees
—5A 48
Castle Vs. Nott —5B 38
Castle Wlk. Nott —2D 36
Caterham Clo. Nott —2D 34
Cat & Fiddle La. W Hal
—3B 30
Catfoot La. Lamb —5F 17
Catherine Av. Ilk —3B 32

Catherine Clo. Nott —6G 13
Catherine St. Nott —5G 13
Catkin Dri. Gilt —5E 11
Catlow Wlk. Nott —5G 15
Cator Clo. Ged —4F 27
Cator La. Bees —5D 46
Cator La. N. Bees —5D 46
Catriona Cres. Arn —3C 16
Catterley Hill Rd. Nott
—3C 38
Cattle Mkt. Rd. Nott —1H 49
Catton Rd. Arn —5C 16
Caulton St. Nott —3D 36
Caunton Av. Nott —6A 26
Causeway M. Nott —1F 49
Cavan Ct. Nott —2G 49
Cavell Clo. Nott —3B 58
Cavell Ct. Nott —1B 48
Cavendish Av. Ged —5F 27
Cavendish Av. Nott —4H 25
Cavendish Clo. Huck —5G 5
Cavendish Ct. Nott —4B 26
Cavendish Ct. Park
—5E 37 (4A 2)
Cavendish Cres. Carl —5E 27
Cavendish Cres. S'fd —1F 45
Cavendish Cres. N. Nott
—5E 37
Cavendish Cres. S. Nott
—6E 37 (4A 2)
Cavendish Dri. Carl —1G 39
Cavendish M. Nott
—5E 37 (4A 2)
Cavendish Pl. Bees —5F 47
Cavendish Pl. Nott —5E 37
Cavendish Rd. Carl —5E 27
Cavendish Rd. Ilk —3B 32
Cavendish Rd. Long E
—3E 55
Cavendish Rd. E. Nott
—5E 37 (4A 2)
Cavendish Rd. W. Nott
—5E 37
Cavendish St. Arn —5A 16
Cavendish St. Lent —2C 48
Cavendish Vale. Nott —4H 25
Caversham Way. W Hal
—1B 30
Cawdron Wlk. Nott —3C 58
Cawston Gdns. Nott —5H 13
Caxmere Dri. Nott —4F 25
Caxton Clo. N'fld —2A 40
Caythorpe Cres. Nott —3G 25
Caythorpe Rise. Nott —3G 25
Cecil St. Nott —6D 36
Cedar Av. Bees —4G 47
Cedar Av. Long E —2E 65
Cedar Av. Nut —3F 23
Cedar Clo. Bing —5G 43
Cedar Clo. Sand —4D 44
Cedar Ct. Bees —4G 47
Cedar Dri. Keyw —5C 70
Cedar Gro. Arn —5D 16
Cedar Gro. Huck —6F 5
Cedar Gro. Nott —5F 35
Cedarland Cres. Nut —3F 23
Cedar Lodge. Nott
—5E 37 (4A 2)
Cedar Rd. Bees —6E 47
Cedar Rd. Nott —1E 37
Cedars Pk. Ilk —1A 32
Cedars, The. Nott —3H 25
Cedar Tree Rd. Arn —4F 15
Celandine Clo. Nott —6C 14
Celia Dri. Carl —2F 39
Cemetery Rd. S'fd —4G 45
Central Av. Arn —6B 16
Central Av. Bees —2E 47
Central Av. Chil —5D 46
(in two parts)
Central Av. Huck —5E 5
Central Av. Map —3D 26
Central Av. New B —6E 25
Central Av. Sand —5D 44
Central Av. S'fd —3G 45
Central Av. W Bri —3B 50
Central Av. S. Arn —6B 16
Central Ct. Nott —2D 48
Central St. Nott —3A 38

Centre Way. Rad T —5E 41
Centurion Way. Nott —3D 48
Cernan Ct. Nott —2F 23
Cerne Clo. Nott —5D 58
Chaceley Way. Nott —2F 48
Chadborn Av. Got —6H 67
Chaddesden, The. Nott
—2G 37
Chad Gdns. Nott —3E 15
Chadwick Rd. Nott —2C 36
Chain La. Nott —2C 48
Chalfield Clo. Nott —4B 58
Chalfont Dri. Nott —3A 36
Chalons Clo. Ilk —6B 20
Chalons Way. Ilk —6B 20
Chamberlain Clo. Nott
—4A 58
Chambers Av. Ilk —2D 32
Chancery, The. Bees —4C 46
Chandos Av. N'fld —1A 40
Chandos St. N'fld —2A 40
Chandos St. Nott —2A 38
Chantrey Rd. W Bri —4A 50
Chantry Clo. Bees —1D 56
Chantry Clo. Kimb —2A 22
Chantry Clo. Long E —3C 54
Chapel Bar. Nott
—5F 37 (4C 2)
Chapel La. Arn —5A 16
Chapel La. Bing —2D 42
Chapel La. Cotg —2F 63
Chapel M. Ct. Bram —3B 44
Chapel Pl. Kimb —1H 21
Chapel St. Bees —3B 46
Chapel St. E'wd —4B 10
Chapel St. Hean —5E 9
Chapel St. Huck —4E 5
Chapel St. Ilk —6B 20
(in two parts)
Chapel St. Kimb —1H 21
Chapel St. Long E —6G 55
Chapel St. Nott —4E 37
Chapel St. Rud —1G 69
Chapel St. Pl. Ilk —6B 20
Chapman Ct. Nott —2H 35
Chapter Dri. Kimb —2A 22
Chard St. Nott —5D 24
Chard Ter. Nott —5D 24
Charlbury Ct. Bees —6B 34
Charlbury Rd. Nott —3G 35
Charlecote Dri. Nott —6D 34
Charlecote Pk. Dri. W Bri
—1G 59
Charles Av. Chil —2C 56
Charles Av. E'wd —3D 10
Charles Av. Lent A —2G 47
Charles Av. Sand —5D 44
Charles Av. S'fd —3H 45
Charles Clo. Ged —5H 27
Charles Clo. Ilk —3D 32
Charles St. Arn —6A 16
Charles St. Long E —1F 65
Charles St. Rud —6G 59
Charlesworth Av. Nott
—1C 36
Charlock Clo. Nott —6C 14
Charlock Gdns. Bing —6D 42
Charlotte Clo. Arn —3A 16
Charlotte Gro. Bees —2D 46
Charlotte St. Ilk —4A 20
Charlton Av. Long E —4H 55
Charlton Gro. Bees —1F 57
Charnock Av. Nott —6B 36
Charnwood Av. Bees —5D 46
Charnwood Av. Keyw —5C 70
Charnwood Av. Long E
—3D 65
Charnwood Av. Sand —1C 54
Charnwood Gdns. Nott
—6F 25
Charnwood Gro. Bing —5D 42
Charnwood Gro. Huck —4B 4
Charnwood Gro. W Bri
—4A 50
Charnwood La. Arn —1C 26
Charnwood Way. Wdbgh
—6H 7
Charter Pk. Ilk —2A 32

Chartwell Av. Rud —6F **59**
Chartwell Gro. Nott —2E **27**
Chatham Clo. Nott —1A **24**
Chatham St. Nott —3G **37**
Chatsworth Av. Bees —3C **56**
Chatsworth Av. Carl —1G **39**
Chatsworth Av. Long E
—1A **66**
Chatsworth Av. Nott —5D **24**
Chatsworth Av. Rad T
—5G **41**
Chatsworth Clo. Sand
—1D **54**
Chatsworth Ct. Huck —5E **5**
Chatsworth Ct. W Hal
—1B **30**
Chatsworth Dri. Huck —5E **5**
Chatsworth Rd. W Bri
—3D **50**
Chaucer St. Ilk —6B **20**
Chaucer St. Nott
—4F **37** (2B **2**)
Chaworth Av. Nut —4A **12**
Chaworth Rd. Bing —5D **42**
Chaworth Rd. Colw —3H **39**
Chaworth Rd. W Bri —5A **50**
Cheadle Clo. Bilb —1D **34**
Cheadle Clo. Map —5D **26**
Cheapside. Nott
—5G **37** (4E **3**)
Cheddar Rd. Nott —5C **58**
Chedington Av. Nott —1F **27**
Chediston vale. Nott —5F **15**
Chedworth Clo. Nott —4B **38**
Chelmsford Rd. Nott —1A **24**
*Chelmsford Ter. Nott —5D **24***
(off Chelmsford Rd.)
Chelsbury Ct. Arn —6A **16**
Chelsea St. Nott —6D **24**
Cheltenham Clo. Tot —3H **55**
Cheltenham St. Nott —3C **24**
Chennel Nook. Cotg —3G **63**
Chepstow Rd. Nott —5C **58**
Cherhill Clo. Nott —6B **58**
Cheriton Dri. Ilk —4G **19**
Cherry Av. Huck —6F **5**
Cherry Clo. Arn —5A **16**
Cherry Clo. Breas —5A **54**
Cherry Hill. Keyw —4D **70**
Cherry Orchard. Cotg —2E **63**
Cherry Orchard Mt. Nott
—1F **25**
Cherry St. Bing —5F **43**
Cherry Tree Clo. Ilk —3H **31**
Cherry Tree Clo. Rad T
—1F **53**
Cherry Tree La. Edw —2D **60**
Cherry Wood Dri. Nott
—2H **35**
Cherrywood Gdns. Nott
—1C **38**
Chertsey Clo. Nott —6B **26**
Chertsey Ct. W Hal —1B **30**
Cherwell Ct. Nott —1F **23**
Chesham Clo. Nut —4D **22**
Chesham Dri. Bees —1B **46**
Chesham Dri. Nott —5F **25**
Chesil Av. Nott —4B **36**
Chesil Cotts. Nott —4B **36**
Cheslyn Dri. Nott —1A **36**
Chesterfield Av. Bing —5E **43**
Chesterfield Av. Ged —4F **27**
Chesterfield Av. Long E
—6H **55**
Chesterfield Ct. Ged —4F **27**
Chesterfield Dri. Bur J
—2G **29**
Chesterfield St. Carl —2F **39**
Chester Grn. Bees —4G **47**
Chesterman Dri. Aws —3D **20**
Chester Rd. Nott —4D **38**
Chestnut Av. Bees —5F **47**
Chestnut Av. Bing —5E **43**
Chestnut Av. Nott —5D **26**
Chestnut Bank. Hean —4B **8**
Chestnut Dri. Nut —6B **12**
Chestnut Gro. Arn —4C **16**
Chestnut Gro. Bur J —3F **29**
Chestnut Gro. Ged —6H **27**

Chestnut Gro. Huck —1H **13**
Chestnut Gro. Nott —2G **37**
Chestnut Gro. Rad T —5F **41**
Chestnut Gro. Sand —4C **44**
Chestnut Gro. W Bri —4H **49**
Chestnut La. Bart —1E **67**
Chestnut Rd. Lan M —2E **9**
Chestnuts, The. Long E
—5C **54**
Chestnuts, The. Nott —6B **26**
Chestnut, The. Rad T —6E **41**
Chettles Ind. Est. Nott
—4B **36**
Chetwin Rd. Nott —4D **34**
Chetwynd Rd. Chil —2B **56**
Chetwynd Rd. Tot —3A **56**
Cheverton Ct. Nott —2G **37**
Cheviot Clo. Arn —3F **15**
Cheviot Ct. Bees —2C **56**
Cheviot Rd. Long E —4C **54**
Chewton Av. E'wd —4C **10**
Chewton St. E'wd —4B **10**
Cheyny Clo. Nott —2G **49**
Chichester Clo. Ilk —1C **32**
Chichester Clo. Nott —6C **14**
Chichester Dri. Cotg —1E **63**
Chidlow Rd. Nott —2D **34**
Chigwell Clo. Nut —5D **22**
Chillon Way. Huck —5B **4**
Chiltern Clo. Arn —3F **15**
Chiltern Dri. W Hal —1C **30**
Chiltern Gdns. Long E
—4C **54**
Chiltern Way. Nott —1F **25**
Chilton Dri. Wat —6A **12**
Chilvers Clo. Nott —6E **15**
Chilwell Ct. Nott —6B **14**
Chilwell La. Bram —4B **46**
Chilwell Retail Pk. Bees
(in two parts) —4C **56**
Chilwell Rd. Bees —6F **47**
Chilwell St. Nott —6D **36**
Chine Gdns. W Bri —6G **49**
Chingford Rd. Nott —1E **35**
Chippendale St. Nott —6D **36**
Chippenham Rd. Nott —1F **25**
Chisbury Grn. Nott —6B **58**
Chisholm Way. Nott —1E **25**
Chiswick Ct. Nott —4G **25**
Christchurch Rd. Huck
—1D **12**
Christina Av. Nott —3A **24**
Christina Cres. Nott —3A **24**
Christine Clo. Huck —2G **5**
Christine Ct. Nott —2C **38**
Christopher Clo. Nott —3F **35**
Church Av. Day —6A **16**
Church Av. Long E —3C **54**
Church Av. Nott —6D **36**
Church Clo. Bing —4F **43**
Church Clo. Day —6A **16**
Church Clo. Nott —3G **37**
Church Clo. Trow —5E **33**
Church Ct. Rad T —6E **41**
Church Cres. Bees —1A **56**
Church Cres. Nott —6H **15**
Church Croft. W Bri —3B **50**
Churchdale Av. S'fd —2G **45**
Church Dri. Day —6H **15**
Church Dri. Huck —4E **5**
Church Dri. Ilk —2H **19**
Church Dri. Keyw —4D **70**
Church Dri. Nott —6F **25**
Church Dri. Sand —4D **44**
Church Dri. W Bri —4B **50**
Church Dri. E. Day —6A **16**
Churchfield Ct. Nott —4F **15**
Churchfield La. Nott —2C **36**
Churchfield Ter. Nott —5C **24**
Churchfield Way. Nott
—4E **15**
Church Ga. Clip —5C **62**
Church Gro. Nott —6C **36**
Church Hill. Kimb —1H **21**
Church Hill. Plum —6G **61**
Churchill Clo. Arn —1B **26**
Churchill Dri. Rud —6F **59**

Churchill Dri. S'fd —3G **45**
Churchill Pk. Colw —4H **39**
Church La. Arn —4A **16**
Church La. Att —4D **56**
Church La. Bart —1E **67**
Church La. Bing —4F **43**
Church La. Bulw —6A **14**
Church La. Coss —5E **21**
Church La. Cotg —2E **63**
Church La. Lin & Huck —1E **5**
Church La. Plum —6G **61**
Church La. S'fd —4F **45**
Church La. Thrum —4B **66**
Church Meadow. Calv —4D **6**
Church M. Nott —2H **49**
Churchmoor La. Arn —4A **16**
Church Rd. B Vil —1C **14**
Church Rd. Bur J —3F **29**
Church Rd. Greas —3G **11**
Church Rd. Nott —2H **37**
Churchside Gdns. Nott
—1C **36**
Church Sq. Hean —4D **8**
Church Sq. Nott —6D **36**
Church St. Arn —5B **16**
Church St. Bees —5F **47**
Church St. Bing —5F **43**
Church St. Bram —3B **46**
Church St. Carl —2G **39**
Church St. E'wd —4A **10**
Church St. Got —6H **67**
Church St. Hean —4D **8**
Church St. Ilk —3H **19**
Church St. Lent —6C **36**
Church St. Old B —5C **24**
Church St. Rud —6G **59**
Church St. Sand —4D **44**
Church St. Shelf —6H **29**
Church St. S'fd —4F **45**
Church View. Ged —6H **27**
Church View. Ilk —2A **32**
Church View. Los —1A **8**
Church View Clo. Arn —4F **15**
Church Wlk. Carl —2G **39**
Church Wlk. E'wd —3B **10**
Church Wlk. S'fd —4F **45**
Church Wlk. Wdbgh —6G **7**
Church Way. Ilk —3H **19**
Churnet Clo. Nott —1C **58**
Churston Ct. Bees —5G **47**
Cinderhill Footway. Nott
—3B **24**
Cinderhill Gro. Ged —5G **27**
Cinderhill Rd. Nott —3H **23**
Cinderhill Wlk. Nott —1H **23**
Citadel St. Nott —4C **36**
City Rd. Bees —4G **47**
City Rd. Nott —2B **48**
City, The. Bees —4G **47**
Clandon Dri. Nott —5F **25**
Clanfield Rd. Nott —2E **35**
Clapham St. Nott —4C **36**
Clara Mt. Rd. Hean —4E **9**
Clarborough Dri. Arn —1C **26**
Clare Clo. Nott —3C **24**
Clarehaven. S'fd —6G **45**
Claremont Av. Bees —3C **46**
Claremont Av. Huck —6E **5**
Claremont Dri. W Bri —2G **59**
Claremont Gdns. Nott —6F **25**
Claremont Rd. Nott —6F **25**
Claremont Ter. Nott
—3E **37** (1A **2**)
Clarence Ct. Nott —4A **38**
Clarence Rd. Bees —3D **56**
Clarence Rd. Long E —1E **65**
Clarence St. Nott —4A **38**
Clarendon Chambers. Nott
—4F **37** (2B **2**)
Clarendon Ct. Nott —1F **37**
Clarendon Pk. Nott —1F **37**
Clarendon St. Nott
—4F **37** (2B **2**)
Clare St. Nott —4G **37** (3E **3**)
Clare Valley. Nott
—5F **37** (5B **2**)
Clarewood Gro. Nott —6C **58**
Clarges St. Nott —1A **24**
Clarke Av. Arn —5B **16**

Clarke Av. Los —3A **8**
Clarke Dri. Long E —3C **64**
Clarke Rd. Nott —1A **50**
Clarke's La. Bees —1D **56**
Clarkson Dri. Bees —5H **47**
Claude St. Nott —2C **48**
Claxton St. Hean —3B **8**
Claxton Ter. Hean —3B **8**
Clay Av. Nott —4C **26**
Claye St. Long E —6G **55**
Clayfield Clo. Nott —1G **23**
Clay La. Hean —3D **8**
Claypole Rd. Nott —2D **36**
Clayton Ct. Bees —4G **47**
Clayton Croft. Nott —4D **36**
Clayton Gro. Los —1A **8**
Clether Rd. Nott —3E **35**
Cleve Av. Bees —6D **46**
Cleveland Av. Long E —4H **55**
Cleveland Clo. Nott —4C **36**
Cleveley's Rd. Bees —2G **55**
Clevely Way. Nott —2C **58**
Cliff Boulevd. Kimb —6H **11**
Cliff Cres. Rad T —5F **41**
Cliff Dri. Rad T —4G **41**
Cliffe Hill Av. S'fd —4F **45**
Cliffgrove Av. Bees —5D **46**
Cliffmere Wlk. Nott —4B **58**
Clifford Av. Bees —3E **47**
Clifford Clo. Keyw —3D **70**
Clifford Clo. Long E —3C **64**
Clifford Ct. Nott —4D **36**
Clifford St. Long E —6G **55**
Clifford St. Nott —3D **36**
Cliff Rd. Carl —3F **39**
Cliff Rd. Nott —5H **37** (5F **3**)
Cliff Rd. Rad T —4G **41**
Cliffs, The. Rad T —4G **41**
Cliff, The. Nott —2D **48**
Cliff Way. Rad T —5F **41**
Clifton Av. Long E —6A **56**
Clifton Av. Rud —5G **59**
Clifton Boulevd. Nott —1B **48**
Clifton Cres. Att —2E **57**
Clifton Grn. Nott —3B **58**
Clifton Gro. Ged —5G **27**
Clifton La. Rud —5E **59**
Clifton M. Nott —5E **37**
Clifton Rd. Rud —6F **59**
Clifton St. Bees —5G **47**
Clifton Ter. Nott
—6E **37** (6A **2**)
Clinton Av. Nott —1F **37**
Clinton Ct. Nott
—4G **37** (2D **2**)
Clinton St. Arn —6A **16**
Clinton St. Bees —4E **47**
Clinton St. E. Nott
—4G **37** (3E **3**)
Clinton St. W. Nott
—4G **37** (3E **3**)
Clinton Ter. Nott —4E **37**
Clipstone Av. Map —3C **26**
Clipstone Av. Nott
—3G **37** (1D **2**)
Clipstone Av. Strel —5D **22**
Clipston La. Plum —6H **61**
Clive Cres. Kimb —2A **22**
Cliveden Grn. Nott —4B **58**
Cloister Sq. Nott —1C **48**
Cloisters, The. Bees —3G **47**
Cloister St. Nott —1C **48**
Close Quarters. Bees —3C **46**
Close, The. Bees —1D **56**
Close, The. Nott —4G **25**
Cloud Av. S'fd —4H **45**
Clouds Hill. Nott —5C **58**
Cloudside Rd. Sand —4D **44**
Clough Ct. Nott —2H **35**
Cloverdale. Cotg —3G **63**
Cloverfields. Calv —2E **7**
Clover Grn. Nott —4B **24**
Cloverlands. W Bri —2G **59**
Cloverlands Dri. Wat —6A **12**
Cloverlands Dri. Wat —6A **12**
Clover Rise. Newt —4D **10**
Club Row. Ilk —1A **32**
Clumber Av. Bees —6D **46**
Clumber Av. Map —3C **26**

Clumber Av. N'fld —2A **40**
Clumber Av. Sher R —1F **37**
Clumber Ct. Ilk —2B **20**
Clumber Ct. Nott —6E **37**
Clumber Cres. N. Nott
—5E **37**
Clumber Cres. S. Nott
—6E **37** (6A **2**)
Clumber Dri. Rad T —4G **41**
Clumber Rd. W Bri —4B **50**
Clumber Rd. E. Nott
—5E **37** (5A **2**)
Clumber Rd. W. Nott —5E **37**
Clumber St. Huck —5G **5**
Clumber St. Long E —6F **55**
Clumber St. Nott
—4G **37** (3E **3**)
Clyde Ter. Nott
—3E **37** (1A **2**)
Coach Dri. E'wd —1B **10**
Coachways. M'ley —4D **18**
Coates Av. Huck —2D **4**
Coatsby Rd. Kimb —6H **11**
Cobden Chambers. Nott
—5G **37** (4E **3**)
Cobden St. Long E —6F **55**
Cobden St. Nott —4C **36**
Cockayne Clo. Sand —2D **54**
Cockerhouse Rd. E'wd
—1A **10**
Cockington Rd. Nott —4C **34**
Cockleys. Long E —1E **65**
Codrington Gdns. Nott
—5G **15**
Cogenhoe Wlk. Arn —3B **16**
Cogley La. Bing —5G **43**
Cohen Clo. Arn —1D **26**
Cokefield Av. Nut —4F **23**
Colborn St. Nott —2B **38**
Colchester Rd. Nott —6E **23**
Coleby Av. Nott —1C **48**
Coleby Rd. Nott —1C **48**
Coledale. W Bri —5E **51**
Coleridge Cres. Day —6H **15**
Coleridge St. Nott —3D **36**
Colesbourne Rd. Nott
—3D **58**
Coles Wlk. Nott —5E **15**
Colin Broughton Ct. Nott
—6B **14**
Colinwood Av. Nott —4C **14**
College Dri. Nott —3B **58**
College Rd. Bees —2E **47**
College St. Long E —2D **54**
College St. Nott
—4F **37** (3B **2**)
Colley Moor Leys La. Nott
—3D **58**
Colliers Way. Nott —3G **23**
Colliery Clo. Nott —2F **49**
Collin Av. Sand —1D **54**
Collin Grn. Nott —3H **25**
Collington St. Bees —5E **47**
Collington Way. W Bri
—6H **49**
Collingwood Clo. Nott
—1C **58**
Collingwood Rd. Long E
—1F **65**
Collins Clo. Nott —2F **23**
Collins Homes. Bees —2E **47**
Collin St. Bees —5F **47**
Collin St. Nott —6G **37** (6E **3**)
Collison St. Nott —3D **36**
Collyer Rd. Calv —2B **6**
Colly Ga. Kimb —2A **22**
Collygate Rd. Nott —2H **49**
Colmon Clo. Nott —6E **15**
Colmon Wlk. Nott —6E **15**
Colonsay Clo. Trow —6F **33**
Colston Cres. W Bri —1H **59**
Colston Ga. Cotg —2F **63**
Colston Rd. Nott —5A **14**
Colville Ct. Nott —2F **37**
Colville St. Nott —2F **37**
Colville Ter. Nott —2F **37**
Colville Vs. Nott —2F **37**
Colwick Bus. Pk. Colw
—4H **39**

Colwick Ind. Est. Colw
(in two parts) —4H **39**
Colwick Lodge. Carl —3H **39**
Colwick Loop Rd. Colw
—4G **39**
Colwick Mnr. Farm. Colw
—4G **39**
Colwick Pk. Clo. Colw
—4G **39**
Colwick Rd. Nott —6B **38**
(in two parts)
Colwick Rd. W Bri —2A **50**
Colwick Wood Ct. Nott
—5C **38**
Comery Av. Nott —2C **38**
Comfrey Clo. Nott —6C **14**
Commerce Sq. Nott
—5H **37** (5F **3**)
Commercial Av. Bees —5F **47**
Commercial Rd. Keyw
—5C **70**
Commercial Rd. Nott —6H **13**
Commodore Gdns. Nott
—5A **24**
Common La. Bees —5A **46**
Common La. Huck —5A **4**
Common La. Stan —4A **30**
Common La. Wat —6B **12**
Commons Clo. Newt —5C **10**
Common, The. Huck —5A **4**
Compton Acres. W Bri
—5F **49**
Compton Acres Shopping Cen.
W Bri —6G **49**
Compton Rd. Nott —4F **25**
Comyn Gdns. Nott
—3H **37** (1F **3**)
Conduit Clo. Nott —1G **49**
Coney Wlk. Nott —5D **14**
Conifer Cres. Nott —6C **58**
Conifer Wlk. Nott —2C **38**
Coningsby Gdns. E. Wd'p
—3B **26**
Coningsby Rd. Wd'p —2B **26**
Coningswath Rd. Carl —5E **27**
Conisborough Ter. Nott
—2G **49**
Coniston Av. Ilk —4H **31**
Coniston Av. Nott —5A **24**
Coniston Clo. Gam —4E **51**
Coniston Rd. Bees —2D **46**
Coniston Rd. Huck —3D **4**
Coniston Rd. Long E —3C **54**
Connelly Clo. Arn —1E **27**
Connelly Ct. Bulw —2B **24**
Connery. Huck —3E **5**
Connery M. Bees —4B **56**
Constance St. Nott —6E **25**
Convent St. Nott
—4H **37** (3F **3**)
Conway Av. Carl —2A **40**
Conway Clo. Nott —2G **37**
Conway Cres. Carl —1A **40**
Conway Gdns. Arn —1A **26**
Conway Rd. Carl —2H **39**
Conway Rd. Huck —2D **12**
Conway St. Long E —5G **55**
Conway Wlk. Nott —2G **37**
Cook Dri. Ilk —3C **32**
Cookson Av. Ged —5F **27**
Coombe Clo. Nott —6A **36**
Co-operative Av. Huck —3F **5**
Co-operative St. Long E
—6G **55**
Cooper Clo. Arn —1E **27**
Cooper Clo. Nott —1F **23**
Coopers Grn. Nott —1E **47**
Cooper St. N'fld —3A **40**
Copeland Av. S'fd —3G **45**
Copeland Gro. Bing —4C **42**
Copeland Rd. Huck —3G **5**
Copenhagen Ct. Nott —6H **25**
Cope St. Nott —3D **36**
Coppice Av. Ilk —2H **19**
Coppice Clo. Huck —6C **4**
Coppice Ct. Hean —6D **8**
Coppice Dri. E'wd —2H **9**
Coppice Dri. Hean —6D **8**

Coppice Gro. Nott —5B **26**
Coppice Rd. Arn —5B **16**
Copplestone Dri. Nott —1E **27**
Copse Clo. Bur J —2F **29**
Copseside Clo. Long E
—5C **54**
Copse, The. Bees —3B **46**
Copse, The. Huck —5G **5**
Copse, The. Ilk —2H **19**
Corben Gdns. Nott —6F **13**
Corby Rd. Nott —6A **26**
Corfield Av. Hean —6D **8**
Coriander Dri. Nott —4B **24**
Corn Clo. Cotg —3E **63**
Cornell Dri. Arn —5D **16**
Cornfield Rd. Kimb —6G **11**
Cornfields, The. Nott —5F **15**
Cornhill Rd. Carl —1D **38**
Cornwall Av. Bees —1A **58**
Cornwall Av. Long E —5A **56**
Cornwallis Clo. Long E
—1F **65**
Cornwall Rd. Arn —6G **15**
Coronation Av. Nott —3F **49**
Coronation Av. Sand —4C **44**
Coronation Rd. B Vil —1C **14**
Coronation Rd. Coss —5D **20**
Coronation Rd. Huck —3D **4**
Coronation Rd. M'ley —4D **18**
Coronation Rd. Nott —4B **26**
Coronation Rd. Nut —2B **22**
Coronation Rd. Stan —3A **30**
Coronation St. Ilk —1B **32**
Coronation Wlk. Ged —6A **28**
Corporation Cotts. Bul
—2H **29**
Corporation Oaks. Nott
—2G **37**
Corporation Rd. Ilk —2C **38**
Corrington Gdns. Nott
—5G **15**
Corsham Gdns. Nott —2C **38**
Cosby Rd. Nott —6B **38**
Cossall Rd. Trow —2E **33**
Costock Av. Nott —3F **25**
Cotgrave Av. Ged —5H **27**
Cotgrave Clo. Strel —5E **23**
Cotgrave La. Toll —2H **61**
Cotgrave Rd. Cotg —5H **63**
Cotgrave Rd. Plum —6H **61**
Cotmanhay Rd. Ilk —4A **20**
Coton Clo. Nott —2E **59**
Cotswold Clo. Long E
—5D **54**
Cotswold Ct. Bees —2D **46**
Cotswold Rd. Nott —6E **23**
Cottage Clo. Ilk —4H **19**
Cottage Garden La. Hean
—3B **8**
Cottage Meadow. Colw
—5H **39**
Cottage Ter. Nott
—4E **37** (3A **2**)
Cottam Dri. Nott —5D **14**
Cottam Gdns. Nott —5D **14**
Cottesmore Rd. Nott —5D **36**
County Bus. Pk. Nott —6A **38**
County Rd. Ged —4E **27**
County Rd. Nott —1A **50**
Court Cres. Nott —5F **35**
Courtenay Gdns. Nott
—2H **37**
Court Gdns. W Bri —1F **59**
Courtleet Way. Nott —2H **23**
Courtney Clo. Nott —4E **35**
Court St. Nott —2D **36**
Court View. Nott
—5E **37** (4A **2**)
Court Yd. Bees —3B **46**
Covedale Rd. Nott —2G **25**
Coventry Ct. Nott —2A **24**
Coventry Rd. Bees —4G **47**
Coventry Rd. Nott —6H **13**
(in two parts)
Covert Clo. Bur J —2E **29**
Covert Clo. Huck —5G **5**
Covert Clo. Keyw —3D **70**

Covert Cres. Rad T —6H **41**
Covert Rd. W Bri —5D **50**
Cowdrey Gdns. Arn —1D **26**
Cowen St. Nott
—4H **37** (3F **3**)
Cowlairs. Nott —6C **14**
Cow La. Bees —3B **46**
Cowley St. Old B —4B **24**
Cowper Rd. Newt —5C **10**
Cowper Rd. Wd'p —3A **26**
Coxmoor Ct. Nott —4E **15**
Coxmore Clo. Edw —1E **61**
Crabtree Field. Nott —5F **39**
Crabtree Rd. Nott —1G **23**
Cragdale Rd. Nott —2G **25**
Cragmoor Rd. Bur J —4E **29**
Craig St. Long E —6G **55**
Crammond Clo. Nott —1F **49**
Crampton Ct. Nott —5E **15**
Cramworth Gro. Nott —4H **25**
Cranberry Clo. W Bri —5F **49**
Cranborne Clo. Trow —1F **45**
Cranbourne Gro. Huck —4C **4**
Cranbrook St. Nott
—4H **37** (3F **3**)
Cranfield Wlk. Nott —3D **58**
Cranfleet Way. Long E
—6D **54**
Cranford Gdns. W Bri
—1G **59**
Cranmer Gro. Nott —2G **37**
Cranmer St. Ilk —6B **20**
Cranmer St. Long E —5F **55**
Cranmer St. Nott —2G **37**
Cranmore Clo. Arn —3C **16**
Cransley Av. Nott —6D **34**
Cranston Av. Arn —4B **16**
Cranston Rd. Bees —2C **46**
Cranthorne Dri. Nott —3E **39**
Crantock Gdns. Keyw
—4D **70**
Cranwell Ct. Nott —1F **23**
Cranwell Rd. Nott —6G **13**
Craster Dri. Arn —3C **16**
Craster Dri. Nott —5F **13**
Craven Rd. Nott —2C **36**
Crawford Av. S'fd —3F **45**
Crawford Clo. Nott —4E **35**
Crawford Rise. Arn —5E **17**
Creeton Grn. Nott —5D **58**
Crescent Av. Carl —6G **27**
Crescent, The. Chil —2C **56**
Crescent, The. Nott —1H **37**
Crescent, The. Rad T —6G **41**
Crescent, The. Ris —2A **54**
Crescent, The. Stan C
—1A **30**
Crescent, The. S'fd —2G **45**
Crescent, The. Tot —3A **56**
Crescent, The. Wd'p —3A **26**
Cresswell Rd. Bees —6B **46**
Cressy Rd. Nott —3D **58**
Cresta Gdns. Nott —5H **25**
Crest View. Nott —4F **25**
Crewe Clo. Nott —3D **36**
Cribb Clo. Nott —4F **49**
Crich View. Nott —5G **25**
Cricketers Ct. W Bri —2B **50**
Criftin Rd. Bur J —3G **29**
Critchley St. Ilk —6B **20**
Critch's Flat. Kimb —1H **21**
Crocus Pl. Nott —6H **37**
Crocus St. Nott —1G **49**
Croft Av. Huck —6E **5**
Croft Cres. Aws —2E **21**
Crofton Clo. Bees —5D **46**
Crofton Clo. Nott —3H **35**
Crofton Rd. Bees —5D **46**
Croft Rd. Arn —5B **16**
Croft Rd. Edw —1C **60**
Croft Rd. Keyw —4B **70**
Crofts, The. Bing —5E **43**
Cromarty Ct. Nott —1F **49**
Cromdale Clo. Arn —4E **17**
Cromer Rd. Nott —2B **38**
Cromford Av. Carl —1F **39**
Cromford Clo. Lan M —1F **9**
Cromford Clo. Long E —2C **64**

Cromford Rd. Lan M —1D **8**
Cromford Rd. W Bri —5D **50**
Cromford Rd. Ind. Est. Lan M
—1F **9**
Crompton Rd. Ilk —1D **44**
Cromwell Av. Ilk —4C **32**
Cromwell Cres. Lamb —5B **16**
Cromwell Rd. Bees —4E **47**
Cromwell St. Carl —2G **39**
Cromwell St. Gilt —5D **10**
Cromwell St. Nott
—4E **37** (2A **2**)
Cromwell Ter. Ilk —4B **20**
Crookdole La. Calv —3D **6**
Cropston Clo. W Bri —1A **60**
Cropton Cres. Nott —3H **35**
Cropton Gro. Bing —5C **42**
Cropwell Gdns. Rad T
—1G **53**
Cropwell Grn. Nott —3B **38**
Cropwell Rd. Rad T —6F **41**
Crosby Rd. W Bri —2B **50**
Crossdale Dri. Keyw —3C **70**
Crossdale Wlk. Nott —5C **14**
Crossfield Ct. Nott —5E **15**
Crossfield Dri. Nott —5E **15**
Crossgate Dri. Nott —2E **49**
Crosshill. Cotg —2G **63**
Crosshill Dri. Ilk —4G **31**
Crosslands Meadow. Colw
—5H **39**
Crossley St. Nott —5F **25**
Crossman St. Nott —5F **25**
Cross St. Arn —5H **15**
Cross St. Bees —4F **47**
Cross St. Carl —1F **39**
Cross St. E'wd —3C **10**
Cross St. Long E —5G **55**
Cross St. N'fld —2A **40**
Cross St. Sand —5A **44**
Cross, The. Cotg —2E **63**
Crowborough Av. Nott
—1E **47**
Crow Ct. Bing —5G **43**
Crowcroft Way. Long E
—3D **54**
Crow Hill Rd. Carl —2H **39**
Crowley Clo. Nott —3C **34**
Crown Clo. Long E —6C **54**
Crown Hill Way. Stan C
—1A **30**
Crow Pk. Dri. Bur J —4E **29**
Crowthorne Clo. Nott —4C **14**
Crowthorne Gdns. Nott
—4C **14**
Croxall Clo. Nott —1C **58**
Croydon Rd. Nott —4C **36**
Crummock Clo. Bees —3C **46**
Crusader Ct. Nott —4A **58**
Cuillin Clo. Long E —4C **54**
Cuillin Clo. Nott —3D **14**
Culbert Lodge. Nott —6D **24**
Culbert Pl. Nott —6D **24**
Culdrose Wlk. Nott —6A **26**
Cullens Ct. Nott —5G **25**
Cumberland Av. Bees —5D **46**
Cumberland Pl. Nott
—5F **37** (4C **2**)
Curie Ct. Nott —1C **48**
Curlew Clo. Nott —4E **39**
Curlew Wharf. Nott —1D **48**
Cursley Way. Bees —3C **56**
Curtis St. Huck —5E **5**
Curzon Av. Carl —2D **38**
Curzon Ct. Nott —3H **37**
Curzon Gdns. Nott —3H **37**
Curzon Pl. Nott
—4H **37** (2F **3**)
Curzon St. Got —6H **67**
Curzon St. Long E —3D **54**
Curzon St. N'fld —2A **40**
Curzon St. Nott
—4H **37** (2F **3**)
Cutthrough La. Nott —3H **47**
Cuxton Clo. Nott —6D **22**
Cycle Rd. Nott —5C **36**
Cypress Ct. Huck —6A **4**
Cyprus Av. Bees —4F **47**
Cyprus Dri. Bees —4F **47**

Cyprus Rd. Nott —1G **37**
Cyril Av. Bees —4E **47**
Cyril Av. Nott —1B **36**
Cyril Av. S'fd —4F **45**
Cyril Rd. W Bri —3C **50**

Dabell Av. Nott —5F **13**
Dagmar Gro. Bees —5G **47**
Dagmar Gro. Nott —6H **25**
Daisy Clo. Cotg —3E **63**
Daisy Farm Rd. Newt —5D **10**
Daisy Rd. Nott —6C **26**
Dakeyne St. Nott
—4A **38** (3H **3**)
Dalbeattie Clo. Arn —4D **16**
Dalby Sq. Nott —6A **36**
Dale Av. Carl —2E **39**
Dale Av. Long E —4F **55**
Dale Av. Map —5C **26**
Dalebrook Cres. Huck —5A **4**
Dale Clo. Huck —5A **4**
Dale Clo. W Bri —4D **50**
Dale Farm Av. Nott —4C **38**
Dale Gro. Nott —5B **38**
Dalehead Rd. Nott —4B **58**
Dale La. Bees —5E **47**
Dalemoor Gdns. Nott —1H **35**
Dale Rd. Carl —2E **39**
Dale Rd. Keyw —4C **70**
Dale Rd. Kimb —1H **21**
Dale Rd. Stan —4A **30**
Dale Rd. Stan D —2A **44**
Daleside. Cotg —3E **63**
Daleside Rd. Nott —6B **38**
Daleside Rd. E. Nott —5D **38**
Dales Shopping Cen. W Hal
—2C **30**
Dale St. Ilk —2B **32**
Dale St. Nott —5A **38**
Dale Ter. Nott —5B **38**
Dale View. Ilk —3A **32**
Dale View Rd. Nott —2D **38**
Dalkeith Ter. Nott —2D **36**
Dallas-York Rd. Bees —5H **47**
Dalley Clo. S'fd —4G **45**
Dallimore Rd. Ilk —5H **31**
Dalton Clo. S'fd —6G **45**
Daltons Clo. Lan M —1E **9**
Damson Wlk. Nott —1D **38**
Danbury Mt. Nott —5H **25**
Dane Clo. Nott —3H **37** (1F **3**)
Dane Ct. Nott —3H **37** (1F **3**)
Danes Clo. Arn —5H **15**
Danethorpe Vale. Nott
—3G **25**
Daniels Way. Huck —1E **13**
Darfield Dri. Hean —3E **9**
Darkey La. S'fd —6H **45**
Dark La. Bing —5G **43**
Dark La. Calv —4C **6**
Darley Av. Bees —2G **55**
Darley Av. Carl —6G **27**
Darley Av. Nott —2C **36**
Darley Dri. Long E —2C **64**
Darley Dri. W Hal —1C **30**
Darley Rd. Nott —2C **36**
Darley Sq. Ilk —2A **20**
Darlton Dri. Arn —6C **16**
Darnall Clo. Nott —6C **14**
Darnhall Cres. Nott —2D **34**
Daron Gdns. Nott —6E **15**
Dartmeet Ct. Nott —2B **36**
Darvel Clo. Nott —3H **35**
Darwin Clo. Nott —5C **14**
Darwin Rd. Ilk —2A **32**
Darwin Rd. Long E —2D **64**
David Gro. Bees —2E **47**
David La. Nott —4B **24**
Davidson Clo. Arn —6E **17**
Davidson St. Nott —6B **38**
Davies Rd. W Bri —4B **50**
Dawlish Clo. Huck —5B **4**
Dawlish Ct. E'wd —2H **9**
Dawlish Dri. Nott —2F **25**
Dawn Clo. Huck —2G **5**
Dawn View. Trow —1F **45**
Dawson Clo. Newt —4C **10**
Dawver Rd. Kimb —1H **21**

Daybrook Av. Nott —4G **25**
Daybrook Bus. Cen. Nott
—1H **25**
Daybrook St. Nott —4G **25**
Deabill St. N'fld —3A **40**
Dead La. Coss —6F **21**
Deakins Pl. Nott —4C **36**
Deal Gdns. Nott —6F **13**
Dean Av. Nott —4D **26**
Dean Clo. Nott —4D **34**
Dean Rd. Wd'p —2A **26**
Deanscourt. Cotg —2G **63**
Deans Croft. Bees —2B **46**
Dean St. Lan M —2G **9**
Debdale La. Keyw —4B **70**
Deddington La. Bees —1C **46**
Deepdale Av. S'fld —5F **45**
Deepdale Av. S'fld —5F **45**
Deepdale Clo. Gam —4D **50**
Deepdale Ct. Hean —4C **8**
Deepdale Rd. Long E —1C **64**
Deepdale Rd. Nott —5D **34**
Deepdene Clo. Nott —5G **23**
Deepdene Way. Nott —5G **23**
Deep Furrow Av. Carl —1F **39**
Deering Ct. Nott —1F **49**
Deerleap Dri. Arn —6G **15**
Deer Pk. Clo. Nott —5E **35**
Deer Pk. Dri. Arn —5G **15**
Delia Av. Huck —2G **5**
Dell Way. Nott —3D **58**
Dellwood Clo. Carl —5E **27**
Delta St. Nott —6D **24**
Delves Ct. Hean —5C **8**
Delves Rd. Hean —5B **8**
Delville Av. Keyw —3C **70**
Denacre Av. Long E —4H **55**
Denehurst Av. Nott —6A **24**
Denewood Av. Bees —1C **46**
Denewood Cres. Nott —1E **35**
Denholme Rd. Nott —4D **34**
Denison St. Bees —4E **47**
Denison St. Nott —3D **36**
Denman St. Nott —4D **36**
Denman St. Central. Nott
—4C **36**
Denmark Gro. Nott —1H **37**
Dennett Clo. Nott
—3A **38** (2H **3**)
Dennis Av. Bees —3E **47**
Dennis St. N'fld —2A **40**
Denstone Rd. Nott —4A **38**
Dentdale Dri. Nott —5B **34**
Denton Av. Sand —5C **44**
Denton Dri. W Bri —1H **59**
Denton Grn. Nott —5F **23**
Denver Ct. S'fld —1G **45**
(Crescent, The)
Denver Ct. S'fld —2G **45**
(Melbourne Rd.)
Deptford Cres. Nott —1A **24**
(in two parts)
Derby Gro. Nott —4D **36**
Derby Rd. Bram & Nott
—3A **46** (3A **2**)
Derby Rd. E'wd —2G **9**
Derby Rd. Hean —4B **8**
Derby Rd. Ilk —2G **31**
Derby Rd. Long E —5C **54**
Derby Rd. Ris & Sand
—1A **54**
Derby Rd. Stan —4A **30**
Derby Rd. S'fld —6E **45**
Derby Rd. Ind. Est. Hean
—4B **8**
Derbyshire Av. Trow —5F **33**
Derbyshire Av. W Hal
—1C **30**
Derbyshire Clo. W Hal
—1C **30**
Derbyshire Cres. Nott
—4G **35**
Derbyshire Dri. Ilk —3A **32**
Derbyshire La. Huck —4E **5**
Derby St. Arn —6B **16**
Derby St. Bees —4F **47**
Derby St. Ilk —1B **32**
Derby St. Nott —4F **37** (3B **2**)

Derby Ter. Nott —4E **37**
Dereham Dri. Arn —1B **26**
Derry Dri. Arn —3B **16**
Derry Hill Rd. Arn —4A **16**
Derry La. Bing —5H **43**
Derwent Av. Ilk —5H **19**
Derwent Av. W Hal —1C **30**
Derwent Clo. Att —2E **57**
Derwent Clo. Gam —4E **51**
Derwent Ct. Nott —3E **37**
Derwent Cres. Arn —1C **26**
Derwent Dri. Huck —1G **13**
Derwent St. Long E —1E **65**
Derwent Ter. Nott —5G **25**
Desford Clo. Nott —3E **25**
De Vere Gdns. Wd'p —2B **26**
Devitt Dri. Huck —2G **5**
Devon Cir. Red —4H **15**
Devon Clo. Sand —6D **44**
Devon Dri. Nott —5F **25**
Devon Dri. Rud —5H **59**
Devonshire Av. Bees —5F **47**
Devonshire Av. Long E
—5A **56**
Devonshire Clo. Ilk —2A **20**
Devonshire Cres. Nott
—5F **25**
Devonshire Dri. E'wd —3B **10**
Devonshire Dri. S'fld —1F **45**
Devonshire Promenade. Nott
—6C **36**
Devonshire Rd. Nott —5F **25**
Devonshire Rd. W Bri
—5A **50**
Devon St. Ilk —4C **32**
Devon St. Nott —4B **38**
Dewberry La. Rad T —1H **53**
Dial, The. Cotg —3E **63**
Dickens Ct. Newt —2D **10**
Dickson Dri. Rud —1H **69**
Didcot Dri. Nott —6B **24**
Digby Av. Nott —4B **38**
Digby Av. Woll —5H **35**
Digby Ct. Nott —6D **36**
Digby Hall Dri. Ged —4E **27**
Digby St. Ilk —6C **20**
Digby St. Kimb —1F **21**
Dirac Clo. Nott —5A **58**
Diseworth Gro. Nott —2H **49**
Distillery St. Rud —1G **69**
Dockholm Rd. Long E
—3E **55**
Dodford Ct. Hean —4E **9**
Dogwood Av. Nott —6F **13**
Dolphin Ct. Nott —5E **15**
Donbas Clo. Bulw —3H **23**
Doncaster Av. Sand —5D **44**
Doncaster Gro. Long E
—4H **55**
Doncaster Ter. Nott —6D **36**
Donington Rd. Nott —4C **58**
Donner Cres. Ilk —2A **20**
Dooland Dri. Nott —6B **26**
Dorchester Gdns. W Bri
—2A **60**
Dorchester Rd. Kimb —6H **11**
Doris Ct. Bees —3A **56**
Doris Rd. Ilk —2C **32**
Dormy Clo. Bees —4C **46**
Dormy Clo. Rad T —6H **41**
Dormy Ct. Nott —6B **14**
Dornoch Av. Nott —5H **25**
Dorothy Av. Huck —2F **5**
Dorothy Av. Newt —2C **10**
Dorothy Av. Sand —6D **44**
Dorothy Courts. Ilk —1A **32**
Dorothy Gro. Nott —3B **36**
Dorset Gdns. W Bri —6G **49**
Dorset St. Nott —4B **36**
Dorterry Cres. Ilk —4C **32**
Douglas Av. Aws —2E **21**
Douglas Av. Carl —3G **39**
Douglas Av. Hean —3A **8**
Douglas Clo. Rad T —1F **53**
Douglas Ct. Bees —3A **56**
Douglas Cres. Carl —3G **39**

Douglas Rd. Bing —5H **43**
Douglas Rd. Long E —3D **54**
Douglas Rd. Nott —4D **36**
Douro Dri. Arn —4D **16**
Dovecote Dri. Nott —5E **35**
Dovecote La. Bees —5F **47**
Dovecote Rd. E'wd & Newt
—3D **10**
Dovecotes, The. Bees —6F **47**
Dovedale Av. Long E —1C **64**
Dovedale Circ. Ilk —2A **20**
Dovedale Ct. Long E —1D **64**
Dovedale Rd. Nott —3E **39**
Dovedale Rd. W Bri —6C **50**
Dove La. Long E —4E **55**
Dovenby Rd. Nott —2D **58**
Dover Beck Clo. Calv —3E **7**
Dover Beck Dri. Wdbgh
—6G **7**
Doveridge Av. Carl —1A **40**
Doveridge Rd. Carl —1A **40**
Dove St. Nott —6H **13**
Downes Clo. Nott —6G **13**
Downham Clo. Arn —1C **26**
Downing Gdns. Nott —5H **13**
Downing St. Nott —5H **13**
Downs, The. Nott —2E **59**
Dowson St. Nott —3B **38**
Doyne Ct. Nott —2G **49**
Drakemyre Clo. Arn —4D **16**
Drake Rd. Carl —4B **40**
Draycott Clo. Los —1A **8**
Draycott Ct. Ilk —4B **20**
Draycott Rd. Long E —2B **64**
Drayton St. Nott —5G **25**
Drift, The. Nott —2C **58**
Dronfield Pl. Ilk —2A **20**
Drummond Av. N'fld —2B **40**
Drummond Dri. Nut —3D **22**
Drummond Rd. Ilk —6A **20**
Drury Wlk. Nott
—5G **37** (5E **3**)
Dryden Ct. S'fld —2G **45**
Dryden St. Nott
—3F **37** (1C **2**)
Drysdale Clo. Nott —2H **23**
Duchess Gdns. Nott —6H **13**
Duchess St. Nott —5H **13**
Dudley Ct. Bees —3A **46**
Duffield Clo. Long E —2C **64**
Duffield Ct. Nott —5D **14**
Duke Clo. Nott —2F **23**
Duke Cres. Gilt —4E **11**
Dukes Pl. Ilk —3A **20**
Dukes Pl. Nott
—5H **37** (4G **3**)
Duke St. Arn —6H **15**
Duke St. Bulw —6H **13**
Duke St. Huck —4F **5**
Duke St. Ilk —4B **32**
Duke St. Nott —1D **36**
Duke St. E. Huck —4F **5**
Duke William Mt. Nott
—5E **37**
Dulverton Vale. Nott —4G **23**
Dulwich Rd. Nott —4C **36**
Dumbles Clo. Ilk —3G **31**
Dunblane Rd. Rud —1G **69**
Duncombe Clo. Nott —2A **38**
Duncroft Av. Ged —6H **27**
Dundas Clo. Nott
—3G **37** (1D **2**)
Dunelm Dri. Calv —3E **7**
Dungannon Rd. Nott —5C **58**
Dunholme Clo. Nott —5H **13**
Dunkery Rd. Nott —5D **58**
Dunkirk Rd. Nott —1C **48**
Dunlin Wharf. Nott —1E **49**
Dunlop Av. Nott —5C **36**
Dunoon Clo. Nott —3C **14**
Dunsby Clo. Nott —4C **58**
Dunsford Dri. Nott —1E **27**
Dunsil Dri. Nott —3E **49**
Dunsmore Clo. Bees —1H **57**
Dunstan St. N'fld —3A **40**
Dunster Rd. Newt —3D **10**
Dunster Rd. W Bri —5C **50**
Dunston Clo. Long E —6H **55**
Dunvegan Dri. Nott —3D **14**

Durham Av. Nott —5B **38**
Durham Chambers. Nott
—5G **37** (4E **3**)
Durham Clo. Nott —5B **38**
Durham Cres. Nott —1A **24**
Durham St. Ilk —6B **20**
Durlston Clo. W Bri —6F **49**
Durnford St. Nott —5D **24**
Dursley Clo. Nott —2H **23**
Dyce Clo. Nott —6F **13**
Dylan M. Nott —1E **35**
Dylan Thomas Rd. Nott
—5F **15**

Eagle Clo. Arn —6C **16**
Eagle Clo. Bees —3D **46**
Eagle Ct. Nott —6B **14**
Eagle Rd. Ilk —5B **32**
Ealing Av. Nott —3B **24**
Eardley Rd. Nott —1C **24**
Earl Cres. Ged —4H **27**
Earl Dri. Gilt —4E **11**
Earls Clo. Nott —4C **34**
Earlsfield Dri. Nott —4B **14**
Earlswood Dri. Edw —1D **60**
Easedale Clo. Gam —4E **51**
Easegill Ct. Nott —5D **14**
(off Old Farm Rd.)
East Acres. Cotg —2F **63**
E. Circus St. Nott
—5F **37** (4C **2**)
Eastcliffe Av. Ged —4F **27**
East Clo. Keyw —5C **70**
Eastcote Av. Bees —1B **46**
East Cres. Bees —6H **47**
East Croft. Nott —6H **37**
Eastdale Rd. Nott —3E **39**
East Dri. Nott —2A **48**
Eastglade Rd. Nott —1D **24**
East Gro. Bing —5F **43**
East Gro. Nott —1E **37**
Eastham Clo. Nott —3A **38**
Eastham Rd. Arn —1E **27**
Eastholme Croft. Nott
—4F **39**
Easthorpe Cotts. Rud —6H **59**
Easthorpe St. Rud —6G **59**
East Moor. Cotg —3G **63**
Eastmoor Dri. Carl —1H **39**
E. Nelson St. Hean —3C **8**
East St. Bing —5F **43**
East St. Got —6H **67**
East St. Hean —5E **9**
East St. Ilk —1B **32**
East St. Long E —5H **55**
East St. Nott —4H **37** (3F **3**)
East St. Rud —1G **69**
East View. W Bri —5H **49**
Eastwell St. Huck —3E **5**
Eastwood. Cotg —3G **63**
Eastwood Clo. Huck —1E **13**
Eastwood Rd. Kimb —6F **11**
Eastwood Rd. Rad T —6G **41**
Eastwood St. Nott —2A **24**
Eaton Av. Arn —6C **16**
Eaton Av. Ilk —3H **31**
Eaton Clo. Bees —5H **47**
Eaton Grange Dri. Long E
—5C **54**
Eatons Rd. S'fld —5F **45**
Eaton St. Nott —4B **26**
Eaton Ter. Nott —5B **26**
Ebenezer St. Ilk —4B **20**
Ebenezer St. Lan M —2F **9**
Ebers Gro. Nott —1G **37**
Ebers Rd. Nott —6G **25**
Ebony Wlk. Nott —1D **38**
Ebury Rd. Nott —6F **25**
Eckington Clo. W Hal —1C **30**
Eckington Ter. Nott —6G **25**
Ecton Clo. Nott —4D **14**
Edale Clo. Huck —5A **4**
Edale Clo. Long E —1D **64**
Edale Rise. Bees —2G **55**
Edale Rd. Nott —4C **38**
Edale Sq. Ilk —2A **20**
Eddlestone Dri. Nott —4D **58**
Edenbridge Ct. Nott —1D **46**

Eden Clo. Arn —1B **26**
Edenhall Gdns. Nott —3D **58**
Eder Dri. Arn —4A **16**
Edern Clo. Nott —6E **15**
Edern Gdns. Nott —6E **15**
Edgbaston Gdns. Nott
—1B **36**
Edgecote Way. Nott —1E **25**
Edge Hill Ct. Long E —3G **65**
Edge Way. Nott —6D **22**
Edgewood Dri. Huck —6B **4**
Edgington Clo. Cotg —3G **63**
Edginton St. Nott —2B **38**
Edginton Ter. Nott —3B **38**
Edgware Rd. Nott —6B **14**
Edgwood Rd. Kimb —1H **21**
Edinbane Clo. Nott —4D **14**
Edinboro Row. Kimb —6G **11**
Edinburgh Dri. Bing —4D **42**
Edingale Ct. Bees —3B **34**
Edingley Av. Nott —3G **25**
Edingley Sq. Nott —3F **25**
Edison Village. High S
—2B **48**
Edith Ter. Nott —3C **36**
Edlington Dri. Nott —6C **34**
Edmond Gro. Huck —3G **5**
Edmonds Clo. Arn —3E **15**
Ednaston Rd. Nott —2B **48**
Edwald Rd. Edw —2G **61**
Edwalton Av. W Bri —4B **50**
Edwalton Clo. Edw —2D **60**
Edwalton Ct. Nott —1C **24**
Edwalton Lodge Clo. Edw
—2C **60**
Edward Av. Nott —1B **36**
Edward Clo. Huck —1D **12**
Edward Rd. E'wd —3C **10**
Edward Rd. Long E —5F **55**
Edward Rd. Nut —2C **22**
Edward Rd. W Bri —2B **50**
Edwards Ct. Nott —2F **25**
Edwards La. Nott —1F **25**
Edward St. Lan M —1F **9**
Edward St. S'fld —4F **45**
Edwinstowe Av. W Bri
—4B **50**
Edwinstowe Dri. Nott —3G **25**
Edwin St. Day —1H **25**
Eelwood Rd. Huck —1D **12**
Egerton Dri. S'fld —1F **45**
Egerton Rd. Wd'p —3H **25**
Egerton St. Nott —2G **37**
Egerton Wlk. Nott —2G **37**
Egling Croft. Colw —5H **39**
Egmont Ct. Nott —1G **49**
Egreaves Av. Los —1A **8**
Egypt Rd. Nott —6D **24**
Eighth Av. Lent —6B **48**
Eisele Clo. Nott —1F **23**
Ekowe St. Nott —5D **24**
Eland St. Nott —6D **24**
Elder Clo. Arn —4C **16**
Elder Gdns. Nott —5E **15**
Elder Gro. Huck —1H **13**
Eldon Chambers. Nott
—5G **37** (4D **2**)
Eldon Rd. Att —4C **56**
Eleanor Av. Ilk —4C **32**
Eleanor Cres. S'fld —4H **45**
Electric Av. Nott —3E **49**
Elford Rise. Nott —4B **38**
Elgar Dri. Long E —2D **64**
Elgar Gdns. Nott —3B **38**
Eliot Clo. Long E —2D **64**
Eliot Dri. Ilk —4H **31**
Eliot Wlk. Nott —5A **58**
Elizabeth Clo. Huck —6C **4**
Elizabeth Clo. W Hal —1B **30**
Elizabeth Ct. Ilk —6H **19**
Elizabeth Gro. Ged —5G **27**
Ella Bank Rd. Hean —4D **8**
Ella Rd. W Bri —2B **50**
Ellastone Av. Nott —4D **14**
Ellerby Av. Nott —3C **58**
Ellerslie Gro. Sand —6C **44**
Ellesmere Clo. Arn —6D **16**
Ellesmere Dri. Trow —4E **33**
Ellesmere Rd. W Bri —1B **60**

Ellington Rd. Arn —3C **16**
Elliot St. Nott —4E **37** (3A **2**)
Ellis Av. Huck —5F **5**
Ellis Clo. Long E —1E **65**
Ellis Ct. Nott —3H **37**
Ellis Gro. Bees —6F **47**
Ellsworth Rise. Nott —1D **24**
Ellwood Cres. Nott —4G **35**
Elm Av. Att —3D **56**
Elm Av. Bees —5E **47**
Elm Av. Bing —5G **43**
Elm Av. Carl —2H **39**
Elm Av. Huck —6C **4**
Elm Av. Keyw —5D **70**
Elm Av. Long E —4E **55**
Elm Av. Nott —2G **37**
Elm Av. Nut —1B **22**
Elm Av. Sand —4D **44**
Elm Bank. Nott —1G **37**
Elm Bank Dri. Nott —1G **37**
Elmbridge. Nott —6F **15**
Elm Clo. Keyw —5D **70**
Elm Clo. Nott —2G **37**
Elmdale Gdns. Nott —1H **35**
Elm Dri. Carl —2H **39**
Elm Gro. Arn —4C **16**
Elmhurst Av. Nott —5E **27**
Elmore Ct. Nott —3E **37**
Elms Clo. Rud —1H **69**
Elmsdale Gdns. Bur J
　　　　—3E **29**
Elmsfield Av. Hean —3E **9**
Elms Gdns. Rud —1G **69**
Elmsham Av. Nott —4C **14**
Elms Pk. Keyw —1H **69**
Elms, The. Colw —3H **39**
Elms, The. Wat —6H **11**
Elmsthorpe Av. Nott —5C **36**
Elmswood Gdns. Nott
　　　　—4H **25**
Elm Tree Av. W Bri —4H **49**
Elmtree Rd. Calv —3E **3**
Elnor St. Lan M —3G **9**
Elson St. Nott —1D **36**
Elston Gdns. Nott —1C **58**
Elston M. Nott —2D **38**
Elstree Dri. Nott —3G **35**
Elswick Clo. Nott —5F **15**
Elswick Dri. Bees —1H **57**
Elterwater Dri. Gam —4E **51**
Eltham Clo. Nott —4F **23**
Eltham Dri. Nott —4F **23**
Eltham Rd. W Bri —4B **50**
Elton Clo. S'fd —3G **45**
Elton M. Nott —6F **25**
Elton Rd. N. Nott —6F **25**
Elton Ter. Nott —2D **36**
Elvaston Ct. Nott —4F **23**
Elvaston Dri. Long E —3B **64**
Elvaston Rd. Nott —4G **35**
Elveden Dri. Ilk —4G **19**
Elwes Lodge. Carl —3H **39**
Emerys Rd. Ged —1B **40**
　　(in four parts)
Emmanuel Av. Arn —4E **15**
Emmanuel Av. Nott —6C **26**
Emneth Clo. Nott —1B **38**
Empingham Clo. Bees
　　　　—3B **56**
Emsworth Clo. Ilk —4H **19**
Ena Av. Nott —4B **38**
Enderby Gdns. Red —4A **16**
Enderby Sq. Bees —3F **47**
Endsleigh Gdns. Bees —4F **47**
Endsleigh Gdns. Edw —1C **60**
Enfield Chambers. Nott
　　　　—5G **37** (5E **3**)
Enfield St. Bees —5E **47**
Engine La. Newt —1D **10**
England Cres. Hean —3E **9**
Ennerdale Clo. Gam —4E **51**
Ennerdale Rd. Long E
　　　　—3D **54**
Ennerdale Rd. Nott —2H **25**
Ennismore Gdns. Nott
　　　　—3A **36**
Ennismore M. W Bri —2G **59**
Enthorpe St. Nott —3H **35**
Epperstone Rd. Epp —1F **7**

Epperstone Rd. W Bri
　　　　—3A **50**
Epsom Rd. Bees —2G **55**
Erdington Way. Bees —2G **55**
Erewash Ct. Long E —4F **55**
Erewash Dri. Ilk —3C **32**
Erewash Gdns. Nott —5E **15**
Erewash Gro. Bees —3H **55**
Erewash Sq. Ilk —3C **32**
Erewash St. Long E —5G **55**
Eric Av. Huck —2D **4**
Erith Clo. Nott —6D **22**
Ernest Rd. Carl —1D **38**
Ernhale Ct. Arn —5A **16**
Erskine Rd. Nott —6F **25**
Esher Gro. Nott —6G **25**
Eskdale Clo. Long E —2D **64**
Eskdale Ct. Gam —4E **51**
Eskdale Dri. Bees —1A **56**
Eskdale Dri. Nott —1H **35**
Essex St. Ilk —5B **20**
Essex St. Ilk —6B **20**
　　(off Stamford St.)
Estwic Av. E'wd —2B **10**
Ethel Av. Huck —2F **5**
Ethel Av. Nott —6C **26**
Ethel Rd. W Bri —4B **50**
Ethel Ter. Nott —6E **25**
Eton Ct. W Hal —1B **30**
Eton Gro. Nott —5H **35**
Eton Rd. W Bri —5A **50**
Eucalyptus Av. Nott —4A **58**
Eugene Gdns. Nott —1H **49**
Eugene St. Nott —6H **37**
Europa Way. Nott —2G **59**
Evans Rd. Nott —4B **24**
Evedon Wlk. Nott —4F **15**
Evelyn St. Bees —4H **47**
Evelyn St. Nott
　　　　—5A **38** (5H **3**)
Eversley Wlk. Nott —5F **15**
Evesham Ct. Bees —4A **56**
Ewart Rd. Nott —1D **36**
Ewe Lamb Clo. Bees —2H **45**
Ewe Lamb La. Bees —2H **45**
Ewell Rd. Nott —4E **35**
Exbourne Rd. Nott —6F **23**
Exbury Gdns. W Bri —1F **59**
Exchange Arc. Nott —4E **3**
Exchange Rd. W Bri —4B **50**
Exchange Wlk. Nott
　　　　—5G **37** (4E **3**)
Excise Chambers. Nott —4F **3**
Exeter Clo. Ged —5H **27**
Exeter Rd. Nott —1E **37**
Exeter Rd. W Bri —5B **50**
Extension St. Ilk —1B **32**
Exton Rd. Nott —4E **25**
Eyam Clo. Bees —6C **34**
Eyre's Gdns. Ilk —5B **20**
Eyre St. Nott —5A **38** (4H **3**)

Fabis Dri. Nott —1C **58**
Factory La. Bees —6E **47**
Factory La. Ilk —3A **20**
Failsworth Clo. Nott —2C **58**
Fairbank Cres. Nott —5H **25**
Fairburn Clo. Bram —4B **46**
Fairburn Clo. Nott —5C **34**
Faircroft Av. Sand —6D **44**
Fairdale Dri. Newt —3D **10**
Fairfax Clo. Nott —5D **24**
Fairfield Clo. Nott —6F **49**
Fairfield Cres. Long E —3C **64**
Fairfield St. Bing —5E **43**
Fairham Av. Got —6H **67**
Fairham Clo. Rud —5F **59**
Fairham Ct. Nott —2B **58**
Fairham Dri. Nott —5B **36**
Fairham Rd. Keyw —4B **70**
Fairholm Ct. Nott —3A **38**
Fairisle Clo. Nott —4E **59**
Fairland Cres. W Bri —1H **59**
Fairlawn Pl. Sher —5H **25**
Fair Lea Clo. Long E —1F **65**
Fairlight Way. Nott —6F **15**
Fairmaid Gro. Nott —3C **58**
Fairmead Clo. Nott —1C **38**

Fairnley Rd. Nott —1D **34**
Fairview Ct. W Bri —3H **59**
Fairview Rd. Wd'p —3A **26**
Fairway. Keyw —4D **70**
Fairway Cres. Nwtn —1B **42**
Fairway Dri. Bees —5D **46**
Fairway Dri. Nott —6B **14**
Falcon Clo. Lent —5C **36**
Falcon Ct. Ilk —6H **19**
Falconers Wlk. Arn —5G **15**
Falcon Gro. Nott —6E **25**
Falcon St. Nott —6E **25**
Falconwood Gdns. Nott
　　　　—4A **58**
Fallow Clo. Nott —3C **58**
Fall Rd. Hean —2C **8**
Falstaff M. New B —6E **25**
Falston Rd. Nott —3G **35**
Faraday Building. High S
　　　　—2B **48**
Faraday Ct. S'fd —2G **45**
Faraday Rd. Nott —5C **36**
Farfield Av. Bees —3E **47**
Farfield Gro. Bees —3E **47**
Farleys La. Huck —5E **5**
Farley St. Nott —6H **13**
Farm Av. Huck —1D **12**
Farm Clo. Ilk —1C **32**
Farm Clo. Long E —2G **65**
Farm Clo. Nott —3C **58**
Farm Rd. Arn —6D **16**
Farm Rd. Bees —6D **46**
Farnborough Rd. Nott
　　　　—5B **58**
Farndale Clo. Long E —2C **64**
Farndale Dri. Nott —5B **34**
Farndon Dri. Bees —2H **55**
Farndon Grn. Nott —5A **36**
Farndon M. Carl —3A **40**
Far New Clo. Sand —6D **44**
Farnham Wlk. W Hal —1B **30**
Farnsfield Av. Bur J —2G **29**
Farnsworth Clo. Wat —4A **12**
Far Pastures Clo. Keyw
　　　　—5C **70**
Farriers Grn. Clif —3A **58**
Farringdon Clo. Nut —4D **22**
Far Rye. Nott —4F **35**
Far St. Bradm —4H **69**
Farthing Ct. Long E —6D **54**
Farwells Clo. Nott —4A **24**
Faulconbridge Clo. Nott
　　　　—1H **23**
Fearn Chase. Carl —2G **39**
Fearn Clo. Breas —6C **54**
Fearnleigh Dri. Nott —5B **24**
Featherstone Clo. Ged
　　　　—4F **27**
Felen Clo. Nott —6E **15**
Felley Clo. Huck —6C **4**
Fellows Rd. Bees —4E **47**
Fellows Yd. Plum —6G **61**
Fell Side. Wd'p —2C **26**
Fellside Clo. Gam —5E **51**
Felstead Ct. Bees —2C **46**
Felstead Rd. Nott —3H **35**
Felton Clo. Bees —6B **46**
Felton Rd. Nott —2H **49**
Fenchurch Clo. Arn —4E **15**
Fenimore Ct. Rad T —6H **41**
Fenroth Clo. Nott —5F **13**
Fenton Ct. Nott —3D **24**
Fenton Dri. Nott —3A **14**
Fenton Rd. Nott —3D **24**
Fenwick Clo. Nott —5F **23**
Fenwick Rd. Nott —5F **23**
Fergus Clo. Nott —5D **58**
Ferguson Clo. Bees —3C **56**
Fern Av. Nott —6F **25**
Fern Clo. Bees —4C **46**
Fern Cres. E'wd —2A **10**
Ferndale Clo. Att —3E **57**
Ferndale Gro. Nott —3D **38**
Ferndale Rd. Nott —3D **38**
Ferngill Clo. Nott —2F **49**
Fernilee Clo. W Hal —1C **30**
Fern Lea Av. Cotg —5A **63**
Fernleigh Av. Nott —5D **26**
Fernwood Cres. Nott —5C **34**

Fernwood Dri. Rad T —5F **41**
Fernwood Dri. Wat —5A **12**
Ferny Hollow Clo. Nott
　　　　—5C **14**
Ferrers Wlk. Nott
　　　　—4A **38** (2H **3**)
Ferriby Ter. Nott —2G **49**
Ferry Lodge. Carl —3G **39**
Festival Rd. Ilk —4G **31**
Festus Clo. Nott —3H **37**
Festus St. N'fld —2A **40**
Field Av. Huck —1D **12**
Field Clo. Bees —1B **56**
Field Clo. Breas —6B **54**
Field Clo. Ged —5H **27**
Field Ho. Clo. Nott —4D **34**
Field La. Bees —1A **56**
Field La. Wdbgh —6G **7**
Field Maltings. Ilk —2B **32**
Fields Av. Rud —2G **69**
Fields Farm Rd. Long E
　　　　—2E **65**
Fieldway. Nott —1F **59**
Fiennes Cres. Nott
　　　　—5G **37** (4E **3**)
　　　　—6E **37** (6A **2**)
Fifth Av. Lent —5A **48**
Filey St. Nott —5A **14**
Finch Clo. Nott —3D **48**
Finchley Clo. Nott —4A **58**
Findern Grn. Nott —3C **38**
Fingal Clo. Nott —4D **58**
Finsbury Av. Nott —5B **38**
Finsbury Pk. Clo. W Bri
　　　　—6G **49**
Finsbury Rd. Arn —3E **15**
Finsbury Rd. Bees —6C **34**
Firbank Ct. Bees —6B **46**
Firbeck Rd. Arn —5C **16**
Firbeck Rd. Nott —5C **34**
Fir Clo. Nott —6F **13**
Fircroft Av. Nott —1E **35**
Fircroft Dri. Huck —6A **4**
Fir Dale. Cotg —2G **63**
Firfield Av. Breas —5A **54**
Firs Av. Bees —4F **47**
Firsby Rd. Nott —5F **23**
Firs Rd. Edw —1C **60**
Firs St. Long E —3C **64**
First Av. Bees —3E **47**
First Av. Carl —2E **39**
First Av. Colw —4G **39**
First Av. Ged —6H **27**
First Av. Ilk —2B **32**
First Av. Lent —5A **48**
First Av. Nott —1F **37**
First Av. Ris —6B **44**
Firs, The. Nott —4H **25**
Firth Clo. Arn —4E **17**
Firth Dri. Bees —3C **56**
Fir Wlk. Nott —2D **38**
Fisher Av. Wd'p —2B **26**
Fisher Ct. Ilk —3B **20**
Fisher Ga. Nott
　　　　—5H **37** (5G **3**)
Fisher La. Bing —5E **43**
Fisher St. Nott —1D **36**
Fishpond Dri. Nott
　　　　—6E **37** (6A **2**)
Five Acres. Nott —1E **59**
Flagholme. Cotg —3F **63**
Flamingo Ct. Nott —1E **49**
Flamstead Av. Lamb —1B **28**
Flamstead Av. Los —1A **8**
Flamstead Rd. Ilk —6B **20**
Flamsteed Rd. Nott —6D **22**
Flatts La. Calv —2C **6**
Flatts, The. Bees —6B **46**
Flawforth Av. Rud —6H **59**
Flawforth La. Rud —6H **59**
Flaxendale. Cotg —3G **63**
Flaxton Way. Nott —6D **14**
Fleam Rd. Nott —1C **58**
Fleeman Gro. W Bri —2C **50**
Fleet Clo. Nott —3B **36**
Fleetway Clo. Newt —4D **10**
Fleetwith Clo. W Bri —6E **51**
Fleming Dri. Wat —5A **12**
Fleming Dri. Carl —2E **39**
Fleming Gdns. Nott —4A **58**

Fletcher Ga. Nott
　　　　—5G **37** (4E **3**)
Fletcher Rd. Bees —4G **47**
Fletcher St. Hean —3C **8**
Fletcher St. Long E —5F **55**
Flewitt Gdns. Nott —3A **38**
Flintham Dri. Nott —3F **25**
Flixton Rd. Kimb —6H **11**
Florence Av. Long E —4H **55**
Florence Boot Clo. Nott
　　　　—3H **47**
Florence Ct. Ilk —6B **20**
Florence Cres. Ged —1B **40**
Florence Gro. Nott —2C **38**
Florence Rd. Ged —6B **28**
Florence Rd. Nott —6C **26**
Florence Rd. W Bri —3C **50**
Florence St. Huck —6E **5**
Florey Ct. Nott —1C **48**
Florey Wlk. Nott —5A **58**
Florin Gdns. Long E —6D **54**
Flowers Clo. Arn —1D **26**
Flying Horse Wlk. Nott
　　　　—5G **37** (4E **3**)
Foljambe Ter. Nott
　　　　—4H **37** (2G **3**)
Folkton Gdns. Nott —6B **26**
Forbes Clo. Long E —2G **65**
Force Hill. Bees —1D **56**
Ford Av. Los —1A **8**
Fordham Grn. Nott —5C **58**
Ford St. Nott —6E **25**
Ford St. N. Nott —6E **25**
Foredrift Clo. Got —6H **67**
Forest Clo. Cotg —2E **63**
Forest Cotts. Nott —4B **14**
Forest Ct. Nott —3E **37**
　　(Gamble St.)
Forest Ct. Nott —2F **37**
　　(N. Sherwood St.)
Forester Clo. Bees —1C **56**
Forester Gro. Carl —2F **39**
Forester Rd. Nott —1C **38**
Forester St. N'fld —2A **40**
Forest Gro. Nott —2F **37**
　　(Colville St.)
Forest Gro. Nott —3E **37**
　　(Mt. Hooton Rd.)
Forest La. Pap —1H **5**
Forest Rd. Bing —5C **42**
Forest Rd. Calv —2B **6**
Forest Rd. E. Nott —3E **37**
Forest Rd. W. Nott —3E **37**
Forest View Ind. & Retail Est.
　　　　Nott —4A **14**
Forge Av. Calv —2D **6**
Forge Mill Gro. Huck —6H **5**
Forge, The. Trow —4D **32**
Forman St. Nott
　　　　—4G **37** (3D **2**)
Forster St. Nott —3C **36**
Forsythia Gdns. Nott —1C **48**
Fosbrooke Dri. Long E
　　　　—2F **65**
Fosse, The. Cotg —6H **63**
Fosse Wlk. Cotg —3G **63**
Foss Way. Bing —6A **42**
Foster Av. Bees —5F **47**
Fosters La. Bing —5F **43**
Fothergill Ct. Nott —2G **37**
Fountaindale Ct. Nott —2H **37**
Fountains Clo. W Bri —5D **50**
Fountains Ct. Bees —5G **47**
Fourth Av. Carl —1D **38**
Fourth Av. Lent —5A **48**
Fourth Av. Nott —1F **37**
Fowler St. Nott —1H **37**
Fox Clo. Long E —2F **65**
Fox Covert. Colw —5H **39**
Fox Covert La. Nott —5H **57**
Foxearth Av. Nott —3E **59**
Foxes Clo. Nott —4E **2**
Foxglove Rd. Newt —5D **10**
Foxgloves, The. Bing —6D **42**
Fox Gro. Nott —4C **24**
Fox Gro. Ct. Nott —4C **24**
Foxhall Rd. Nott —1E **37**
Fox Hill. Cotg —3E **63**
Foxhill Rd. Bur J —2E **29**

Foxhill Rd. Carl —1E 39
Foxhill Rd. Central. Carl
　　—1D 38
Foxhill Rd. E. Carl —1F 39
Foxhill Rd. W. Carl —1C 38
Foxhollies Gro. Nott —4F 25
Fox Meadow. Huck —5D 4
Fox Rd. W Bri —2B 50
Foxton Clo. Ilk —4G 19
Foxton Clo. Nott —5F 13
Foxton Gdns. Nott —2G 35
Foxwood Clo. Calv —3D 6
Foxwood La. Wdbgh —4D 6
Fradley Clo. Nott —3A 14
Frampton Rd. Nott —2G 35
Frances Gro. Huck —2F 5
Francis Gro. Nott —4C 24
Francis Rd. Carl —1H 39
Francis St. Nott
　　—3E 37 (1A 2)
(in two parts)
Franklin Clo. Nott —5G 15
Franklin Dri. Toll —4F 61
Franklyn Gdns. Keyw —3C 70
Franklyn Gdns. Nott —3A 36
Fraser Cres. Carl —6D 26
Fraser Rd. Carl —6D 26
Fraser Rd. Nott —3H 49
Fraser Sq. Carl —6D 26
Freckingham St. Nott
　　—4H 37 (4H 3)
Freda Av. Ged —5F 27
Freda Clo. Ged —4F 27
Frederic Av. Hean —6D 8
Frederick Av. Carl —2D 38
Frederick Av. Ilk —4C 32
Frederick Gro. Nott —6D 36
Frederick Rd. S'fd —4F 45
Frederick St. Long E —6H 55
Freeland Clo. Bees —2H 55
Freemans Rd. Carl —1A 40
Freemans Ter. Carl —1H 39
Freemantle Wlk. Nott —5C 14
Freeston Dri. Nott —5F 13
Freeth Ct. Nott —1B 50
Freeth St. Nott —1A 50
Freiston St. Nott —2C 36
Fremount Dri. Nott —2G 35
French St. Ilk —3C 32
Fretwell St. Nott —2C 36
Friar La. Nott —5F 37 (5C 2)
Friars Ct. Ilk —3G 31
Friars Ct. Nott —6E 37 (6A 2)
Friar St. Long E —6F 55
Friar St. Nott —1C 48
Friar Wlk. Nwtn —1C 42
Friary Clo. Nott —1C 48
Friary, The. Nott —1C 48
Friday La. Ged —5H 27
Friesland Dri. Sand —6B 44
Frinton Rd. Nott —6E 23
Frisby Av. Long E —1G 65
Frobisher Gdns. Nott —1C 14
Frogmore St. Nott —3G 37
Front St. Arn —5B 16
Frost Av. Lan M —1E 9
Fryar Rd. E'wd —1B 10
Fryma Ho. Nott —3D 36
Fulforth St. Nott
　　—3G 37 (1D 2)
Fuller St. Rud —1G 69
Fullwood Av. Ilk —6A 20
Fullwood St. Ilk —6A 20
Fulwood Clo. Bees —1C 56
Fulwood Cres. Nott —6G 23
Fulwood Dri. Long E —6C 54
Furlong Av. Arn —6A 16
Furlong Clo. S'fd —3F 45
Furlong St. Arn —6A 16
Furnace La. Los —1A 8
Furnace Rd. Ilk —2D 32
Furness Clo. W Bri —4D 50
Furness Rd. Nott —4A 24
Furze Gdns. Nott —2H 37
Fylde Clo. Bees —3G 55
Fylingdale Way. Nott —6B 34

Gables, The. Nott —6E 25

Gabor Clo. Nott —4A 58
Gabor Ct. Nott —4A 58
Gabrielle Clo. Nott —3B 24
Gadd St. Nott —3D 36
Gadwall Cres. Nott —1E 49
Gainsborough Clo. Long E
　　—2G 65
Gainsborough Clo. S'fd
　　—5G 45
Gainsborough Ct. Bees
　　—4G 47
Gainsford Clo. Nott —2D 24
Gainsford Cres. Nott —2D 24
Gala Way. Nott —1C 24
Gale Clo. Bees —5H 47
Galena Dri. Nott —2C 38
Galen Ct. Nott —1C 48
Gallows Inn Clo. Ilk —4C 32
Gallows Inn Ind. Est. Ilk
　　—3D 32
Galway Rd. Arn —5H 15
Galway Rd. Nott —6D 36
Gamble St. Nott —3E 37
Gamston Cres. Nott —4G 25
Ganton Clo. Nott —6B 26
Garden Av. Carl —2F 39
Garden Av. Ilk —4B 32
Garden City. Carl —1G 39
Gardendale Av. Nott —4B 58
Gardenia Clo. Bees —3A 56
Gardenia Cres. Nott —5D 26
Gardenia Gro. Nott —5D 26
Garden Rd. Bing —4D 62
Garden Rd. E'wd —2B 10
Garden Rd. Huck —4D 4
Garden Rd. S'fd —4F 45
Gardens Ct. W Bri —4C 50
Gardens, The. Los —1A 8
Garden St. Nott —4D 36
Garfield Clo. S'fd —2D 45
Garfield Ct. Nott —4D 36
Garfield Rd. Nott —4D 36
Garforth Clo. Nott —1C 36
Garners Hill. Nott
　　—5H 37 (5F 3)
Garnet Ct. Nott —4A 38
Garnet St. N'fld —2H 39
Garnett Av. Hean —3D 8
Garrett Gro. Nott —3A 66
Garsdale Clo. Gam —5E 51
Garsdale Dri. Nott —2E 58
Garton Clo. Bees —6B 46
Garton Clo. Nott —2H 23
Gas St. Sand —5E 45
Gatcombe Clo. Rad T
　　—6G 41
Gatcombe Gro. Sand —2C 54
Gateford Clo. Bees —1B 46
Gatehouse Ct. Bees —6D 46
Gateside Rd. Nott —2E 49
Gatling St. Nott —4C 36
Gaul St. Nott —6H 13
Gauntley Ct. Nott —1D 36
Gauntley St. Nott —1C 36
Gautries Clo. Nott —5E 15
Gavin M. Nott —1D 36
Gawthorne St. Nott —6D 24
Gayhurst Grn. Nott —2C 24
Gayhurst Rd. Nott —2C 24
Gaynor Ct. Nott —3H 35
Gayrigg Ct. Bees —1B 56
Gayton Clo. Nott —1D 14
Gaywood Clo. Nott —5D 58
Gedling Gro. Arn —6B 16
Gedling Gro. Nott
　　—3E 37 (1A 2)
Gedling Rd. Arn —6B 16
Gedling Rd. Carl —1H 39
Gedling St. Nott
　　—5H 37 (4G 3)
Gedney Av. Nott —1B 36
Gell Rd. Bees —1A 56
George Av. Bees —6F 47
George Av. Long E —4H 55
George Grn. Ct. Snei —5B 38
(off Sneinton Boulevd.)
George Rd. Carl —2F 39
George Rd. W Bri —4A 50
George's La. Calv —5A 6

George St. Arn —1A 26
George St. Huck —3E 5
George St. Lan M —2F 9
George St. Nott
　　—4H 37 (3F 3)
Georgia Dri. Arn —3A 16
Georgina Rd. Bees —6F 47
Gerrard Clo. Arn —3E 15
Gertrude Rd. W Bri —3C 50
Ghost Ho. La. Bees —6B 46
Gibbons Av. S'fd —5F 45
Gibbons St. Lent —3C 48
Gibb St. Long E —6G 55
Gibson Rd. Nott —1E 37
Gifford Gdns. Nott —1G 49
Gilbert Av. Got —6H 67
Gilbert Gdns. Nott —3C 38
Gilbert St. Huck —4E 5
Gilead St. Nott —6H 13
Giles Av. W Bri —5H 49
Gillian Ct. S'fd —5G 45
Gilliver La. Clip —4C 62
Gillot St. Hean —5E 9
Gillotts Clo. Bing —4E 43
Gill St. Nott —3F 37 (1C 2)
Gilpet Av. Nott —1B 38
Giltbrook Cres. Gilt —5E 11
Gilt Hill. Kimb —6F 11
Giltway. Gilt —6E 11
Gimson Clo. Ilk —4G 19
Gin Clo. Way. Aws —1E 21
Gipsy La. Nott —4A 58
Girton Rd. Nott —4E 25
Gisburn Clo. Nott —1E 59
Glade Av. Nott —4A 36
Gladehill Rd. Nott —6G 15
Glade, The. Nott —6C 58
Gladstone Av. Got —6H 67
Gladstone Av. Hean —3C 8
Gladstone St. Bees —6E 47
Gladstone St. Carl —2F 39
Gladstone St. Hean —3C 8
Gladstone St. Ilk —2B 32
(in two parts)
Gladstone St. Lan M —2G 9
Gladstone St. Long E —1F 65
Gladstone St. Nott —1D 36
Gladys St. Nott —6E 25
Glaisdale Dri. E. Nott —3D 34
Glaisdale Dri. W. Nott
　　—4D 34
Glaisdale Pk. Ind. Est. Nott
　　—3D 34
Glaisdale Parkway Nott
　　—4D 34
Glamis Rd. Nott —5E 25
Glanton Way. Arn —3C 16
Glapton La. Nott —3B 58
Glapton Rd. Nott —2G 49
Glaramara Clo. Nott —2F 49
Glasshouse St. Nott
　　—4G 37 (2E 3)
Glebe Cotts. Nott —3F 49
Glebe Cres. Ilk —2C 32
Glebe Cres. Stan —3A 30
Glebe Dri. Bur J —4D 28
Glebe Farm Clo. W Bri
　　—1G 59
Glebe Farm View. Ged
　　—4H 27
Glebe La. Rad T —6F 41
Glebe Rd. Carl —5E 27
Glebe Rd. Nut —1C 22
Glebe Rd. W Bri —4B 50
Glebe St. Huck —3E 5
Glebe St. Nott —4D 36
Glebe, The. Coss —3D 20
Glen Av. E'wd —4D 10
Glenbrook. Cotg —2G 63
Glenbrook Cres. Nott —2G 35
Glencairn Dri. Nott —1G 35
Glencairn St. Nott —6G 23
Glencoe Rd. Nott —4E 59
Glencoyne Rd. Nott —5C 58
Glendale Clo. Carl —5F 27
Glendale Ct. Bees —5E 15
Glendale Gdns. Arn —6C 16
Glendoe Gro. Bing —5C 42

Glendon Dri. Huck —6E 5
Glendon Dri. Nott —4E 25
Glendon Rd. Ilk —5G 31
Gleneagles Ct. Edw —2D 60
Gleneagles Dri. Arn —4D 16
Glenfield Av. Kimb —6F 11
Glenfield Rd. Long E —2F 65
Glenhelen. Colw —3H 39
Glenlivet Gdns. Nott —4D 58
(in two parts)
Glenloch Dri. Nott —5D 58
Glenmore Rd. W Bri —5D 50
Glenorchy Cres. Nott —5C 14
Glenparva Av. Red —4A 16
Glenridding Clo. W Bri
　　—6F 51
Glen Rd. Bur J —2E 29
Glensford Gdns. Nott —5C 14
Glenside. Wd'p —2D 26
Glenside Rd. Bees —2C 46
Glenstone Ct. Nott —1D 36
Glen, The. Nott —4C 58
Glentworth Rd. Nott —3C 36
Glenwood Av. Nott —5D 34
Glins Rd. Nott —5D 14
Gloucester Av. Bees —6F 47
Gloucester Av. Nott —5C 36
Gloucester Av. Nut —4F 23
Gloucester Av. Sand —1C 54
Glover Av. Nott —5D 34
Glue La. Los —2A 8
Goatchurch Ct. Nott —4E 15
Goathland Clo. Nott —5F 15
Godber Rd. Huck —6C 4
Godfrey Dri. Ilk —4G 31
Godfrey St. Hean —4C 8
Godfrey St. N'fld —3A 40
Godkin Dri. Lan M —1E 9
Goldcrest Rd. Nott —3H 23
Goldham Rd. Nott —6D 22
Goldsmith Sq. Nott
　　—4F 37 (2C 2)
Goldsmith St. Nott
　　—4F 37 (2C 2)
Goldswong Ter. Nott —2G 37
Golf Club Rd. Stan D —2C 44
Golf Course Rd. Keyw
　　—5F 71
Golf Rd. Rad T —6G 41
Goodall Cres. Huck —5G 5
Goodall St. Nott —2D 36
Goodliffe St. Nott —1D 36
Goodman Clo. Gilt —5E 11
Goodwin Clo. Sand —5C 44
Goodwin Dri. Kimb —1G 21
Goodwin St. Nott
　　—3E 37 (1A 2)
Goodwood Av. Arn —5A 16
Goodwood Cres. Ilk —5H 31
Goodwood Dri. Bees —3H 55
Goodwood Rd. Nott —5D 34
Goole Av. Ilk —4H 31
Goosegate. Cotg —2E 63
Goose Ga. Nott
　　—5H 37 (4F 3)
Gordon Clo. Att —3D 56
Gordon Gro. Nott —6D 24
Gordon Rise. Nott —5A 26
Gordon Rd. Bur J —2G 29
Gordon Rd. Nott —3A 38
Gordon Rd. W Bri —4B 50
Gordon Sq. W Bri —4B 50
Gordon St. Ilk —6B 20
Gordon St. Nott —3B 24
Gorman Ct. Arn —6D 16
Gorse Clo. Calv —3B 6
Gorse Clo. Long E —3D 64
Gorse Clo. Newt —4D 10
Gorse Ct. Nott —2C 24
Gorse Rd. Keyw —4B 70
Gorse Wlk. Nott —2D 38
Gorsey Rd. Nott —2H 37
Gosforth Ct. Nott —2H 49
Gothic Clo. Nott —3C 24
Goverton Sq. Nott —2B 24
Gowan Clo. Bees —3C 56
Goyden Clo. Nott —5E 15
G P T Bus. Pk. Bees —6G 47
Grace Av. Bees —5H 47

Grace Cres. Hean —3D 8
Grace Dri. Nott —1B 36
Grafton Av. Wd'p —2A 26
Grafton Ct. Nott —4E 37
Graham St. Ilk —2B 32
Graham St. Nott —4D 36
Grainger Av. W Bri —2A 60
Graingers Ter. Huck —6F 5
Grainger St. Nott —1A 50
Grampian Dri. Arn —3F 15
Grampian Way. Long E
　　—5C 54
Granby Ct. Bing —5D 42
Granby St. Ilk —5B 20
Granby Vs. Nott —5B 38
Grandfield Av. Rad T —5F 41
Grandfield Cres. Rad T
　　—5F 41
Grandfield St. Los —1A 8
Grange Av. Bees —5F 47
Grange Av. Breas —5A 54
Grange Av. Rud —5F 59
Grange Clo. Nott —3F 49
Grange Cres. Ged —4H 27
Grange Dri. Long E —5H 55
Grangelea Gdns. Bees
　　—3C 46
Grangemoor. Pap —2H 5
Grange Pk. Long E —5H 55
Grange Pk. W Bri —6D 50
Grange Rd. Edw —1C 60
Grange Rd. Long E —5H 55
Grange Rd. Stock —4B 24
Grange Rd. Wd'p —3A 26
Grange View. E'wd —2B 10
Grange View Rd. Ged —5H 27
Grangewood Av. Ilk —2B 32
Grangewood Ct. Nott —6C 34
Grangewood Rd. Nott
　　—6C 34
Grannis Dri. Nott —1G 35
Grantham Clo. Gilt —6E 11
Grantham Rd. Bing —5F 43
Grantham Rd. Rad T —1D 52
Grantleigh Clo. Nott —4F 35
Granton Av. Nott —5D 58
Grant St. Nott —4D 36
Granville Av. Long E —4F 55
Granville Ct. Nott —4B 38
Granville Cres. Rad T —1E 53
Granville Gro. Nott —4B 38
Grasby Wlk. Nott —3B 58
Grasmere Av. Nott —5A 24
Grasmere Clo. Huck —3D 4
Grasmere Ct. Long E —3D 54
Grasmere Gdns. Got —5H 67
Grasmere Rd. Bees —3D 46
Grasmere Rd. Long E
　　—3D 54
Grasmere St. Sand —6D 44
Grassingdale Clo. Carl —5F 27
Grassington Rd. Nott —4A 34
Grassmere. Cotg —2G 63
Grass Rd. Carl —2A 28
Grass St. Ilk —4A 20
Grassy La. Bees —6G 47
Graveney Gdns. Arn —1D 26
Graylands Rd. Nott —2D 34
Grazingfield. Nott —1E 59
Greasley Av. Newt —3E 11
Greasley St. Nott —6H 13
Gt. Freeman St. Nott
　　—3G 37 (1E 3)
Gt. Hoggett Dri. Bees —5A 46
Gt. Northern Clo., The. Nott
　　—6H 37 (6G 3)
Gt. Northern Rd. E'wd —3H 9
Gt. Northern Way. N'fld
　　—3B 40
Greaves Clo. Arn —2D 34
Greaves Clo. Nott —6D 22
Greek St. Nott —4E 37
Greenacre. Bur J —2E 29
Greenacre. Edw —1D 60
Greenacre. Nott —4B 34
Greenacre Av. Hean —2E 9
Greenacres Caravan Pk. W Bri
　　—2F 51

Greenacres Clo. Newt —3E **11**
Green Av. N'fld —2A **40**
Greenbank. Carl —3F **39**
Greenbank Ct. Nott —5G **25**
Greenburn Clo. Gam —5F **51**
Green Clo. Huck —6G **5**
Green Clo. Plum —3D **70**
Greencroft. Nott —3C **58**
Greendale Gdns. Nott
　—1H **35**
Greendale Rd. Arn —1B **26**
Greendale Rd. Nott —3E **39**
Greenfield Gro. Carl —1D **38**
Greenfields. Lan M —1E **9**
Greenfields Dri. Cotg —3F **63**
Greenfield St. Nott —2B **48**
Greenford Dri. Nut —4D **22**
Greengates Av. Nott —4B **26**
Greenhill Cres. Carl —3G **39**
Greenhill Rise. Carl —3G **39**
Greenhill Rd. Carl —3G **39**
Greenhills Av. Car —2C **10**
Greenhills Rd. E'wd —2B **10**
Greenland Cres. Bees —1C **56**
Green La. Ilk —2C **32**
Green La. Nott —3B **58**
Green Leys. W Bri —1G **59**
Green Platt. Cotg —2E **63**
Greens Ct. Ilk —6H **19**
Greens Farm La. Ged —5A **28**
Greenside Clo. Long E
　—6G **55**
Greenside Wlk. Nott —3E **39**
Greens La. Kimb —1H **21**
Green St. Bart —3E **67**
Green St. Nott —3H **49**
Green, The. Bees —1E **57**
Green, The. Rad T —6E **41**
Green, The. Rud —1G **69**
Greenway Clo. Rad T —6E **41**
Greenway, The. Sand —5D **44**
Greenwich Av. Nott —3A **24**
Greenwich Pk. Clo. W Bri
　—6G **49**
Greenwood Av. Huck —3D **4**
Greenwood Av. Ilk —2C **32**
Greenwood Av. Nott —4F **39**
Greenwood Ct. Bees —6D **46**
Greenwood Cres. Carl
　—3G **39**
Greenwood Gdns. Rud
　—1H **69**
Greenwood Rd. Nott & Carl
　—4D **38**
Greenwood Vale. Huck —3C **4**
Greet Ct. Nott —2B **36**
Greetwell Clo. Nott —3G **35**
Gregg Av. Hean —3D **8**
Gregory Av. Lan M —2E **9**
Gregory Av. Lent —6D **36**
Gregory Av. Map —5C **26**
Gregory Boulevd. Nott
　—2C **36**
Gregory Clo. S'fd —3H **45**
Gregory Ct. Bees —1B **56**
Gregory Ct. Lent —6D **36**
Gregory Ct. Nott —1D **36**
Gregory St. Ilk —1A **32**
Gregory St. Nott —3C **24**
Gregson Gdns. Bees —4B **56**
Grenay Ct. Rud —5F **59**
Grenfell Ter. Nott —3C **24**
Grenville Dri. Ilk —4B **20**
Grenville Dri. S'fd —3G **45**
Grenville Rise. Arn —4B **16**
Grenville Rd. Bees —1H **57**
Gresham Clo. W Bri —4G **49**
Gresham Gdns. W Bri
　—4H **49**
Gresham Gdns. Wd'p —2C **26**
Gresley Rd. Ilk —6B **20**
Gretton Rd. Nott —3C **26**
Greyfriar Ga. Nott
　—6G **37** (6D **2**)
Greyhound St. Nott
　—5G **37** (3E **3**)
Greys Rd. Wd'p —3B **26**
Greystoke Dri. Nott —2C **34**
Grey St. Newt —4C **10**

Greythorn Dri. W Bri —1H **59**
Grierson Av. Nott —5F **15**
Griffs Hollow. Carl —2G **39**
Grimesmoor Rd. Calv —2E **7**
Grimsby Ter. Nott
　—3G **37** (1E **3**)
Grimston Rd. Nott —3C **36**
Grindon Cres. Nott —3A **14**
Grindslow Av. W Hal —1C **30**
Grinsbrook. Lent —5C **36**
Gripps Comn. Cotg —3F **63**
Grisedale Ct. Bees —1A **56**
Gritley M. Nott —1F **49**
Grizedale Gro. Bing —5B **42**
Groome Av. Los —1A **8**
Grosvenor Av. Breas —5B **54**
Grosvenor Av. Long E
　—3C **64**
Grosvenor Av. Nott —1G **37**
Grosvenor Ct. Nott —1G **37**
Grosvenor Rd. E'wd —3B **10**
Grouville Dri. Wd'p —2C **26**
Grove Av. Bees —5E **47**
Grove Clo. Bur J —2F **29**
Grove Ct. Bees —5D **46**
Grover Av. Nott —4C **26**
Grove Rd. Bing —4F **43**
Grove Rd. Nott —6D **36**
Groveside Cres. Nott —2A **58**
Grove St. Bees —6G **47**
Grove, The. Breas —5B **54**
Grove, The. Calv —3E **7**
Grove, The. Nott —5F **25**
　(Haydn Av.)
Grove, The. Nott —3D **36**
　(Southey St.)
Grundy St. Nott —2C **36**
Guardian Ct. Nott —1A **36**
Guinea Clo. Long E —6C **54**
Gunn Clo. Nott —6G **13**
Gunnersbury Way. Nut
　—4D **22**
Gunthorpe Clo. Nott —4F **25**
Gunthorpe Dri. Nott —4F **25**
Gunthorpe Rd. Ged —4E **27**
Gutersloh Ct. S'fd —3H **45**
Guy Clo. S'fd —5G **45**
Gwenbrook Av. Bees —6E **47**
Gwenbrook Rd. Bees —6E **47**
Gwndy Gdns. Nott —6E **15**

Hackworth Clo. Newt
　—2D **10**
Hadbury Rd. Nott —4D **24**
Hadden Ct. Nott —4D **34**
Haddon Clo. Carl —5F **27**
Haddon Clo. Huck —5E **5**
Haddon Clo. W Hal —1C **30**
Haddon Cres. Bees —2C **56**
Haddon Nurseries. Ilk
　—4A **20**
Haddon Rd. W Bri —5B **50**
Haddon St. Ilk —4A **20**
Haddon St. Nott —5F **25**
Haddon Way. Long E —3B **64**
Haddon Way. Rad T —5G **41**
Hadleigh Clo. Bees —3G **55**
Hadley St. Ilk —4C **32**
Hadrian Gdns. Nott —3E **15**
Hadstock Clo. Sand —1D **54**
Hagg La. D Abb —4B **30**
　(in two parts)
Hagley Clo. Nott —3C **38**
Haileybury Cres. W Bri
　—1B **60**
Haileybury Rd. W Bri —6B **50**
Haise Ct. Nott —2F **23**
Halberton Dri. W Bri —1H **59**
Hales Clo. Cotg —2E **63**
Haley Clo. Kimb —1F **21**
Halifax Ct. Nott —5D **22**
Halifax Pl. Nott
　—5H **37** (5F **3**)
Halina Ct. Bees —4F **47**
Hallam Ct. Ilk —4B **20**
Hallam Fields Rd. Ilk —5C **32**
Hallam Rd. Bees —5F **47**

Hallam Rd. Nott —5C **26**
Hallam's La. Arn —6B **16**
Hallams La. Bees —1D **56**
Hallam Way. W Hal —1B **30**
Hall Clo. Rad T —6E **41**
Hall Ct. W Hal —2C **30**
Hall Croft. Bees —6F **47**
Hallcroft Rd. Ilk —1B **32**
Hall Dri. Bees —6D **46**
Hall Dri. Got —6G **67**
Hall Dri. Nott —6E **35**
Hall Dri. Sand —5D **44**
Hall Farm Clo. Toll —4F **61**
Hallfields. Edw —2D **60**
Hall Gdns. Bees —4B **46**
Hallington Dri. Hean —4B **8**
Hallowell Dri. Nott —3F **23**
Hall Rd. Lan M —1G **9**
Halls La. Newt —5C **10**
Halls Rd. S'fd —5F **45**
Hall St. Nott —4H **25**
Hall View Dri. Nott —3D **34**
Halstead Clo. Bees —1C **56**
Halstead Clo. Nott —4H **23**
Haltham Wlk. Nott —5B **58**
Hambledon Dri. Nott —4H **35**
Hambleton. Long E
　—4C **54**
Hambling Clo. Nott —6G **13**
Hamilton Clo. Arn —4E **17**
Hamilton Clo. Bees —5H **55**
Hamilton Clo. Clif —2D **58**
Hamilton Ct. Nott
　—6F **37** (6B **2**)
Hamilton Dri. Nott
　—6F **37** (6B **2**)
Hamilton Dri. Rad T —5F **41**
*Hamilton Gdns. Nott —6F **25***
　(off Alexandra St.)
Hamilton Pl. Nott —5B **38**
Hamilton Rd. Long E —4F **55**
Hamilton Rd. Nott —1F **37**
Hamilton, The. Nott —1C **48**
Hamlet, The. Hean —2C **8**
Hampden Gro. Bees —5E **47**
Hampden St. Gilt —5D **10**
Hampden St. Lan M —2F **9**
Hampden St. Nott
　—3F **37** (1C **2**)
Hampshire Dri. Sand —6D **44**
*Hampstead Ct. Nott —4G **25***
　(off Daybrook St.)
Hampstead Rd. Nott —6A **26**
Hampton Clo. Bees —2F **55**
Hampton Clo. W Hal —1B **30**
Hampton Rd. W Bri —5A **50**
Handel St. Nott
　—4A **38** (3H **3**)
Hand's Rd. Hean —4D **8**
Hankin St. Huck —5G **5**
Hanley Av. Bees —3B **46**
Hanley St. Nott
　—4F **37** (3C **2**)
Hannah Cres. Nott —4H **35**
Hanover Ct. Nott —3D **34**
Hanslope Cres. Nott —3D **34**
Hanson Cres. Huck —4E **5**
Hanworth Gdns. Arn —5H **15**
Harberton Clo. Red —4A **16**
Harby Dri. Nott —5A **36**
Harcourt Cres. Nut —4F **23**
Harcourt Rd. Nott —1E **37**
Harcourt St. Bees —5E **47**
Harcourt Ter. Nott
　—4H **37** (2G **3**)
Harden Ct. Nott —5A **58**
Hardstaff Almshouses. Ged
　—5G **27**
Hardstaff Rd. Nott —4C **38**
Hardwick Av. W Hal —1C **30**
Hardwicke Rd. Bees —2C **56**
Hardwick Gro. Bing —4D **42**
Hardwick Gro. Nott —1B **48**
Hardwick Gro. W Bri —2B **50**
Hardwick Pl. Ilk —4G **31**
Hardwick Rd. Sher —4G **25**
Hardwick Rd. Park —6E **37**
Hardwood Clo. Nott —6G **13**

Hardy Barn. Ship —5E **9**
Hardy Clo. Kimb —6H **11**
Hardy Clo. Long E —1F **65**
Hardy's Dri. Ged —6H **27**
Hardy St. Kimb —6H **11**
Hardy St. Nott —3E **37**
Harewood Av. Nott —2B **24**
Harewood Clo. Rad T
　—6G **41**
Harewood Clo. Sand —1C **54**
Harkstead Rd. Nott —4F **15**
Harlaxton Dri. Long E
　—4A **56**
Harlaxton Dri. Nott —5D **36**
Harlaxton Wlk. Nott —3G **37**
Harlech Clo. Ilk —4G **19**
Harlech Rise. Bees —1G **56**
Harlequin Clo. Rad T —6H **41**
Harlequin Ct. E'wd —2H **9**
Harley St. Nott —6D **36**
Harlow Ct. W Hal —2B **30**
Harlow Gro. Ged —5G **27**
Harmston Rise. Nott —3D **24**
　(in two parts)
Harnett Clo. Nott
　—5H **37** (5F **3**)
Harold Av. Lan M —1F **9**
Harold Ct. Nott —5A **38**
Harold St. Nott —5A **38**
Harpenden Sq. Nott —4G **23**
Harpole Wlk. Arn —3B **16**
Harrier Gro. Huck —1E **13**
Harriett St. S'fd —4F **45**
Harrimans Dri. Breas —5B **54**
Harrimans La. Lent —3B **48**
Harrington Clo. Ged —6B **28**
Harrington Dri. Nott —5D **36**
Harrington St. Long E
　—2D **64**
Harris Clo. Nott —4F **35**
Harrison Rd. S'fd —3F **45**
Harris Rd. Bees —5D **46**
Harrogate Rd. Nott —4E **39**
Harrogate St. N'fld —2H **39**
Harrowby Rd. Nott —5D **36**
Harrow Gdns. Nott —5A **36**
Harrow Rd. Huck —6B **4**
Harrow Rd. Nott —5G **35**
Harrow Rd. W Bri —6A **50**
Harry Peel Ct. Bees —5G **47**
Hart Av. Sand —5C **44**
Hartcroft Rd. Nott —1F **35**
Hartford Clo. Nott —1H **49**
Hartington Av. Carl —6F **27**
Hartington Av. Huck —5A **4**
Hartington Clo. W Hal
　—1C **30**
Hartington Pl. Ilk —2A **20**
Hartington Rd. Nott —4G **25**
Hart Lea. Sand —5D **44**
Hartley Ct. Nott —3D **36**
Hartley Dri. Bees —5H **47**
Hartley Rd. Nott —3C **36**
Hartness Rd. Nott —4A **58**
Hartside Clo. Gam —4E **51**
Hartside Gdns. Long E
　—4C **54**
Hart St. Lent —6D **36**
Hartwell St. Nott —3H **37**
Hartwood Dri. S'fd —2F **45**
Harvest Clo. Bing —5D **42**
Harvest Clo. Nott —5D **14**
Harvey Clo. Rud —2H **69**
Harvey Ct. Nott —1C **48**
Harvey Croft. Trow —5E **33**
Harvey Rd. Nott —1F **35**
Harwich Clo. Nott —5G **13**
Harwill Cres. Nott —5H **23**
Harwood Clo. Arn —5D **16**
Haslam St. Nott
　—6F **37** (6C **2**)
Haslemere Rd. Long E
　—5D **54**
Haslemere Rd. Nott —1B **36**
Hassock La. N. Ship —6F **9**
Hassock La. S. Ship —1G **19**
Hassocks La. Bees —4H **47**
Hassocks, The. Bees —4H **47**
Hastings St. Carl —2E **39**

Haswell Rd. Nott —2H **23**
Hatfield Av. Sand —1D **54**
Hatfield Dri. W Bri —1G **59**
Hatfield Rd. Nott —6G **25**
Hatherleigh Clo. Nott —1H **35**
Hathern Clo. Long E —2F **65**
Hathern Grn. Bees —3G **47**
Hathersage Av. Long E
　—2B **64**
Hatley Clo. Nott —2F **49**
Hatton Clo. Arn —3E **15**
Hatton Crofts. Long E
　—1E **65**
Havelock St. Ilk —2B **32**
Haven Clo. W Bri —6H **49**
Havenwood Rise. Nott
　—5B **58**
Haverhill Cres. Nott —3B **14**
Haversham Clo. Nott —5B **24**
Hawarden Ter. Nott —2D **36**
Hawkhurst Dri. Nott —1D **46**
Hawkins Ct. Ilk —3B **20**
Hawkridge Gdns. Nott
　—4A **38** (2H **3**)
Hawkridge St. Nott
　—4H **37** (2H **3**)
Hawkshead Clo. W Bri
　—6F **51**
Hawksley Gdns. Nott —3A **58**
Hawksley Rd. Nott —2C **36**
Hawks Wood Clo. Chil
　—1B **56**
Hawksworth Av. Nott —3H **25**
Hawksworth Rd. W Bri
　—2B **50**
Hawksworth St. Nott —4A **38**
Hawley Mt. Nott —4B **26**
Haworth Ct. Nott —4A **58**
Hawthorn Av. Breas —5B **54**
Hawthorn Av. Cotg —3F **63**
Hawthorn Av. Huck —4D **4**
Hawthorn Clo. Edw —1D **60**
Hawthorn Clo. Keyw —5C **70**
Hawthorn Clo. Nott —2F **49**
Hawthorn Clo. Wdbgh —6H **7**
Hawthorn Cres. Arn —4C **16**
Hawthorne Av. Long E
　—1E **65**
Hawthorne Av. S'fd —1H **45**
Hawthorne Gro. Bees —5H **47**
Hawthorne Rise. Aws —3D **20**
Hawthorn View. Nott —1F **49**
Hawthorn Wlk. Nott —2D **38**
Hawton Cres. Nott —6A **36**
Hawton Spinney. Nott
　—5A **36**
Hayden La. Huck —1F **5**
Haydn Av. Nott —5F **25**
Haydn Rd. Nott —5E **25**
Haydock Clo. Kimb —6H **11**
Hayes Clo. W Hal —1C **30**
Hayes Rd. Keyw —4B **70**
Hayles Clo. Nott —1F **25**
Hayley Clo. Kimb —1F **21**
Hayling Clo. Ilk —4G **19**
Hayling Dri. Nott —6B **24**
Haynes Av. Trow —4E **33**
Haynes Clo. Nott —2D **58**
Hay's Clo. Ilk —5H **19**
Haywood Ct. Nott
　—5A **38** (4H **3**)
Haywood Rd. Nott —5B **26**
Haywood St. Nott
　—5A **38** (4H **3**)
Hayworth Rd. Sand —6D **44**
Hazelbank Av. Nott —6B **26**
Hazel Clo. Bing —5G **43**
Hazel Clo. Hean —4B **8**
Hazel Dri. Nut —1B **22**
Hazel Gro. Huck —6E **5**
Hazel Gro. Map —3C **26**
Hazel Hill Cres. Nott —6F **15**
Hazelhurst Gdns. Nott
　—6H **13**
Hazel Meadows. Huck —6E **5**
Hazel Rd. Carl —5C **36**
Hazel St. Nott —5H **13**
　(in two parts)

Hazelwood. Cotg —2G **63**
Hazelwood Clo. Newt —3D **10**
Hazelwood Dri. Huck —6A **4**
Hazelwood Rd. Nott —2C **36**
Headingley Gdns. Nott
—1B **36**
Healey Clo. Nott —1G **49**
Heanor Ga. Ind. Est. Hean
(in two parts) —5B **8**
Heanor Ga. Rd. Hean —4A **8**
Heanor Rd. Ilk —2H **19**
Heanor Rd. Los —1A **8**
Heanor Rd. Smal & Hean
—5A **8**
Heard Cres. Bees —3F **47**
Heathcoat Building. High S
—2B **48**
Heathcote St. Nott
—5H **37** (4F **3**)
Heather Clo. Newt —3D **10**
Heather Clo. Nott —2H **37**
Heather Cres. Breas —5B **54**
Heather Croft. W Bri —1G **59**
Heatherington Gdns. Nott
—4E **15**
Heatherley Dri. Nott —3D **24**
Heather Rise. Bees —2E **47**
Heather Rd. Carl —6F **27**
Heathervale. W Bri —5F **49**
Heathfield Av. Ilk —1C **32**
Heathfield Gro. Bees —2D **56**
Heathfield Rd. Nott —3D **24**
Heath Gdns. Breas —5C **54**
Heath, The. Gilt —5D **10**
Heaton Clo. Nott —6B **26**
Heckington Dri. Nott —4H **35**
Hedderley Wlk. Nott
—3H **37** (1F **3**)
Heddington Gdns. Arn
—5G **15**
Hedley St. Nott —1E **37**
Hedley Vs. Nott —6E **25**
Heighington Gro. Nott
—3C **24**
Helen Clo. Bees —5D **46**
Hellebore Clo. Nott —6C **14**
Helm Clo. Nott —6F **13**
Helmsdale. Arn —4D **16**
Helmsdale Clo. Arn —4D **14**
Helston Dri. Nott —5D **22**
Helvellyn Clo. Nott —1G **49**
Helvellyn Way. Long E
—3D **54**
Hemingway Clo. Carl —2E **39**
Hemlock Av. Long E —4F **55**
Hemlock Av. S'fd —3G **45**
Hemlock Gdns. Nott —1F **23**
Hemlock La. Ilk —4H **31**
Hemmingway Clo. Newt
—4E **11**
Hempshill La. Nott —1F **23**
(in two parts)
Hemsby Gdns. Nott —5H **13**
Hemscott Clo. Nott —5F **13**
Hemsley Dri. E'wd —2H **9**
Hemswell Clo. Nott —4C **38**
Hendon Rise. Nott —1B **38**
Hendre Gdns. Nott —6E **15**
Henley Clo. N'fld —3A **40**
Henley Gdns. S'fd —3A **44**
Henley Rise. Nott —4E **25**
Henley Way. W Hal —1B **30**
Henning Gdns. Nott —5G **13**
Henrietta St. Nott —1A **24**
Henry Ct. Nott —1G **49**
Henry Rd. Bees —5G **47**
Henry Rd. Nott —6D **36**
Henry Rd. W Bri —3A **50**
Henry St. Huck —5F **5**
Henry St. Red —3A **16**
Henry St. Snei —5A **38**
Henshaw Av. Ilk —4H **31**
Henshaw Pl. Ilk —3A **20**
Henson Sq. Bees —3B **46**
Hensons Row. Nott —5B **24**
Hepple Dri. Nott —6F **13**
Herald Clo. Bees —4H **47**
Herbert Rd. Nott —6F **25**
Hereford Rd. Ged —4H **27**

Hereford Rd. Nott —4D **38**
Hereford Rd. Wd'p —2A **26**
Hermitage Sq. Nott —5B **38**
Hermitage Wlk. Ilk —4B **32**
Hermitage Wlk. Nott
—6E **37** (6A **2**)
Hermon St. Nott —4E **37**
Heron Dri. Lent —5C **36**
Herons Ct. W Bri —1E **61**
Heron Wharf. Nott —1D **48**
Herrywell La. Cotg —6H **63**
Hervey Grn. Nott —3C **58**
Heskey Clo. Nott —3G **37**
Heskey Wlk. Nott —3G **37**
Heslington Av. Nott —1C **36**
Hethbeth Ct. Nott —1G **49**
Hethersett Gdns. Nott
—5H **13**
Hetley Rd. Bees —3F **47**
Hexham Av. Ilk —5C **32**
Hexham Clo. Nott —5C **50**
Hexham Gdns. Nott —3E **15**
Heyford Ct. Hean —4E **9**
Hickings La. S'fd —3G **45**
Hickling Rd. Nott —5C **26**
Hickling Way. Cotg —4G **63**
Highbank Dri. Nott —5C **58**
Highbury Av. Nott —2B **24**
Highbury Rd. Keyw —3C **70**
Highbury Rd. Nott —6A **14**
Highbury Wlk. Nott —1A **24**
High Chu. St. Nott —6D **24**
(in two parts)
Highclere Dri. Carl —1H **39**
Highcliffe Rd. Nott —4C **38**
Highcroft. Nott —3B **26**
High Croft Clo. Long E
—2G **65**
Highcroft Dri. Nott —4B **34**
High Cross Ct. Nott —3D **36**
High Cross Leys. Nott
—3G **37** (1E **3**)
High Cross St. Nott
—4H **37** (3F **3**)
Highfield Ct. Bees —5F **47**
Highfield Dri. Carl —2F **39**
Highfield Dri. Ilk —4F **31**
Highfield Dri. Nut —3F **23**
Highfield Gro. W Bri —4B **50**
Highfield Rd. Bees —2A **56**
Highfield Rd. Keyw —3C **70**
Highfield Rd. Nott —2B **48**
Highfield Rd. Nut —3E **23**
Highfield Rd. W Bri —4B **50**
Highfields Science Pk. Nott
—2B **48**
Highfield St. Long E —3E **55**
Highgate Clo. Carl —5F **27**
Highgate Dri. Ilk —4G **19**
Highgrove Av. Bees —5D **46**
Highgrove Gdns. Edw
—1C **60**
High Hazles Clo. Ged —4G **27**
High Hill View. Toll —4F **61**
High Holborn. Ilk —4A **20**
High Hurst. Calv —3C **6**
High La. Central. W Hal
—6D **18**
High La. E. W Hal —6E **19**
High La. W. W Hal —1B **30**
High Leys Rd. Huck —6D **4**
High Meadow. Toll —4F **61**
High Pavement. Nott
—5H **37** (5F **3**)
High Rd. Bees —5B **46**
High Rd. Chil —6E **47**
High Rd. Tot —3A **56**
High Spannia. Kimb —6H **11**
High St. Arnold, Arn —5B **16**
High St. Av. Arn —6A **16**
High St. Heanor, Hean —3C **8**
High St. Hucknall, Huck
—4E **5**
High St. Ilkeston, Ilk —1B **32**
High St. Kimberley, Kimb
—1H **21**
High St. Long Eaton, Long E
—5G **55**

High St. Loscoe, Los —1A **8**
High St. Nottingham, Nott
—5G **37** (4E **3**)
High St. Pl. Nott
—5G **37** (4E **3**)
High St. Ruddington, Rud
—6G **59**
High St. Stapleford, S'fd
—4G **45**
Highurst Ct. Nott —4E **37**
Highurst St. Nott —4E **37**
High View Av. Keyw —4D **70**
High View Ct. Nott —1H **37**
Highwood Av. Nott —1F **35**
Highwray Gro. Nott —4B **58**
Hilary Clo. Nott —6D **34**
Hilcot Dri. Nott —6H **23**
Hill Clo. Newt —4E **11**
Hill Clo. W Bri —5D **50**
Hillcrest Clo. Wat —6A **12**
Hillcrest Dri. Huck —5B **4**
Hillcrest Gdns. Bur J —2E **29**
Hill Crest Gro. Nott —4F **25**
Hillcrest Rd. Keyw —3C **70**
Hillcrest View. Carl —6D **26**
Hill Dri. Bing —4D **42**
Hill Farm Ct. Edw —3C **60**
Hillfield Gdns. Nott —3C **14**
Hillfield Rd. S'fd —3H **45**
Hillgrove Gdns. Nott —5E **15**
Hilliers Ct. Nott —5D **14**
Hillingdon Av. Nut —4D **22**
Hillington Rise. Nott —6G **15**
Hill Rise. Trow —5E **33**
Hill Rd. Bees —2B **56**
Hill Rd. B Vil —1C **14**
Hill Rd. Hean —4B **8**
Hillsford Clo. Nott —4G **35**
Hillside. Lan M —2E **9**
Hill Side. Nott —6B **36**
Hillside Av. Nott —2C **36**
Hillside Cres. Bees —3E **47**
Hillside Dri. Bur J —2F **29**
Hillside Dri. Long E —5D **54**
Hillside Gro. Sand —5C **44**
Hillside Rd. Bees —2B **56**
Hillside Rd. Bram —3C **46**
Hillside Rd. Rad T —6G **41**
Hills Rd. Wd'p —3A **26**
Hillview Av. Nott —5H **25**
Hillview Rd. Bees —4A **56**
Hill View Rd. Carl —6C **26**
Hilton Clo. Long E —3B **64**
Hilton Ct. W Bri —6D **50**
Hilton Cres. W Bri —6D **50**
Hilton Rd. Nott —5B **26**
Hinchin Brook. Lent —5C **36**
Hinshelwood Ct. Nott —5A **58**
Hinsley Clo. Arn —5D **16**
Hirst Ct. Nott —4E **37**
Hirst Cres. Nott —5F **35**
Hoare Rd. Bees —3B **56**
Hobart Clo. Nott —2G **49**
Hobart Dri. S'fd —2H **45**
Hobson Dri. Ilk —3A **32**
Hockerwood. Nott —1C **58**
Hockley. Nott —5H **37** (4G **3**)
Hodgkin Clo. Nott —4A **58**
Hodgkinson St. N'fld —3A **40**
Hodson Ho. Nott —5G **25**
Hoefield Cres. Nott —1G **23**
Hoewood Rd. Nott —6G **13**
Hogan Gdns. Nott —4E **15**
Hogarth Clo. S'fd —5G **45**
Hogarth St. Nott —3B **38**
Hoggetts Clo. Bees —5B **46**
Hogg La. Rad T —6E **41**
(in two parts)
Hoggs Field. E'wd —3B **10**
Holbeck Rd. Huck —2F **5**
Holbeck Rd. Nott —3B **36**
Holborn Av. Nott —4B **38**
Holborn Clo. Nut —4D **22**
Holborn Pl. Bulw —6A **14**
Holbrook Ct. Nott —5C **58**
Holbrook St. Hean —3C **8**
Holby Clo. Nott —5D **14**
Holcombe Clo. Nott —5H **23**

Holdale Rd. Nott —3D **38**
Holden Ct. Nott —4E **37**
Holden Cres. Nut —1C **22**
Holden Gdns. S'fd —5G **45**
Holden Rd. Bees —4E **47**
Holden St. Nott
—4E **37** (2A **2**)
Holgate. Nott —3A **58**
Holgate Rd. Nott —2G **49**
Holgate Wlk. Huck —5C **4**
Holkham Av. Bees —6C **46**
Holkham Clo. Arn —1C **26**
Holkham Clo. Ilk —4G **19**
Holland Clo. Got —6H **67**
Holland Meadow. Long E
—2F **65**
Holland St. Nott —2D **36**
Holles Cres. Nott
—6E **37** (6A **2**)
Hollies Dri. Edw —1C **60**
Hollies, The. Sand —6C **44**
Hollington Rd. Nott —3G **35**
Hollinwell Av. Sand
—2D **54**
Hollins, The. Calv —2E **7**
Hollinwell Av. Nott —4H **35**
Hollinwell Ct. Edw —2D **60**
Hollinwood La. Calv —3A **6**
(in two parts)
Hollis St. Nott —6E **25**
Hollows, The. Long E —5A **56**
Hollows, The. Nott —1E **59**
Hollowstone. Nott
—5H **37** (5G **3**)
(in two parts)
Holly Av. Breas —4B **54**
Holly Av. Carl —1F **39**
Holly Av. Thorn —2C **38**
Holly Av. Wilf —3F **49**
Holly Clo. Bing —5G **43**
Holly Clo. Huck —6F **5**
Holly Ct. Bees —3C **46**
Holly Ct. Nott —2B **38**
Hollycroft. W Bri —1C **60**
Hollydale Rd. Nott —3D **38**
Hollydene Clo. Huck —6A **4**
Hollydene Cres. Nott —3F **23**
Hollyfarm Ct. Newt —4E **11**
Holly Gdns. Nott —2B **38**
Hollygate Ind. Pk. Cotg
—1G **63**
Hollygate La. Cotg —2F **63**
Holly La. Bees —6E **47**
Holly Rd. Wat —6H **11**
Hollythorpe Pl. Huck —6A **4**
Holme Clo. Ilk —5H **19**
Holme Clo. Wdbgh —6H **7**
Holme Croft. W Hal —2C **30**
Holmefield Cres. Ilk —1C **32**
Holme Gro. W Bri —1D **50**
Holme Lea. Hol P & Rad T
—6B **40**
Holme Lea. Sand —5D **44**
Holme Lodge. Carl —3G **39**
Holme Rd. Bing —5F **43**
Holme Rd. W Bri —2B **50**
Holmes Clo. Lan M —2E **9**
Holmesfield Dri. Hean —5D **8**
Holmes Rd. Breas —5A **54**
Holmes St. Hean —3B **8**
Holme St. Nott —1A **50**
Holmewood Cres. Nott
—1F **25**
Holmewood Dri. Gilt —5D **10**
Holmfield Rd. Bees —2C **56**
Holmsfield. Keyw —5C **70**
Holroyd Av. Nott —5B **38**
Holt Gro. Calv —2D **6**
Holwood Ct. Nott —1G **23**
Holyoake Dri. Long E —6H **55**
Holyoake Rd. Nott —4E **27**
Holyrood Ct. Bees —2C **46**
Holywell Rd. Ilk —4G **19**
Home Clo. Arn —5H **15**
Home Croft, The. Bees
—4B **46**
Home Farm Clo. Got —6H **67**
Homefield Av. Arn —3C **16**
Homefield Rd. Nott —2B **36**

Holdale Rd. Nott —3D **38**
Homestead. Lan M —1E **9**
Homewell Wlk. Nott —2D **58**
Honeysuckle Clo. Nott
—6E **23**
Honeysuckle Gro. Bing
—6D **42**
Honeysuckle Gro. Nott
—3H **23**
Honeywood Ct. Nott —2C **38**
Honeywood Dri. Nott —2C **38**
Honingham Clo. Arn —2B **26**
Honingham Rd. Ilk —4G **19**
Honister Clo. Gam —4E **51**
Honister Clo. Nott —6B **58**
Honiton Clo. Bees —3A **56**
Honiton Rd. Nott —6E **23**
Hood Cotts. Nott —6E **25**
Hood St. Nott —5H **25**
Hooley Clo. Long E —1D **64**
Hooley Pl. Nott —4H **25**
Hoopers Wlk. Nott —1G **49**
Hooton Rd. Carl —2E **39**
Hooton St. Nott —4B **38**
Hope Clo. Nott —1F **49**
Hopedale Clo. Nott —4C **36**
Hope Dri. Nott —6F **37** (6B **2**)
Hope St. Bees —4E **47**
Hope St. Ilk —2B **32**
Hopewell Clo. Rad T —4G **41**
Hopewell Wlk. Ilk —2B **20**
Hopkins Ct. E'wd —2B **10**
Horace Av. S'fd —4E **45**
Hornbeam Clo. Ilk —2D **32**
Hornbeam Gdns. Nott
—6F **13**
Hornbuckle Ct. Nott —4D **36**
Hornchurch Rd. Nott —1D **34**
Hornsby Wlk. Nott —5C **14**
Horridge St. Ilk —3B **20**
Horsendale Av. Nut —3E **23**
Horsham Dri. Nott —5D **14**
Horsley Cres. Lan M —2E **9**
Hoselett Field Rd. Long E
—2G **65**
Hoten Rd. Nott —6B **38**
Hotspur Clo. Nott —2C **24**
Houghton Clo. Nut —3E **23**
Houldsworth Rise. Arn
—3A **16**
Hound Rd. W Bri —3A **50**
Hounds Ga. Nott
—5G **37** (5C **2**)
(in two parts)
Houseman Gdns. Nott
—1G **49**
Houston Clo. Nott —4C **14**
Hovenden Gdns. Nott
—2C **36**
Hove Rd. Nott —2C **24**
Howard Clo. Long E —4G **55**
Howard St. Nott
—4G **37** (2F **3**)
Howbeck Rd. Arn —5D **16**
Howden Rd. Nott —3A **14**
Howell Jones Rd. Bees
—2B **56**
Howells Clo. Nott —5G **15**
Howick Dri. Nott —5F **13**
Howitt St. Hean —3D **8**
Howitt St. Long E —6G **55**
Hoylake Cres. Nott —2D **34**
Hoylake Wlk. Nott —5E **15**
Hoyland Av. Nott —1C **48**
Hubert St. Nott —3D **36**
Hubert St. Nott —3D **36**
Hucknall By-Pass. Huck
—4C **4**
Hucknall Clo. Strel —5D **22**
Hucknall Cres. Ged —5G **27**
Hucknall La. Nott —5A **14**
Hucknall Rd. Bulw & Nott
—4B **14**
Hudson St. Nott —3B **38**
Hufton's Ct. Hean —6D **8**
Hufton's Dri. Hean —6D **8**
Hugessen Av. Huck —3G **5**
Huggett Gdns. Nott —5C **14**
Humber Clo. Nott —1G **49**
Humber Lodge. Bees —4G **47**

Humber Rd. Bees —4G **47**
Humber Rd. Long E —4E **55**
Humber Rd. S. Bees —5H **47**
Humberston Rd. Nott —6C **34**
Hungerhill La. Wdbgh
—3H **17**
Hungerhill Rd. Nott —2H **37**
Hunger Hill Yd. Ilk —3C **32**
Hungerton St. Nott —6D **36**
Hunston Clo. Nott —2G **35**
Hunt Av. Hean —3C **8**
Hunter Rd. Arn —1E **27**
Hunters Clo. Nott —5E **49**
Huntingdon Dri. Nott
—5F **37** (5B **2**)
Huntingdon St. Nott
—3G **37** (1D **2**)
Huntingdon Wlk. Sand
—6D **44**
Huntingdon Way. Bees
—3H **55**
Huntley Clo. Nott —4E **59**
Hurcomb St. Nott —2B **38**
Hurley Ct. W Hal —1C **30**
Hurst Dri. Stan —3A **30**
Hurts Croft. Bees —1D **56**
Hurt's Yd. Nott
—4G **37** (3D **2**)
Huss's La. Long E —6H **55**
Hutchinson Grn. Nott
—3H **37** (1F **3**)
Hutton Clo. Bees —2D **46**
Hutton St. Nott —6B **38**
Huxley Clo. Nott —2D **34**
Hyde Clo. Nott —1D **58**
Hyde Pk. Clo. W Bri —6G **49**
Hyson Clo. Nott —1D **36**
Hyson St. Nott —2D **36**

Ian Gro. Carl —1H **39**
Ilam Sq. Ilk —2A **20**
Ilford Clo. Ilk —4H **19**
Ilingfield Ct. Nott —6D **34**
Ilkeston Rd. Hean —4D **8**
Ilkeston Rd. Ilk —6B **32**
Ilkeston Rd. Nott
—4B **36** (3A **2**)
Ilkeston Rd. Stan D & Sand
—2E **45**
Ilkeston Rd. S'fd —1G **45**
Ilkeston Rd. Trow —4D **32**
Imperial Av. Bees —5E **47**
Imperial Av. Ged —6G **27**
Imperial Rd. Bees —5E **47**
Imperial Rd. Nott —1B **24**
Inchwood Clo. Bees —3H **55**
Incinerator Rd. Nott —1A **50**
Independent St. Nott —3D **36**
Ingham Gro. Nott —6C **36**
Ingham Rd. Long E —3E **55**
Ingleborough Gdns. Long E
—5C **54**
Ingleby Clo. Cotg —3E **63**
Ingleby Clo. Nott —5B **34**
Ingleby Rd. Long E —3B **64**
Inglefield Rd. Ilk —3B **32**
Inglewood Rd. Nott —4C **58**
Ingram Rd. Nott —1B **24**
Ingram Ter. Nott —1B **24**
Inham Cir. Chil —5C **46**
Inham Clo. Bees —6A **46**
Inham Rd. Bees —6A **46**
Innes Clo. Carl —2E **39**
Instow Rise. Nott —3H **37**
Intake Rd. Keyw —4B **70**
Iona Dri. Trow —6F **33**
Iona Gdns. Nott —4E **15**
Ipswich Cir. Nott —4C **38**
Ireland Av. Bees —6G **47**
Ireland Clo. Bees —6G **47**
Iremonger Rd. Nott —1H **49**
Irene Ter. Nott —5D **24**
Ireton Gro. Att —4D **56**
Ireton St. Bees —5E **47**
Ireton St. Nott —4E **37** (2A **2**)
Irwin Dri. Nott —1G **23**
Isaac Newton Cen. High S
—2B **48**

Isaacs La. S'fd —4F **45**
Isabella St. Nott
—6G **37** (6D **2**)
Isandula Rd. Nott —5D **24**
Island St. Nott
—6H **37** (6G **3**)
Islay Clo. Arn —4B **16**
Islay Clo. Trow —6F **33**
Ives Clo. W Bri —1G **59**
Ivy Clo. Wat —4H **11**
Ivy Gro. Carl —2F **39**
Ivy Gro. Nott —1E **37**
Ivy La. E'wd —3A **10**

Jacklin Gdns. Nott —4E **15**
Jackson Av. Ilk —6A **20**
Jackson Av. Sand —5C **44**
James St. Arn —5A **16**
James St. Kimb —1H **21**
Japonica Dri. Nott —3H **23**
Jardines, The. Bram —2C **46**
Jarrow Gdns. Nott —3D **14**
Jarvis Av. Nott —3D **38**
Jasmine Clo. Bees —2D **46**
Jasmine Clo. Clif —4A **58**
Jasmine Clo. Strel —6E **23**
Jasmine Rd. Nott —4C **24**
Jasper Clo. Rad T —1E **53**
Jayne Clo. Ged —5A **28**
Jayne Clo. Nott —3E **35**
Jebb's La. Bing —5F **43**
Jedburgh Clo. Kimb —6G **11**
Jedburgh Clo. Nott —3H **37**
Jedburgh Wlk. Nott —3H **37**
Jenned Rd. Arn —3C **16**
Jenner St. Nott —1F **37**
Jenness Av. Nott —4C **14**
Jennison St. Nott —6A **14**
Jenny Burton Way. Huck
—6G **5**
Jermyn Dri. Arn —4E **15**
Jersey Gdns. Nott —3A **38**
Jervis Ct. Ilk —4B **20**
Jesmond Rd. Nott —1B **24**
Jessamine Ct. Bees —5G **47**
Jessops La. Ged —5H **27**
Joan Av. Hean —3C **8**
John Carroll Ct. Nott —3B **38**
John Quinn Ct. Nott —6D **24**
Johnson Av. Huck —6F **5**
Johnson Dri. Hean —3D **8**
Johnson Rd. Nott —5C **36**
John's Pl. Hean —4B **8**
Johns Rd. Rad T —6G **41**
John St. Hean —3B **8**
John St. Ilk —6B **20**
John St. New B —6D **24**
Jona Gdns. Nott —4E **15**
Joyce Av. Bees —2H **55**
Joyce Av. Nott —3H **25**
Joyce Clo. Nott —3H **25**
Jubilee Ct. Nott —6D **22**
Jubilee Rd. Day —1A **26**
Jubilee St. Kimb —6G **11**
Jubilee St. Nott —3B **38**
Judson Av. S'fd —5H **45**
Julian Rd. W Bri —3D **50**
Julie Av. Hean —4E **9**
Jumelles Dri. Calv —3B **6**
Junction Rd. Long E —1A **66**
Juniper Clo. Nott —4A **58**
Juniper Ct. Gilt —5E **11**
Juniper Gdns. Bing —5G **43**

Kappler Clo. N'fld —2A **40**
Karen Rise. Arn —4C **16**
Katherine Dri. Bees —2H **55**
Kayes Wlk. Nott
—5H **37** (5F **3**)
Keats Clo. Day —6H **15**
Keats Clo. Long E —2D **64**
Keats Clo. Nut —1B **22**
Keats Dri. Huck —5B **4**
Kedleston Clo. Bees —6C **46**
Kedleston Clo. Long E
—2C **64**

Kedlestone Dri. Ilk —4H **19**
Keeling Clo. Newt —4D **10**
Keepers Clo. B Vil —1C **14**
Kegworth Rd. Nott —6F **67**
Keilder Dri. Bing —5C **42**
Kelfield Clo. Nott —2C **24**
Kelham Grn. Nott —3B **38**
Kelham M. Nott —1D **38**
Kelling Clo. Nott —1E **25**
Kelly Wlk. Nott —4F **49**
Kelsey Clo. Att —2E **57**
Kelso Gdns. Nott —1F **49**
Kelstern Clo. Nott —4A **24**
Kelvedon Gdns. Nott —3A **38**
Kelvin Clo. S'fd —6E **45**
Kelvin Rd. Nott —2C **38**
Kemmel Rd. Nott —2B **24**
Kempsey Clo. Nott —5C **14**
Kempson St. Rud —6G **56**
Kempton Clo. Kimb —6G **11**
Kempton Dri. Arn —4C **16**
Kendal Clo. Huck —3D **4**
Kendal Ct. W Bri —3D **50**
Kendal Dri. Bees —3D **46**
Kendale Ct. Nott —1B **38**
Kendleston Wlk. Nott —5E **15**
Kendrew Ct. Nott —4A **58**
Kenia Clo. Carl —1F **39**
Kenilworth Ct. Bees —3G **47**
Kenilworth Ct. Nott
—6F **37** (6B **2**)
Kenilworth Dri. Ilk —4G **31**
Kenilworth Rd. Bees —4G **47**
Kenilworth Rd. Nott
—6F **37** (6B **2**)
Kenmore Gdns. Nott —3H **37**
Kennedy Av. Long E —2E **65**
Kennedy Clo. Day —6H **15**
Kennedy Dri. S'fd —2G **45**
Kenneth Rd. Arn —3B **16**
Kennington Rd. Nott —4B **36**
Kenrick Rd. Nott —6C **26**
(in two parts)
Kenrick St. N'fld —2A **40**
Kensal Ct. W Bri —3A **50**
Kensington Clo. Bees —4A **56**
*Kensington Clo. Nott —4G **25**
(off Daybrook St.)*
Kensington Gdns. Carl
—2G **39**
Kensington Gdns. Ilk —2C **32**
Kensington Pk. Clo. W Bri
—6G **49**
Kensington Rd. Sand —1D **54**
Kensington St. Ilk —3B **32**
Kenslow Av. Nott —2C **36**
Kent Av. Bees —1F **57**
Kenton Av. Nut —4D **22**
Kenton Ct. Nott —2H **49**
Kent Rd. Gilt —4E **11**
Kent Rd. Nott —5B **26**
Kent Rd. S'fd —5F **45**
Kent St. Nott —4H **37** (3F **3**)
Kentwood Rd. Nott —5B **38**
Kenyon Rd. Nott —6B **36**
Keppel Ct. Ilk —4B **20**
Kersall Ct. Nott —2B **24**
Kersall Dri. Nott —2B **24**
Kersall Gdns. Huck —4F **5**
Kersall Gdns. Cres. Huck
—4F **5**
Kestrel Clo. Carl —6D **26**
Kestrel Clo. Ilk —5D **32**
Kestrel Rd. Ilk —5B **32**
Keswick Clo. Bees —3D **46**
Keswick Clo. Gam —4E **51**
Keswick Clo. Ilk —4H **31**
Keswick Ct. Long E —3D **54**
Keswick Ct. Nott
—5A **38** (4H **3**)
Keswick St. Nott
—5A **38** (4H **3**)
Kett St. Nott —6H **13**
Keverne Clo. Nott —5A **24**
Kevin Rd. Nott —1D **46**
Kew Clo. W Bri —2G **59**
Kew Cres. Hean —4F **9**
Keys Clo. Nott —6G **13**

Key St. Nott —4B **38**
Keyworth La. Bradm —5A **70**
Keyworth Rd. Ged —4F **27**
Kibworth Clo. Nott —3D **24**
Kiddier Av. Arn —6D **16**
Kilbourne Rd. Arn —4D **16**
Kilbourn St. Nott —3G **37**
Kilburn Clo. Bees —1B **46**
Kilburn Dri. Ilk —4H **19**
Kilby Av. Nott —3C **38**
Kilby Ho. Long E —6F **55**
Kildare Rd. Nott —1B **38**
Kildonan Clo. Nott —5D **22**
Killerton Grn. Nott —6D **58**
Killerton Pk. Dri. W Bri
—1F **59**
Killisick Ct. Arn —5D **16**
Killisick La. Arn —3D **16**
Killisick Rd. Arn —4D **16**
Kilnbrook Av. Arn —4D **16**
Kiln Clo. W Hal —6C **18**
Kilnwood Clo. Nott —2C **38**
Kilsby Rd. Nott —3D **58**
Kilverton Clo. Nott —1B **46**
Kilvington Rd. Arn —6D **16**
Kimber Clo. Nott —3D **34**
Kimberley Clo. Kimb —2H **21**
Kimberley Eastwood By-Pass.
E'wd —3H **9**
Kimberley Rd. Nut —2B **22**
Kimberley St. Nott —5C **38**
Kimbolton Av. Nott —4D **36**
Kindlewood Dri. Bees —4B **56**
King Charles St. Nott
—5F **37** (5C **2**)
King Edward Ct. Nott
—4H **37** (3F **3**)
King Edward St. Huck —5E **5**
King Edward St. Nott
—4H **37** (3F **3**)
King Edward St. Sand
—5D **44**
Kingfisher Clo. Bees —6H **47**
Kingfisher Clo. Nott —3B **24**
Kingfishers Ct. W Bri —1E **61**
Kingfishers Wharf. Nott
—1E **49**
King George Av. Ilk —1A **32**
King John's Arc. Nott —4E **3**
King John's Chambers. Nott
—4E **3**
Kinglake Pl. Nott —1G **49**
Kingrove Av. Bees —5D **46**
Kings Av. Ged —5G **27**
Kingsbridge Av. Nott —1E **27**
Kingsbridge Way. Bram
—5C **46**
Kingsbury Dri. Nott —1G **35**
Kingsdale Clo. Long E
—2C **64**
Kingsdown Mt. Nott —1E **47**
Kingsford Av. Nott —3C **36**
Kingsley Cres. Long E
—3D **64**
Kingsley Dri. N'fld —2A **40**
Kingsley Rd. Nott —5C **38**
Kingsmead Av. Trow —1F **45**
King's Meadow Rd. Nott
—1E **49**
Kingsmoor Clo. Nott —1G **35**
King's Pl. Nott —5H **37** (4F **3**)
Kings Rd. Sand —5D **44**
Kingsthorpe Clo. Nott —6B **26**
Kingston Av. Ilk —5C **32**
Kingston Ct. Nott —5A **38**
Kingston Ct. W Hal —1B **30**
Kingston Dri. Colg —1E **63**
Kingston Rd. W Bri —5A **50**
King St. Bees —5G **47**
King St. E'wd —3B **10**
King St. Ilk —6B **20**
King St. Long E —5F **55**
King St. Nott —5G **37** (4D **2**)
Kings Wlk. Nott
—4G **37** (3D **2**)
Kingsway. Hean —3B **8**
Kingsway. Ilk —4D **32**
Kingsway. Rad T —1E **53**
Kingsway Gdns. Huck —1E **13**

Kingsway Rd. Huck —1E **13**
Kingswell Rd. Arn —6B **16**
Kingswood Clo. W Bri
—6H **49**
Kingswood Rd. Nott —4H **35**
Kingswood Rd. W Bri
—6H **49**
Kinlet Rd. Nott —1E **25**
Kinross Cres. Nott —3G **35**
Kinsale Wlk. Nott —1C **58**
Kipling Clo. Nott —5A **58**
Kippis St. Nott —4H **37** (3F **3**)
Kirby Clo. Newt —2C **10**
Kirby Rd. Newt —2C **10**
Kirkbride Ct. Bees —1B **56**
Kirkby Av. Ilk —3B **32**
Kirkby Gdns. Nott —1H **49**
Kirk Clo. Bees —1D **56**
Kirk Cotts. Nott —3C **24**
Kirkdale Clo. Nott —5B **34**
Kirkdale Gdns. Long E
—1D **64**
Kirkdale Rd. Long E —2D **64**
Kirkdale Rd. Nott —3D **38**
Kirkewhite Ct. Nott —1H **49**
Kirkewhite St. W. Nott
—1G **49**
Kirkewhite Wlk. Nott —1G **49**
Kirkfield Dri. Breas —5A **54**
Kirkham Clo. Hean —4B **8**
Kirkham Dri. Bees —3H **55**
Kirkhill. Bing —4E **43**
Kirkland Dri. Bees —3C **56**
Kirk La. Rud —6G **59**
Kirkley Gdns. Arn —5C **16**
Kirkman Rd. Los —1A **8**
Kirk Rd. Nott —5C **26**
Kirkstead Gdns. Nott —2D **36**
Kirkstead St. Nott —2D **36**
Kirkstone Ct. Long E —3D **54**
Kirkstone Dri. Gam —4E **51**
Kirkwhite Av. Long E —6F **55**
Kirtle Clo. Nott —1H **35**
Kirtley Dri. Nott —1E **49**
Kirton Av. Long E —6F **55**
Kittiwake M. Lent —5C **36**
Kiwi Dri. Huck —6B **4**
Knapp Av. E'wd —4B **10**
Kneesall Gro. Huck —4F **5**
Kneeton Clo. Ged —3F **27**
Kneeton Clo. Nott —3G **25**
Kneeton Vale. Nott —3G **25**
Knighton Av. Nott —3C **36**
Knighton Rd. Wd'p —2H **25**
Knightsbridge Ct. Nott
—4G **25**
Knightsbridge Dri. W Bri
—1G **59**
Knightsbridge Gdns. Huck
—2D **4**
Knights Clo. Nott —5D **14**
Knight's Clo. W Bri —2G **59**
Knight St. N'fld —3H **39**
Kniveton Pk. Ilk —2H **31**
Knole Rd. Nott —4E **35**
Knoll Av. Huck —6B **4**
Knowle Hill. Kimb —2A **22**
Knowle La. Kimb —2A **22**
Knowle Pk. Kimb —2A **22**
Knowles Wlk. Arn —5G **15**
Kozi Kots. N'fld —2H **39**
Krebs Clo. Nott —4A **58**
Kyle View. Nott —4E **15**
Kyme St. Nott —4D **36**
Kynance Gdns. Nott —6F **49**

Labray Rd. Calv —2C **6**
Laburnum Av. Keyw —5E **71**
Laburnum Clo. Sand —4D **44**
Laburnum Gdns. Nott
—2C **24**
Laburnum Gro. Bees —6H **47**
Laburnum Gro. Huck —6F **5**
Laburnum St. Nott —2H **37**
Lace Rd. Bees —4F **47**
Lace St. Nott —2B **48**
Lacey Av. Huck —6E **5**
Lacey Fields Rd. Hean —4E **9**

Ladbrooke Cres. Nott —4A 24
Ladybank Rise. Arn —5E 17
Lady Bay Av. W Bri —2B 50
Lady Bay Bri. Nott & W Bri
—1A 50
Lady Bay Ct. W Bri —2C 50
Lady Bay Rd. W Bri —2C 50
Ladybridge Rd. Att —2E 57
Ladycroft Av. Huck —4E 5
Ladylea Rd. Long E —3C 64
Ladysmith St. Nott —5C 38
Ladysmock Gdns. Nott
—1H 49
Ladywood Rd. Ilk —5E 31
Lake Av. Los —1A 8
Lakehead Ho. Nott —4C 58
Lakeland Av. Huck —6G 5
Lakeside Av. Long E —3E 65
Lakeside Cres. Long E
—2E 65
Lake St. Nott —3D 36
Lamartine St. Nott
—4H 37 (2G 3)
Lamb Clo. Dri. Newt —1D 10
Lambert Gdns. Nott —1A 36
Lambert St. Nott —2C 36
Lambeth Ct. Bees —4H 47
Lambeth Rd. Arn —5E 17
Lambie Clo. Nott —4A 36
Lambley Almshouses. Nott
—1H 37
Lambley Av. Nott —4D 26
Lambley Bridle Rd. Bur J
—1D 28
Lambley Ct. Nott —4B 26
Lambley La. Bur J —2D 28
Lambley La. Ged —4H 27
Lambley St. Nott —6H 13
Lambourne Dri. Nott —4F 35
Lambourne Gdns. Wd'p
—2C 26
Lambton Clo. Ilk —4A 20
Lamcote Gdns. Rad T
—6E 41
Lamcote Gro. Nott —2H 49
Lamcote M. Rad T —6E 41
Lamcote St. Nott —2H 49
Laming Gap La. Keyw
—3G 71
Lamins La. B Vil —1F 15
Lammas Gdns. Nott —1H 49
Lamorna Gro. Nott —5F 49
Lamplands. Cotg —2E 63
Lamp Wood Clo. Calv —3C 6
Lanark Clo. Nott —4A 36
Lancaster Av. Sand —1C 54
Lancaster Av. S'fd —5G 45
Lancaster Ct. Nott —2D 38
Lancaster Rd. B Vil —1C 14
Lancaster Rd. Huck —1D 12
Lancaster Rd. Nott —2D 38
Lancaster Way. Nott —5D 22
Lancelot Dri. Wat —4H 11
Lancelyn Gdns. W Bri
—1A 60
Landcroft Cres. Nott —1E 25
Landmere Clo. Ilk —4G 19
Landmere Gdns. Nott —6B 26
Landmere La. Rud & Edw
Landmere La. W Bri —2F 59
Landsdown Gro. Long E
—4H 55
Landseer Clo. Nott —3C 36
Laneham Av. Arn —6C 16
Laneside Av. Bees —3G 55
Lane, The. Aws —3E 21
Laneward Clo. Ilk —3H 19
Langar Clo. Nott —3G 25
Langar Rd. Bing —6A 68
Langbank Av. Nott —4C 14
Langdale Dri. Long E —1C 64
Langdale Gro. Bing —5B 42
Langdale Rd. Nott —4A 48
Langden Ct. Long E —1G 65
Langdon Clo. Long E —4C 54
Langdown Clo. Nott —5G 13

Langford Rd. Arn —6D 16
Langham Av. Nott —3C 38
Langham Dri. Bur J —2F 29
Langley Av. Arn —1B 26
Langley Av. Ilk —2H 19
Langley Mill By-Pass. Lan M
—1G 9
Langstrath Rd. Nott —4C 58
Langtree Gdns. Bing —4F 43
Langtry Gro. Nott —6E 25
Lansdown Clo. Bees —1B 56
Lansdowne Dri. W Bri
—1H 59
Lansdowne Rd. Nott —3C 38
Lansing Clo. Nott —5D 58
Lanthwaite Clo. Nott —4D 58
Lanthwaite Rd. Nott —4D 58
Lapford Clo. Nott —1F 27
Larch Clo. Bing —5G 43
Larch Clo. Huck —6F 5
Larch Cres. Bees —5D 46
Larch Cres. E'wd —3A 10
Larchdene Av. Nott —6D 34
Larch Dri. Sand —4D 44
Larch Gdns. Nott —6G 13
Larch Way. Keyw —5E 71
Largs Clo. Nott —4C 14
Lark Clo. Bees —6A 46
Larkdale St. Nott
—3E 37 (1A 2)
Larkfield Rd. Nut —2B 22
Larkland's Av. Ilk —2C 32
Larkspur Av. Red —3A 16
Larwood Gro. Nott —3G 25
Lascelles Av. Ged —5F 27
Latham St. Nott —6H 13
Lathkill Av. Ilk —2A 20
Lathkill Clo. Nott —6H 13
Lathkilldale Cres. Long E
Latimer Clo. Nott —1A 24
Latimer Dri. Bees —6B 34
Laughton Av. W Bri —1G 59
Laughton Cres. Huck —1E 13
Launceston Cres. Nott
—1E 59
Launder St. Nott —1G 49
Laurel Av. Keyw —5D 70
Laurel Cres. Long E —1E 65
Laurel Rd. Carl —1F 37
Laurie Av. Nott —1E 37
Laurie Clo. Nott —1E 37
Lauriston Dri. Nott —3A 24
Lavender Clo. Nott —6E 23
Lavender Cres. Carl —6F 27
Lavender Gro. Bees —6H 47
Lavender Wlk. Nott —2H 37
Laver Clo. Arn —6D 16
Lawdon Rd. Arn —4C 16
Lawley Av. Bees —2G 47
Lawn Clo. Hean —3D 8
Lawn Hill Rd. Kimb —6G 11
Lawn Mill Rd. Kimb —6G 11
Lawn Ter. Ilk —1A 32
Lawrence Av. Aws —3E 21
Lawrence Av. Breas —5A 54
Lawrence Av. Colw —4G 39
Lawrence Av. E'wd —3B 10
Lawrence Clo. Cotg —2F 63
Lawrence St. Long E —5F 55
Lawrence St. Sand —4D 44
Lawrence St. S'fd —5F 45
Lawrence Way. Nott —1E 49
Lawson Av. Long E —6G 55
Lawson St. Nott —3E 37
Lawton Dri. Nott —4A 14
Laxton Av. Nott —2B 24
Laxton Dri. Huck —5C 4
Leabrook Clo. Nott —2A 58
Leabrook Gdns. Huck —3G 5
Leacroft Rd. Nott —3B 58
Leadale Av. Huck —3G 5
Leafield Grn. Nott —3C 58
Leafy La. Hean —4D 8
Leahurst Gdns. W Bri —6D 50

Leahurst Rd. W Bri —6C 50
Leahy Gdns. Nott —1D 24
Leake Rd. Got —6H 67
Leamington Dri. Bees
—1C 56
Leander Clo. Nott —4F 49
Leas, The. Bul —2H 29
Lechlade Clo. W Hal —1B 30
Lechlade Rd. Nott —1E 25
Ledbury Vale. Nott —6H 23
Leech Ct. Gilt —6D 10
Lee Cres. Ilk —1D 32
Lee La. Hean —4F 9
Leen Clo. B Vil —1D 14
Leen Clo. Huck —3G 5
Leen Ct. Nott —1C 48
Leen Dri. Bulw —4A 14
Leen Dri. Huck —2F 5
Leen Ga. Nott —1C 48
Leen Mills La. Huck —2F 5
Leen Pl. Nott —4C 36
Leen Valley Way. Huck
—6G 5
Leen View Ct. Nott —1G 23
Lee Rd. Bur J —2G 29
Lee Rd. Calv —2F 6
Lees Barn Rd. Rad T —1D 52
Lees Hill Footpath. Nott
—6A 38
Lees Hill St. Nott —5A 38
Lee St. Nott —6C 26
Leicester Ho. S'fd —3H 45
Leicester St. Long E —6H 55
Leigh Clo. W Bri —5G 49
Leigh Rd. Bees —2H 55
Leighton St. Nott —3B 38
Leiston Gdns. Nott —5E 15
Leivers Av. Arn —5B 16
Lema Clo. Nott —5B 14
Lendal Ct. Nott —4C 30
Lendrum Ct. Bur J —3F 29
Leniscar Av. Los —1A 8
Lennox St. Nott
—4H 37 (3G 3)
Lenton Av. Nott —5E 37
Lenton Av. Toll —4E 61
Lenton Boulevd. Nott —4C 36
Lenton Cir. Toll —4E 61
Lenton Ct. Nott —6E 37
(Lenton Av.)
Lenton Ct. Nott —5D 36
(Lombard Clo.)
Lenton Hall Dri. Nott —2H 47
Lenton La. Nott —1D 48
(in two parts)
Lenton Mnr. Nott —6C 36
Lenton Rd. Nott
—6E 37 (6A 2)
Lenton St. Sand —4E 45
Leonard Av. Nott —5F 25
Leonard St. Bulw —2H 23
Leopold St. Long E —5F 55
Le Page Ct. Nott —1G 35
Leroy Wallace Av. Nott
—3D 36
Lerwick Clo. Nott —4E 59
Leslie Av. Bees —6F 47
Leslie Av. Kimb —1E 21
Leslie Av. Nott —1E 37
Leslie Gro. Calv —3D 6
Leslie Rd. Nott —1E 37
Letchworth Cres. Bees
—1C 56
Letcombe Rd. Nott —2C 58
Leverton Ct. W Bri —6B 50
Leverton Grn. Nott —3C 58
Leverton Wlk. Arn —5C 16
Levick Ct. Nott —1G 49
Lewcote La. Ilk —6E 19
Lewindon Ct. Wd'p —3A 26
Lewis Clo. Nott
—3H 37 (1F 3)
Lexington Gdns. Nott
—3H 25
Leybourne Dri. Nott —1C 24
Leyland Clo. Bees —3H 55
Leys Ct. Rud —1G 69
Leys Rd. Rud —1G 69
Leys, The. Nor W —6H 61

Leys, The. Nott —3B 58
Ley St. N'fld —2A 40
Leyton Cres. Bees —6H 47
Lichfield Clo. Bees —2G 55
Lichfield Clo. Long E —6H 55
Lichfield Rd. Nott —5C 38
Liddell Gro. Nott —4F 35
Liddington St. Nott —6D 24
Lilac Av. Carl —1E 39
Lilac Clo. Keyw —5E 71
Lilac Clo. Nott —6E 23
Lilac Cres. Bees —6H 47
Lilac Gro. Bees —6H 47
Lilac Gro. Sand —6H 47
Lilac M. Ilk —4H 19
Lilac Rd. Huck —6F 5
Lilacs, The. Nott —5F 47
Lilian Hind Ct. Nott —5F 13
Lilleker Rise. Arn —4A 16
Lillie Ter. Nott —5B 38
Lillington Rd. Nott —6H 13
Lily Av. N'fld —2A 40
Lily Gro. Bees —6H 47
Lime Av. Lan M —3G 9
Lime Clo. Nut —1A 22
Lime Clo. Rad T —6F 41
Limefield Ct. W Bri —2C 50
Lime Gro. Long E —5F 55
Lime Gro. Sand —5D 44
Lime Gro. S'fd —6F 45
Lime Gro. Av. Bees —6E 47
Lime La. Arn —1A 16
Limes, The. Bart —1E 67
Limes, The. M'ley —4C 18
Lime St. Ilk —2B 32
Lime St. Nott —6H 13
Lime Ter. Long E —5F 55
Lime Tree Av. Nott —4H 23
Lime Tree Av. Woll —6H 35
Limetree Clo. Keyw —5D 70
Lime Tree Ct. Bees —2G 47
Limetree Ct. Ilk —3G 31
Limetree Rise. Ilk —3G 31
Lime Tree Rd. Huck —1H 13
Limmen Gdns. Nott —3A 38
Limpenny St. Nott —3E 37
Linby Av. Huck —4F 5
Linby Clo. Ged —5G 27
Linby Clo. Nott —2H 25
Linby Dri. Strel —5D 22
Linby Gro. Huck —3F 5
Linby La. Lin & Pap —1G 5
Linby Rd. Huck —3F 5
Linby St. Nott —5A 14
Linby Wlk. Huck —3E 5
Lincoln Av. Sand —1C 54
Lincoln Cir. Nott —5E 37
Lincoln Clo. S'fd —2G 45
Lincoln Clo. Nott —2E 35
Lincoln Gro. Rad T —6F 41
Lincoln St. Nott
—4G 37 (3E 3)
Lincoln St. Old B —4C 24
Lindale Clo. Gam —5E 51
Lindbridge Rd. Nott —5F 23
Linden Av. Nott —4A 58
Linden Ct. Bees —6G 47
Linden Gro. Bees —6G 47
Linden Gro. Ged —6B 28
Linden Gro. Sand —4C 44
Linden Gro. S'fd —5G 45
Linden St. Nott —2H 37
Lindfield Clo. Nott —5G 23
Lindfield Rd. Nott —5F 23
Lindisfarne Gdns. Nott
—4E 15
Lindley St. Newt —1D 10
Lindley Ter. Nott —2C 36
Lindrick Clo. Edw —1E 61
Lindsay St. Nott —2D 36
Lindum Gro. Nott —6B 38
Lindum Rd. Nott —4B 24
Linette Clo. Nott —6E 25
Linford Ct. Bees —3B 34
Ling Cres. Rud —5G 59
Lingfield Ct. Nott —6D 34
Lingford. Cotg —2G 63
Lingford St. Huck —5F 5
Lingmell Clo. W Bri —5E 51

Lingwood La. Wdbgh —6G 7
Linkin Rd. Bees —5C 46
Linkmel Clo. Nott —2E 49
Linkmel Rd. E'wd —2G 9
Linksfield Ct. W Bri —3G 59
Linnell St. Nott —3B 38
Linsdale Clo. Nott —4B 34
Linsdale Gdns. Ged —3F 27
Linton Rise. Nott —3C 38
Linwood Cres. E'wd —4B 10
Lion Clo. Nott —4A 24
Lismore Clo. Nott —4C 36
Lissett Av. Ilk —2A 32
Lister Clo. Nott —1C 48
Listergate. Nott
—5G 37 (5E 3)
Listergate S. Nott
—5G 37 (5E 3)
Listowel Cres. Nott —5C 58
Litchen Clo. Ilk —5B 32
Litchfield Rise. Arn —3A 16
Littlegreen Rd. Wd'p —2B 26
Lit. Hallam Hill. Ilk —4A 32
Lit. Hallam La. Ilk —3B 32
Lit. Hayes. W Bri —1G 59
Lit. John Wlk. Nott —2H 37
Little La. Calv —3B 6
Little La. Kimb —2H 21
Little La. Toll —2G 61
Lit. Lime La. Arn —1A 16
Lit. Lunnon. Bart —1E 67
Lit. Meadow. Cotg —3G 63
Littlemore La. Bradm —4H 69
Lit. Oakwood Dri. Nott
—3B 14
Lit. Ox. Colw —5H 39
Lit. Tennis St. Nott —6C 38
Lit. Tennis St. S. Nott
—1C 50
Littlewell La. Stan D —1B 44
Littlewood Gdns. Nott
—4C 34
Litton Clo. Ilk —3A 20
Litton Clo. Wd'p —3A 26
Liverpool St. Nott
—4A 38 (3H 3)
Llanberis Gro. Nott —5A 24
Lloyd St. Nott —5G 25
Loach Ct. Nott —4A 36
Lobelia Clo. Nott —2H 37
Lock Clo. Bees —2G 57
Lock Clo. Ilk —3G 31
Lockerbie St. Carl —3H 39
Lockton Av. Hean —4C 8
Lockwood Clo. Bees —1A 58
Lockwood Clo. Nott —4E 15
Lodge Clo. Nott —1B 36
Lodge Clo. Red —3A 16
Lodge Farm La. Arn —4A 16
Lodge Rd. Long E —2F 65
Lodge Rd. M'ley —4C 18
Lodge Rd. Newt —5C 10
Lodgewood Clo. Nott —1G 23
Lodore Clo. W Bri —5E 51
Logan Sq. Nott —3C 24
Logan St. Nott —1A 24
Lois Av. Nott —6D 36
Lombard Clo. Nott —6D 36
Lombardy Lodge. Bees
—4A 56
London Rd. Nott
—6H 37 (6G 3)
Long Acre. Bing —5E 43
Long Acre. Huck —4B 4
Longacre. Wd'p —3B 26
Long Acre E. Bing —5F 43
Longbeck Av. Nott —6C 26
Longclose Ct. Nott —2G 23
Longdale Rd. Nott —1H 25
Longden Ct. Bees —1H 45
Longden St. Nott
—4A 38 (3H 3)
Longfellows Clo. Nott —5F 15
Longfield Cres. Ilk —4B 32
Longfield La. Ilk —4B 32
Longford Cres. Nott —3A 14

Long Hill Rise. Huck —5D 4
Longlands Clo. Bees —1C 56
Longlands Rd. Bees —1H 57
Long La. Att —3D 56
Long La. Ship —1H 19
Long La. Wat —4A 12
Longleat Cres. Bees —1C 56
Longmead Clo. Nott —1G 25
Longmead Dri. Nott —1G 25
Longmoor Gdns. Long E
—3C 54
Longmoor La. Breas —4A 54
Longmoor La. Sand —2D 54
Longmoor Rd. Long E
—3C 54
Longore Sq. Nott —5B 36
Longridge Rd. Wd'p —2B 26
Long Row. Nott
—5G 37 (4D 2)
Long Row E. Nott
—5G 37 (4E 3)
Long Row W. Nott
—5G 37 (4D 2)
Long Stairs. Nott —5H 37
Longthorpe Ct. Arn —6B 16
Longue Dri. Calv —3B 6
Longwall Av. Nott —2E 49
Longwood Ct. Nott —5D 14
Lonsdale Dri. Bees —3G 55
Lonsdale Rd. Nott —3G 36
Lord Haddon Rd. Ilk —6A 20
Lord Nelson St. Nott —5B 38
Lord St. Nott —5B 38
Lorimer Av. Nott —2E 49
Lorna Ct. Nott —6H 25
Lorne Clo. Nott —2G 37
Lorne Gro. Rad T —6F 41
Lorne Wlk. Nott —2G 37
Lortas Rd. Nott —5D 24
Loscoe-Denby La. Los —1A 8
Loscoe Gdns. Nott —6F 25
Loscoe Grange. Los —2A 8
Loscoe Mt. Rd. Nott —5G 25
Loscoe Rd. Hean —2B 8
Loscoe Rd. Nott —6F 25
Lothian Rd. Toll —4E 61
Lothmore Ct. Nott —1F 49
Lotus Clo. Nott —2A 38
Loughborough Av. Nott
—5B 38
Loughborough Rd. W Bri &
Rud —5A 50
Loughrigg Clo. Nott —2F 49
Louis Av. Bees —4E 47
Louise Av. N'fld —1A 40
Lovel Clo. Ged —6B 28
Lovell Clo. Nott —2F 23
Lowater St. Carl —2D 38
Lowcroft. Wd'p —3B 26
Lowdham La. Wdbgh —6H 7
Lowdham Rd. Ged —4E 27
Lowdham St. Nott
—4A 38 (3H 3)
Lwr. Beauvale. Newt —2C 10
Lwr. Bloomsgrove Rd. Ilk
—5B 20
Lwr. Brook St. Long E
—6G 55
Lwr. Canaan. Rud —5H 59
Lwr. Chapel St. Ilk —4C 20
Lwr. Clara Mt. Rd. Hean
—4E 9
Lower Ct. Bees —4G 47
Lwr. Dunstead Rd. Lan M
—2E 9
Lwr. Eldon St. Nott
—5A 38 (5H 3)
Lwr. Gladstone St. Hean
—3C 8
Lwr. Granby St. Ilk —5B 20
Lwr. Middleton St. Ilk —6C 20
Lwr. Nelson St. Hean —3B 8
Lwr. Orchard St. S'fd —4F 45
Lwr. Park St. S'fd —5E 45
Lwr. Parliament St. Nott
—4H 37 (3E 3)
Lwr. Regent St. Bees —5G 47
Lower Rd. Bees —4H 47
Lwr. Stanton Rd. Ilk —3B 32

Lwr. Whitworth Rd. Ilk
—3B 32
Loweswater Ct. Gam —4E 51
Lowlands Dri. Keyw —3D 70
Lowlands Lea. Hean —3D 8
Low Pavement. Nott
—5G 37 (5E 3)
Lows La. Stan D —1B 44
Low Wood Rd. Nott —2E 23
Loxley Ct. Nott —1H 35
Lucerne Clo. Nott —5F 49
Lucknow Av. Nott —1H 37
Lucknow Ct. Nott —1H 37
Lucknow Dri. Nott —1H 37
Lucknow Rd. Nott —1H 37
Ludford Rd. Nott —5A 14
Ludgate Clo. Arn —3E 15
Ludham Av. Nott —5H 13
Ludlam Av. Gilt —6C 10
Ludlow Av. W Bri —4B 50
Ludlow Clo. Bees —2D 46
Ludlow Hill Rd. W Bri
—6B 50
Lulworth Clo. W Bri —6G 49
Lulworth Ct. Kimb —6H 11
Lune Clo. Att —2E 57
Lupin Clo. Nott —2H 37
Luther Clo. Nott —2A 38
Luton Clo. Nott —6B 24
Lutterell Way. W Bri —6D 50
Lybster M. Nott —1F 49
Lychgate Ct. Wat —5H 11
Lydney Pk. W Bri —5F 49
Lyle Clo. Kimb —6G 11
Lyme Pk. W Bri —6F 49
Lymington Gdns. Nott
—3B 38
Lymn Av. Ged —5H 27
Lynam Ct. Nott —6H 13
Lyncombe Gdns. Keyw
—4D 70
Lyndale Rd. Bees —3A 46
Lynden Av. Long E —1F 65
Lyndhurst Gdns. W Bri
—1H 59
Lyndhurst Gro. Long E
—4F 55
Lyndhurst Rd. Nott —5B 38
Lynmouth Cres. Nott —2C 36
Lynmouth Dri. Ilk —4H 19
Lynncroft. E'wd —2C 10
Lynstead Dri. Huck —6A 4
Lynton Ct. Nott —2B 38
Lynton Gdns. Arn —5C 16
Lynton Rd. Bees —5C 46
Lyons Clo. Rud —5F 59
Lytham Dri. Edw —2E 61
Lytham Gdns. Nott —4E 15
Lythe Clo. Nott —6E 49
Lytton Clo. Nott
—4A 38 (2H 3)

M

Mabel Gro. W Bri —3C 50
Mabel St. Nott —1H 49
Macauley Gro. Nut —1B 22
Machins La. Edw —2C 60
McIntosh Rd. Ged —4F 27
Mackinley Av. S'fd —2G 45
Maclaren Gdns. Rud —1H 69
Maclean Rd. Carl —2E 39
Macmillan Clo. Nott —4B 26
Madford Bus. Pk. Day
—1H 25
Madryn Wlk. Nott —6E 15
Mafeking St. Nott —5C 38
Magdala Rd. Nott —1G 37
Magdalene Way. Huck —3E 5
Magnolia Clo. Nott —6E 23
Magnolia Ct. Bees —2D 46
Magnolia Gro. Huck —1H 13
Magnus Ct. Bees —6G 47
Magnus Rd. Nott —4G 25
Magson Clo. Nott —4A 38
Maiden La. Nott
—5H 37 (4G 3)
Maidens Dale. Arn —5H 15
Maid Marian Way. Nott
—5F 37 (4C 2)

Maidstone Dri. Nott —1D 46
Main Rd. Cotg —4D 52
Main Rd. Ged —6H 27
Main Rd. Lent —5A 48
Main Rd. Plum —6G 61
Main Rd. Rad T —6E 41
Main Rd. Shelf —1H 41
Main Rd. Wat —4A 12
Main Rd. Wilf —5F 49
Main St. Aws —2E 21
Main St. Breas —5A 54
Main St. Bur J —3F 29
Main St. Calv —2A 6
Main St. E'wd —4B 10
Main St. Gam —4E 51
Main St. Keyw —6C 70
Main St. Kimb —1H 21
Main St. Lin —1E 5
Main St. Long E —6G 55
Main St. M'ley —4C 18
Main St. Newt —3E 11
Main St. Stan D —3B 44
Main St. Strel —5B 22
Main St. Wdbgh —6F 7
Main St. Bulwell. Bulw
(in two parts) —1H 23
Maitland Av. Wd'p —3B 26
Maitland Rd. Wd'p —3B 26
Major St. Nott —4G 37 (2D 2)
Malbon Clo. Nott —1B 38
Malcolm Clo. Nott —2G 37
Maldon Clo. Bees —1C 56
Malin Hill. Nott
—5H 37 (5F 3)
Malkin Av. Rad T —5G 41
Mallard Clo. Nott —3D 24
Mallard Ct. Bees —6G 47
Mallard Rd. Carl —3B 40
Malling Wlk. Nott —6A 26
Mallow Way. Bing —6D 42
Malmesbury Rd. Nott —3C 26
Maltby Clo. Nott —5H 23
Maltby Rd. Nott —3C 26
Malt Cotts. Nott —6D 24
Malthouse Clo. E'wd —4B 10
Malting Clo. Rud —1G 69
Maltings, The. Nott —2C 38
Maltmill La. Nott
—5H 37 (5E 3)
Malton Rd. Nott —5D 24
Malt St. Got —6H 67
Malvern Clo. Nott —6A 26
Malvern Ct. Bees —5H 47
Malvern Cres. W Bri —6B 50
Malvern Gdns. Long E
—5C 54
Malvern Rd. Nott —6A 26
Malvern Rd. W Bri —6A 50
Manchester St. Long E
—1F 65
Mandalay St. Nott —3B 24
Manesty Cres. Nott —6C 58
Manifold Gdns. Nott —1G 49
Manly Clo. Nott —5C 14
Manners Av. Ilk —4H 19
Manners Ind. Est. Ilk —6H 19
Manners Rd. Ilk —6A 20
Manners St. Ilk —3C 32
Manning St. Nott —2H 37
Manning View. Ilk —5B 20
Mannion Cres. Long E
—2D 64
Manns Leys. Cotg —3E 63
Mann St. Nott —1D 36
Manor Av. Att —2E 57
Manor Av. Bees —5F 47
Manor Av. S'fd —3F 45
Manor Clo. Edw —2D 60
Manor Ct. Bees —6B 46
Manor Ct. Breas —5A 54
Manor Ct. Carl —2H 39
Manor Cres. Carl —1H 39
Manor Croft. Nott —4C 24
Manor Farm La. Nott —4C 58
Manor Fields Dri. Ilk —2H 31
Manor Grn. Wlk. Carl —1H 39
Manor Ho. Rd. Long E
—6H 55

Manor Leigh. Breas —5A 54
Manor Pk. Rud —6F 59
Manor Rd. Bart —1E 67
Manor Rd. Bing —5F 43
Manor Rd. Calv —3C 6
Manor Rd. Carl —1H 39
Manor Rd. E'wd —4B 10
Manor Rd. Ilk —6A 20
Manor Rd. Keyw —4C 70
Manor St. Nott —5A 38
Manorwood Rd. Cotg —3F 63
Mansell Clo. E'wd —4D 10
Mansfield Ct. Nott —1F 37
Mansfield Gro. Nott
—3F 37 (1C 2)
Mansfield La. Calv —3D 6
Mansfield Rd. E'wd —1B 10
Mansfield Rd. Hean —3D 8
Mansfield Rd. Nott
—2F 37 (1D 2)
Mansfield Rd. Red —1A 16
Mansfield St. Nott —5G 25
Manston M. Nott —3D 36
Manthorpe Cres. Nott
—4B 26
Manton Cres. Bees —3F 47
Manvers Ct. Nott
—5A 38 (4H 3)
Manvers Gro. Rad T —6F 41
Manvers Rd. W Bri —5B 50
Manvers St. N'fld —3A 40
Manvers St. Nott
—5A 38 (4H 3)
Manville Clo. Bees —6B 34
Manville Clo. Nott —3A 36
Maori Clo. Huck —1C 12
Maple Av. Bees —6H 47
Maple Av. Sand —4D 44
Maplebeck Rd. Arn —6C 16
Maple Clo. Bing —5G 43
Maple Clo. Keyw —5E 71
Maple Clo. Rad T —1F 53
Mapledene Cres. Nott
—6C 34
Maple Dri. Ged —5A 28
Maple Dri. Huck —6C 4
Maple Dri. Nut —1B 22
Maple Gdns. Hean —4B 8
Maple Gro. Breas —5B 54
Maples St. Nott —2D 36
Maplestead Av. Nott —5F 49
Mapletree Clo. Nott —6F 15
Maple Way. Nott —1A 60
Mapperley Cres. Nott —5A 26
Mapperley Hall Dri. Nott
—6G 25
Mapperley La. M'ley —5C 18
Mapperley Orchard. Arn
—6D 16
Mapperley Pk. Dri. Nott
—1G 37
Mapperley Plains. Nott
—2D 26
Mapperley Rise. Nott —5A 26
Mapperley Rd. Nott —2G 37
Mapperley St. Nott —5G 25
March Clo. Nott —6C 14
Marchesi Clo. Huck —1E 13
Marchwood Clo. Nott —4B 36
Margaret Av. Ilk —1B 32
Margaret Av. Long E —4H 55
Margaret Av. Sand —1D 54
Margaret Cres. Ged —5G 27
Margaret Pl. Bing —4D 42
Margarets Ct. Bees —3A 46
Mar Hill Rd. Carl —2H 39
Maria Ct. Park —6E 37 (6A 2)
Marie Gdns. Huck —6E 5
Marina Av. Bees —6F 47
Marina Rd. Smal —5A 8
Mariner Ct. Nott —1G 23
Marion Av. Huck —2G 5
Marion Murdock Av. Ged
—5G 27
Maris Clo. Nott —3A 58
Maris Dri. Bur J —3F 29
Market Pl. Bing —5E 43
Market Pl. Bulw —6H 13
Market Pl. Huck —4E 5

Market Pl. Ilk —1A 32
Market Pl. Long E —5G 55
Market St. Bing —5E 43
Market St. Hean —3C 8
Market St. Ilk —1B 32
Market St. Nott
—4G 37 (3D 2)
Markham Cres. Nott —3G 25
Markham Rd. Bees —2D 46
Mark St. Sand —6E 45
Marlborough Ct. Bees —3F 47
Marlborough Ct. W Bri
—4B 50
Marlborough Rd. Bees
—3F 47
Marlborough Rd. Long E
—4H 55
Marlborough Rd. Wd'p
—2H 25
Marldon Clo. Nott —4C 34
Marlow Av. Nott —5C 24
Marlow Cres. W Hal —1B 30
Marl Rd. Rad T —6H 41
Marlwood. Cotg —4G 63
Marmion Rd. Nott —2C 38
Marne Clo. Ilk —5B 20
Marnham Dri. Nott —6A 26
Marple Sq. Nott —2G 37
Marriott Av. Bees —6A 46
Marriott Clo. Bees —6A 46
Marsant Clo. Bees —3A 36
Marshall Dri. Bees —3A 46
Marshall Hill Dri. Nott
—6D 26
Marshall Rd. Nott —6C 26
Marshall St. Hean —3D 8
Marshall St. Nott —5G 25
Marshall Way. Ilk —3H 31
Marston Rd. Nott —2D 38
Martell Ct. Bees —2C 56
Martin Clo. Bulw —5F 13
Martin Ct. Nott —1G 23
Martindale Clo. Gam —4E 51
Martinmass Clo. Nott —1C 48
Martin's Hill. Carl —2G 39
Marton Rd. Bees —2C 56
Marton Rd. Nott —4A 14
Marvin Rd. Bees —5F 47
Marwood Cres. Carl —5E 27
Marwood Rd. Carl —6E 27
Mary Ct. Nott —6A 26
Maryland Ct. S'fd —2G 45
Mary Rd. E'wd —4D 10
Masonic Pl. Nott
—4F 37 (3C 2)
Mason Rd. Ilk —5H 19
Massey Clo. Bur J —4E 29
Massey Gdns. Nott —3A 38
Masson Ct. Nott —4E 15
Matlock Ct. Long E —2B 64
Matlock Ct. Nott
—4G 37 (2D 2)
Matlock St. N'fld —2H 39
Matthews Ct. S'fd —2H 45
Mattingly Rd. Nott —1G 23
Maud St. Nott —6E 25
Maun Av. Nott —3B 36
Maun Gdns. Nott —3B 36
Maurice Dri. Nott —5A 26
Maws La. Kimb —6G 11
Maxtoke Rd. Nott —6E 37
Maxwell Clo. Nott —6D 36
Maxwell St. Long E —6G 55
May Av. Nott —5E 35
May Cotts. Nott —3C 24
May Ct. Nott —6F 25
Maycroft Gdns. Nott —2C 38
Mayes Rise. B Vil —1C 14
Mayfair Gdns. Nott —2D 24
Mayfield Av. Hean —4C 8
Mayfield Ct. Nott —1H 49
Mayfield Dri. S'fd —1H 45
Mayfield Gro. Long E —6G 55
Mayfield Rd. Carl —2D 38
Mayflower Clo. W Bri —4C 50
Mayflower Rd. Newt —5D 10
Mayland Clo. Nott —3C 34
Maylands Av. Breas —5A 54

Mayo Rd. Nott —6E **25**
Maypole. Nott —2C **58**
Maypole Yd. Nott
—4G **37** (3E **3**)
May's Av. Carl —3E **39**
Mays Clo. Carl —3E **39**
May St. Ilk —3A **20**
Maythorn Clo. Nott —2G **59**
Maythorne Wlk. Nott —5G **15**
Meadowbank Ct. E'wd —2H **9**
Meadowbank Way. E'wd
—2H **9**
Meadow Clo. Carl —2A **28**
Meadow Clo. E'wd —1B **50**
Meadow Clo. Huck —6B **4**
Meadow Clo. Nott —1A **50**
Meadow Cotts. N'fld —2H **39**
Meadow Ct. Nott —1B **50**
(Brand St.)
Meadow Ct. Nott —1A **50**
(Meadow Clo.)
Meadow Dri. Keyw —4E **71**
Meadow End. Got —6H **57**
Meadow End. Rad T —6H **41**
Meadow Gdns. Bees —1E **57**
Meadow Gro. Nott —1A **50**
Meadow La. Bur J —3F **29**
Meadow La. Chil —6E **47**
Meadow La. Long E —6H **55**
Meadow La. Nott —1A **50**
Meadow Rise. Nott —1F **23**
Meadow Rd. Aws —2E **21**
Meadow Rd. Bees —6G **47**
Meadow Rd. N'fld —2H **39**
Meadows, The. Hean —4C **8**
Meadows, The. Wdbgh
—6F **7**
Meadow St. Ilk —6B **20**
Meadows Way. Nott —2F **49**
Meadowsweet Hill. Bing
—5C **42**
Meadow Trading Est. Nott
—6A **38**
Meadowvale Cres. Nott
—4C **58**
Medawar Clo. Nott —4A **58**
Medawear Clo. Nott —4A **58**
Medbank Ct. Nott —6E **49**
Meden Clo. Nott —2C **58**
Meden Gdns. Nott —2B **36**
Medina Dri. Toll —4F **61**
Medway Clo. Bees —6C **46**
Medway St. Nott —4B **36**
Meeks Rd. Arn —5D **16**
Meerbrook Pl. Ilk —4G **31**
Meer Rd. Bees —6A **46**
Melbourne Ct. Long E
—3B **64**
Melbourne Ct. Nott —6A **24**
Melbourne Rd. Nott —1H **35**
Melbourne Rd. S'fd —1G **45**
Melbourne Rd. W Bri —2B **50**
Melbury Rd. Nott —1C **34**
Melbury Rd. Wd'p —3B **26**
Meldreth Rd. Nott —2E **35**
Melford Hall Dri. W Bri
—1G **59**
Melford Rd. Nott —1D **34**
Melksham Rd. Nott —5G **15**
Mellers Ct. Nott —2C **38**
Mellon Ter. Nott
—4E **37** (2A **2**)
Mellors Rd. Arn —4B **16**
Mellors Rd. W Bri —6B **50**
Melrose Av. Bees —6G **47**
Melrose Av. Nott —4G **25**
Melrose Gdns. W Bri —1H **59**
Melrose St. Nott —5G **25**
Melton Ct. Sand —6C **44**
Melton Gdns. Edw —1C **60**
Melton Gro. W Bri —4G **49**
Melton Rd. Toll —4C **60**
Melton Rd. W Bri & Edw
—4A **50**
Melville Ct. Nott —1G **37**
Melville Gdns. Nott —3A **38**
Melville St. Nott
—6G **37** (6E **3**)
Melvyn Dri. Bing —5E **43**

Mendip Clo. Long E —4C **54**
Mendip Ct. Nott —5D **14**
Mensing Av. Cotg —2E **63**
Merchant St. Nott —5H **13**
(in two parts)
Mercury Clo. Nott —2C **24**
Mere Clo. Calv —3D **6**
Meredith Clo. Nott —2F **49**
Meredith Ct. S'fd —1H **45**
Meregill Clo. Nott —4E **15**
Merevale Av. Nott —1D **58**
Mere Way. Rud —2H **69**
Meriac St. Nott —5D **14**
Meriden Av. Bees —3G **47**
Merlin Clo. Nott —3C **58**
Merlin Dri. Huck —1E **13**
Merlin Way. Ilk —5B **32**
Merrivale Ct. Nott —1G **37**
Mersey St. Nott —6H **13**
Merton Av. Arn —4D **16**
Merton Ct. S'fd —2G **45**
Metcalf Rd. Newt —2D **10**
Mettham St. Nott —6D **36**
Mevell Ct. Nott
—5E **37** (5A **2**)
Mews La. Calv —3C **6**
Mews, The. Nott —1E **37**
Meynall Gro. Nott —6E **25**
Meynell Rd. Long E —2F **65**
Miall Ct. Nott —4C **36**
Miall St. Nott —4C **36**
Michael Gdns. Nott —6F **25**
Mickleborough Av. Nott
—1B **38**
Mickleborough Way. W Bri
—2G **59**
Mickledon Clo. Long E
—5C **54**
Mickleson Clo. Nott —1F **49**
Micklemoor La. Bing —1H **43**
Middle Av. Carl —1E **39**
Middlebeck Av. Arn —5E **17**
Middlebeck Dri. Arn —5D **16**
Middledale Rd. Carl —3E **39**
Middlefell Way. Nott —4B **58**
Middle Furlong Gdns. Nott
—1F **49**
Middle Furlong M. Nott
—1F **49**
Middle Hill. Nott
—5G **37** (5E **3**)
Middle La. Bees —6E **47**
Middle Nook. Nott —4E **35**
Middle Orchard St. S'fd
—4F **45**
Middle Pavement. Nott
—5G **37** (5E **3**)
Middle St. Bees —5F **47**
Middleton Boulevd. Nott
—5A **36**
Middleton Clo. Nut —1C **22**
Middleton Cres. Bees —2E **47**
Middleton Rd. Ilk —4C **32**
Middleton St. Aws —3E **21**
Middleton St. Bees —4F **47**
Middleton St. Ilk —6C **20**
Midhurst Clo. Bees —1C **56**
Midhurst Way. Nott —3C **58**
Midlame Gdns. Nott —6F **13**
Midland Av. N'fld —2A **40**
Midland Av. Nott —6C **36**
Midland Av. S'fd —6E **45**
Midland Clo. Nott —3B **36**
Midland Cotts. W Bri —4B **50**
Midland Ct. Nott —4B **36**
Midland Cres. Carl —2H **39**
Midland Gro. N'fld —1A **40**
Midland Rd. Carl —2H **39**
Midland Rd. E'wd —3B **10**
Midland Rd. Hean —3C **8**
Midland St. Long E —5G **55**
Midland Ter. Long E —4G **55**
Midway, The. Nott —3C **48**
Mikado Rd. Long E —2E **65**
Milburn Gro. Bing —5C **42**
Mildenhall Cres. Nott —5G **15**
Mile End Rd. Colw —4G **39**
Milford Av. Long E —2D **54**

Milford Clo. Nott —5G **13**
Milford Ct. Day —1H **25**
Milford Dri. Ilk —4H **19**
Milford Dri. Nott —3E **39**
Mill Acre Clo. Ilk —5H **19**
Millbank. Hean —4E **9**
(in two parts)
Millbank Clo. Ilk —4H **19**
Millbank Ct. Nott —1G **23**
Millbeck Av. Nott —5C **34**
Millbeck Clo. Gam —5E **51**
Mill Clo., The. Old B —4C **24**
Mill Cres. Arn —5A **16**
Milldale Clo. Nott —3A **58**
Milldale Rd. Long E —1D **64**
Millennium Way. Nott
—3G **23**
Millennium Way E. Nott
—3G **23**
Millennium Way W. Nott
—3G **23**
Miller Hives Clo. Cotg —2E **63**
Millers Bri. Cotg —3E **63**
Millers Clo. Shelf —6H **29**
Millers Ct. Nott —3C **36**
Millers Dale. Ilk —2A **20**
Mill Field Clo. Bur J —4E **29**
Millfield Clo. Ilk —4G **19**
Millfield Rd. Ilk —2C **32**
Millfield Rd. Kimb —6G **13**
Mill Hill La. Breas —4A **54**
Mill Hill Rd. Bing —6D **42**
Millicent Gro. W Bri —3B **50**
Millicent Rd. W Bri —3A **50**
Mill La. Arn —5A **16**
Mill La. Clip —4D **62**
Mill La. Coss —1D **32**
Mill La. Cotg —1E **63**
Mill La. Sand —5B **44**
Mill Rd. Hean —5E **9**
Mill Rd. Newt —2C **10**
Mill Rd. S'fd —3F **45**
Mill St. Ilk —6B **20**
Mill St. Nott —4B **24**
Millview Clo. Nott —5B **38**
Mill View Ct. Nott —5A **38**
Milner Rd. Long E —5F **55**
Milner Rd. Nott —5G **25**
Milnhay Rd. Lan M —3G **9**
Milton Av. Ilk —3A **20**
Milton Ct. Arn —6D **16**
Milton Ct. Nott —4F **25**
Milton Cres. Att —3D **56**
Milton Rise. Huck —6B **4**
Milton Rd. Ilk —3A **20**
Milton St. Ilk —3B **20**
Milton St. Long E —6F **55**
Milton St. Nott
—4G **37** (2E **3**)
Milton Ter. Long E —6F **55**
Milverton Rd. Nott —5G **15**
Milward Rd. Los —3B **8**
Mimosa Clo. Nott —4A **58**
Minerva St. Nott —5H **13**
(in two parts)
Minster Clo. Huck —3F **5**
Minster Ct. Nott —2F **37**
Minster Gdns. Newt —4D **10**
Mint Gro. Long E —6C **54**
Minver Cres. Nott —4A **24**
Mirberry M. Nott —6C **36**
Miriam Ct. W Bri —4A **50**
Mission St. Nott —5A **26**
Mitchell Av. Lan M —1E **9**
Mitchell Clo. Nott —1G **23**
Mitchell St. Long E —6G **55**
Mitchell Ter. Ilk —4C **32**
Moffat Clo. Nott —2B **38**
Moira Ho. Arn —6B **16**
Mollington Sq. Nott —3H **23**
Mona Rd. W Bri —2C **50**
Mona St. Bees —5H **47**
Monks Clo. Ilk —1C **32**
Monk's La. Got —6H **67**
Monksway. Nott —1E **59**
Monkton Clo. Ilk —4H **19**
Monkton Dri. Nott —2E **35**
Monmouth Clo. Nott —5B **34**
Monroe Wlk. Nott —6E **15**

Monsaldale Clo. Long E
—1D **64**
Monsall Av. Ilk —2A **20**
Monsall St. Nott —6D **24**
Monsell Dri. Red —4A **16**
Montague Rd. Huck —3E **5**
Montague St. Bees —4F **47**
Montague St. Nott —6A **14**
Montfort Cres. Nott —3H **25**
Montfort St. Nott —4E **37**
Montgomery Clo. Bees
—3C **56**
Montgomery St. Nott
—3E **37** (1A **2**)
Montpelier Rd. Nott —2C **48**
Montrose Ct. S'fd —2G **45**
Monyash Clo. Ilk —4A **20**
Moorbridge Cotts. Nott
—3B **14**
Moorbridge Ct. Bing —4E **43**
Moorbridge La. S'fd —2F **45**
Moorbridge Rd. Bing —4E **43**
Moorbridge Rd. E. Bing
—4E **43**
Moore Clo. W Bri —2D **50**
Moore Ga. Bees —5F **47**
Moore Rd. Map —5C **26**
Moores Av. Sand —4E **45**
Moor Farm Caravan Pk. Calv
—4G **7**
Moor Farm Inn La. Bram
—1A **46**
Moorfield Ct. S'fd —3G **45**
Moorfield Cres. Sand —6D **44**
Moorfields Av. E'wd —2B **10**
Moorgate St. Nott —4E **37**
Moorgreen. Newt —1E **11**
Moorgreen Dri. Strel —5D **22**
Moorgreen Ind. Pk. Newt
—1D **10**
Moorhouse Rd. Nott —3E **35**
Moorings, The. Nott —1H **49**
Moorland Av. S'fd —5F **45**
Moorlands Clo. Long E
—3D **54**
Moor La. Bees —1B **46**
Moor La. Bing —4E **43**
Moor La. Bradm —5H **69**
Moor La. Bun —6E **67**
Moor La. Calv —4G **7**
Moor La. D Abb —6D **30**
Moor La. Got —6H **67**
Moor La. Rud —1G **69**
Moor Rd. B Vil —2B **14**
Moor Rd. Calv —3E **7**
Moor Rd. Pap —1H **5**
Moor Rd. Strel —6D **22**
Moorsholm Dri. Nott —5D **34**
Moor St. N'fld —2H **39**
Moor, The. Trow —3A **34**
Moray Ct. Kimb —6H **11**
Morden Clo. Nott —1D **34**
Morden Rd. Gilt —5E **11**
Moreland Ct. Carl —2E **39**
Moreland Ct. Nott —6A **38**
Moreland St. Nott —6B **38**
Morello Av. Carl —2H **39**
Moreton Rd. Nott —6C **58**
Morgan M. Nott —3B **58**
Morkinshire Cres. Cotg
—1F **63**
Morkinshire La. Cotg —1E **63**
Morley Av. Nott —5A **26**
Morley Ct. Nott
—5A **38** (4H **3**)
Morley Dri. Ilk —4H **19**
Morley Gdns. Nott —6F **25**
Morley Rd. Nott —6C **26**
Morley St. Day —1A **26**
Mornington Clo. Sand
—5E **45**
Mornington Cres. Nut
—4D **22**
Morrell Bank. Nott —1D **24**
Morris Rd. Nott —6D **22**
Morris St. N'fld —2A **40**
Morton Gdns. Rad T —6H **41**
Morval Rd. Nott —2E **35**
Morven Av. Huck —5F **5**

Mosley St. Huck —5E **5**
Mosley St. Nott —1D **36**
Moss Clo. Arn —5G **15**
Mosscroft Av. Nott —4B **58**
Mossdale Rd. Nott —2G **25**
Moss Dri. Bram —4B **46**
Moss Rise. Nott —5C **26**
Moss Rd. Huck —4D **4**
Moss Rd. Ilk —2A **32**
Moss Side. Nott —2E **59**
Mosswood Cres. Nott —6F **15**
Mottram Rd. Bees —5C **46**
Mountbatten Ct. Ilk —4B **20**
Mountbatten Gro. Ged
—5G **27**
Mountbatten Way. Bees
—3C **56**
Mountfield Av. Sand —1C **54**
Mountfield Dri. Nott —6E **15**
Mt. Hooton. Nott —3E **37**
Mt. Hooton Rd. Nott —2G **25**
Mt. Pleasant. Carl —2G **39**
Mt. Pleasant. Ilk —3A **20**
Mt. Pleasant. Keyw —4D **70**
Mt. Pleasant. Nott —5B **24**
Mt. Pleasant. Rad T —6E **41**
Mt. Sorrel Dri. W Bri —5D **50**
Mount St. Breas —6B **54**
Mount St. Hean —4C **8**
Mount St. New B —6D **24**
Mount St. Nott
—5F **37** (4C **2**)
(in two parts)
Mount, The. Arc. Nott —4C **2**
Mount, The. B Vil —1C **14**
Mount, The. Carl —5E **27**
Mount, The. Nott —6E **23**
Mount, The. Red —4H **15**
Mount, The. S'fd —5F **45**
Mowbray Ct. Nott
—4H **37** (2G **3**)
Mowbray Gdns. W Bri
—6B **50**
Mowbray Rise. Arn —5B **16**
Moyra Dri. Arn —6G **15**
Mozart Clo. Nott —4C **36**
Mudpie La. W Bri —2D **50**
Muir Av. Toll —5F **61**
Muirfield Rd. Arn —4D **14**
Mulberry Clo. W Bri —6F **49**
Mulberry Gdns. Nott —5G **13**
Mulberry Gro. Huck —1H **13**
Mundella Rd. Nott —2H **49**
Mundy's Dri. Hean —5D **8**
Mundy St. Hean —4C **8**
Mundy St. Ilk —5B **20**
Munford Cir. Nott —4G **23**
Munks Av. Huck —4D **4**
Murby Cres. Nott —5H **13**
Murden Way. Bees —5H **47**
Muriel Rd. Bees —4F **47**
Muriel St. Nott —6H **13**
Muskham Av. Ilk —4B **20**
Muskham St. Nott —2H **49**
Musk Hollows. Huck —3D **4**
Musk View. E'wd —3D **10**
Musters Ct. W Bri —5A **50**
Musters Cres. W Bri —6B **50**
Musters Croft. Colw —6H **39**
Musters Rd. Bing —5D **42**
Musters Rd. Rud —1F **69**
Musters Rd. W Bri —3A **50**
Musters Wlk. Nott —6G **13**
Muston Clo. Nott —6B **26**
Myrtle Av. Long E —1E **65**
Myrtle Av. Nott —1F **37**
Myrtle Av. S'fd —5G **45**
Myrtle Gro. Bees —4G **47**
Myrtle Rd. Carl —1E **39**
Myrtus Clo. Nott —3A **58**

Nabbs La. Huck —5B **4**
Naburn Ct. Nott —6B **24**
Nairn Clo. Arn —4D **16**
Nairn M. Carl —2G **39**
Nanranjan M. Nott —3E **37**
Nansen St. Nott —1A **24**

Naomi Ct. Nott —4A **14**
Naomi Cres. Nott —4A **14**
Narrow La. Wat —4H **11**
Naseby Clo. Nott —3D **24**
Naseby Dri. Long E —3G **65**
Nathaniel Rd. Long E —6H **55**
Nathans La. Rad T —4A **52**
Navenby Wlk. Nott —3C **58**
Naworth Clo. Nott —2C **24**
Naylor Av. Got —6H **67**
Neal Ct. Lan M —2E **9**
Neale St. Long E —6G **55**
Near Meadow. Long E
—2G **65**
Nearsby Dri. W Bri —5D **50**
Needham Rd. Arn —5C **16**
Needham St. Bing —5E **43**
Needwood Av. Trow —1F **45**
Neighwood Clo. Tot —3G **55**
Nell Gwyn Cres. Nott —4G **15**
Nelper Cres. Ilk —4C **32**
Nelson Rd. Bees —1G **57**
Nelson Rd. Day —6A **16**
Nelson Rd. Nott —6A **14**
Nelson St. Ilk —3B **20**
Nelson St. Long E —1F **65**
Nelson St. Nott
—5H **37** (4G **3**)
Nene Clo. Huck —2E **13**
Nesfield Ct. Ilk —6A **20**
Nesfield Rd. Ilk —6A **20**
Neston Dri. Nott —3H **23**
Nethbeth Ct. Nott —1G **49**
Nether Clo. E'wd —2B **10**
Nether Clo. Nott —3C **38**
Netherfield La. Shard —6B **64**
Netherfield Rd. Long E
—3D **64**
Netherfield Rd. Sand —6D **44**
Nethergate. Nott —3A **58**
(in two parts)
Nether St. Bees —5G **47**
Nettlecliff Wlk. Nott —5C **14**
Neville Rd. Calv —4D **6**
Neville Sadler Ct. Bees
—4G **47**
Newall Dri. Bees —3C **56**
Newark Av. Nott —5A **38**
Newark Ct. Nott —2D **24**
Newark Cres. Nott —5A **38**
Newark St. Nott
—5A **38** (5H **3**)
Newbery Av. Long E —1H **65**
Newbridge Clo. W Hal
—1B **30**
Newbury Clo. Nott —3C **26**
Newbury Ct. Nott —1F **37**
Newbury Dri. Nott —4D **22**
Newcastle Av. Bees —5F **47**
Newcastle Av. Ged —6G **27**
Newcastle Chambers. Nott
—5G **37** (4D **2**)
Newcastle Cir. Nott
—5E **37** (5A **2**)
Newcastle Ct. Park —5E **37**
Newcastle Dri. Nott
—5E **37** (3A **2**)
Newcastle Farm Dri. Nott
—6A **24**
Newcastle St. Bulw —5A **14**
Newcastle St. Nott
—4G **37** (3E **3**)
Newcastle Ter. Nott
(Derby Rd.) —4E **37** (3A **2**)
Newcastle Ter. Nott —6B **24**
(Nuthall Rd.)
Newcombe Dri. Arn —6E **17**
New Derby Rd. E'wd —3A **10**
Newdigate Rd. Wat —6A **12**
Newdigate St. Ilk —3C **32**
Newdigate St. Kimb —1A **22**
Newdigate St. Nott —4E **37**
Newdigate St. W Hal —1A **30**
Newdigate Vs. Nott —4E **37**
New Eaton Rd. S'fd —6G **45**
New Farm La. Nut —1C **22**
Newfield Rd. Nott —4E **25**
Newgate Clo. Carl —2G **39**

Newgate Ct. Nott —5D **36**
Newgate St. Bing —4E **43**
Newhall Gro. W Bri —2B **50**
Newham Clo. Hean —4E **9**
Newholm Dri. Nott —6E **49**
Newland Clo. Bees —3A **56**
Newland Clo. Nott —4A **36**
Newlands Clo. Edw —1E **61**
Newlands Dri. Ged —6H **27**
Newlands Dri. Hean —2C **8**
New Lawn Rd. Ilk —1A **32**
Newlyn Dri. Nott —1B **36**
Newlyn Gdns. Nott —1B **36**
Newmanleys Rd. E'wd
—5A **10**
Newmanleys Rd. S. E'wd
—5A **10**
Newman Rd. Calv —2C **6**
Newmarket Rd. Nott —1H **23**
Newmarket Way. Bees
—3H **55**
Newport Dri. Nott —6B **24**
Newquay Av. Nott —2C **36**
New Rd. Bart —1E **67**
New Rd. Newt —1F **11**
New Rd. Nott —3C **36**
New Rd. Rad T —6F **41**
New Rd. S'fd —2F **45**
New Row. Carl —2F **39**
Newstead Av. Nott —5D **26**
Newstead Av. Rad T —5G **41**
Newstead Ct. Nott —2C **24**
Newstead Dri. W Bri —4D **50**
Newstead Gro. Bing —5C **42**
Newstead Gro. Nott —3F **37**
Newstead Ind. Est. Arn
—6C **16**
Newstead Rd. Long E —2E **55**
Newstead Rd. N. Ilk —4H **19**
Newstead Rd. S. Ilk —4H **19**
Newstead St. Sher —4G **25**
Newstead Ter. Huck —3E **5**
Newstead Way. Strel —5D **22**
New St. Carl —4H **39**
New St. Long E —5G **55**
New St. Sher R —6F **25**
New St. Stan —3A **30**
New Ter. Sand —5D **44**
Newthorpe Comn. Newt
—4C **10**
Newthorpe St. Nott —1H **49**
Newton Av. Bing —5D **42**
(in two parts)
Newton Av. Rad T —5G **41**
Newton Clo. Arn —1D **26**
Newtondale Clo. Nott —6B **24**
Newton Dri. S'fd —5G **45**
Newton Dri. W Bri —1G **59**
Newton Gdns. Nwtn —3C **42**
Newton Rd. Ged —4F **27**
Newton's La. Coss —4D **20**
Newton St. Bees —5E **47**
Newton St. Nott —1G **49**
New Tythe St. Long E
—6H **55**
New Vale Rd. Colw —4F **39**
New Windmill Ct. Nott
—5B **38**
Nicholas Rd. Bees —2D **46**
Nicker Hill. Keyw —3G **70**
Nicklaus Ct. Nott —5E **15**
(off Crossfield Dri.)
Nidderdale. Nott —5C **34**
Nidderdale Clo. Nott —6C **34**
Nightingale Clo. Nott —2G **47**
Nightingale Clo. Nut —1D **22**
Nile St. Nott —4H **37** (3G **3**)
Nine Acre Gdns. Nott —5F **13**
Nine Corners. Kimb —1H **21**
Nixon Rise. Huck —6B **4**
Nobel Rd. Nott —5A **58**
Noel St. Kimb —1A **22**
Noel St. Nott —1D **36**
No Man's La. Dray & Sand
—4A **44**
Nook End Rd. Hean —4B **8**
Nook, The. Bees —4G **47**
Nook, The. Calv —3D **6**
Nook, The. Chil —1E **57**

Nook, The. Kimb —2A **22**
Nook, The. Los —1A **8**
Nook, The. Nott —5E **35**
Norbett Clo. Bees —2C **56**
Norbett Ct. Arn —4C **16**
Norbett Rd. Arn —5C **16**
Norbreck Clo. Nott —4H **23**
Norburn Cres. Nott —4D **24**
Nordean Rd. Nott —2C **26**
Norfolk Av. Bees —4A **56**
Norfolk Clo. Huck —6B **4**
Norfolk Pk. Arn —2D **26**
Norfolk Pl. Nott
—4G **37** (3D **2**)
Norfolk Rd. Long E —4H **55**
Norfolk Wlk. Sand —6D **44**
Norland Clo. Nott —2A **38**
Normanby Rd. Nott —6C **34**
Norman Clo. Bees —5C **46**
Norman Clo. Nott —3G **37**
Norman Cres. Ilk —4A **20**
Norman Dri. E'wd —3D **10**
Norman Dri. Huck —1E **13**
Norman Dri. Ilk —3A **20**
Norman Rd. Nott —1C **38**
Norman St. Ilk —1A **20**
Norman St. Kimb —6H **11**
Norman St. N'fld —3A **40**
Normanton La. Keyw —4D **70**
Northall Av. Nott —1H **23**
Northampton St. Nott
—3A **38**
North Av. Sand —5C **44**
N. Church St. Nott
—4G **37** (2D **2**)
N. Circus St. Nott
—4F **37** (3C **2**)
Northcliffe Av. Nott —5D **26**
Northcote St. Long E —6G **55**
Northcote Way. Nott —2A **24**
Northdale Rd. Nott —2D **38**
Northdown Dri. Bees —1C **56**
Northdown Rd. Nott —3A **36**
North Dri. Bees —5E **47**
North Rd. Long E —1H **55**
North Rd. Nott —5E **37**
North Rd. Rud —5F **59**
North Rd. W Bri —5A **50**
N. Sherwood St. Nott
—2F **37** (2D **2**)
Northside Wlk. Arn —3B **16**
North St. Bees —5E **47**
North St. Ilk —6B **20**
North St. Kimb —2A **22**
North St. Lan M —2F **9**
North St. Newt —3E **11**
North St. Nott —5A **38** (4H **3**)
Northumberland Clo. Nott
—3H **37** (1F **3**)
Northville Ct. Nott —2H **37**
Northwold Av. W Bri —5H **49**
Northwood Cres. Nott
—1G **25**
Northwood Rd. Nott —1G **25**
Northwood St. S'fd —3F **45**
Norton St. Nott —3D **36**
(in two parts)
Norwich Gdns. Arn —3B **16**
Norwood Rd. Nott —4C **36**

Notintone Pl. Nott —5A **38**
Notintone St. Nott —5A **38**
Nottingham Airport. Rad T
—6H **51**
Nottingham Rd. Bing —5B **42**
Nottingham Rd. Bul —2G **29**
Nottingham Rd. Bur J
—4D **28**
Nottingham Rd. Day —1A **26**
Nottingham Rd. E'wd & Newt
—3B **10**
Nottingham Rd. Got —6H **67**
Nottingham Rd. Huck —6G **5**
Nottingham Rd. Ilk —2B **32**
Nottingham Rd. Keyw
—5C **70**
Nottingham Rd. Kimb
—1A **22**
Nottingham Rd. Long E & Chil
—5G **55**
Nottingham Rd. Nott —5C **24**
Nottingham Rd. Nut —2D **22**
Nottingham Rd. Rad T
—1D **52**
Nottingham Rd. S'fd —4F **45**
Nottingham Rd. Trow
—5E **33**
Nottingham Rd. Wdbgh
—3F **17**
Nuart Rd. Bees —5F **47**
Nugent Gdns. Nott —3A **38**
Nursery Av. Bees —6C **46**
Nursery Av. Sand —6B **44**
Nursery Av. W Hal —2C **30**
Nursery Clo. Huck —1G **13**
Nursery Clo. Rad T —6H **41**
Nursery Dri. Carl —1F **39**
Nursery Hollow. Ilk —3A **32**
Nursery La. Nott —2C **38**
Nursery Rd. Arn —6B **16**
Nursery Rd. Bing —5H **43**
Nursery Rd. Rad T —6H **41**
Nutbrook Cres. Ilk —5H **31**
Nuthall Circ. Ilk —5G **31**
Nuthall Gdns. Nott —1B **36**
Nuthall Rd. Nott —3H **23**

Oak Acres. Bees —6A **46**
Oak Av. Bing —5G **43**
Oak Av. Lan M —1F **9**
Oak Av. Rad T —5E **41**
Oak Av. Sand —4C **44**
Oakdale Dri. Bees —1C **56**
Oakdale Rd. Arn —5D **16**
Oakdale Rd. Carl —3F **39**
Oakdale Rd. Nott —3D **38**
Oak Dri. E'wd —3A **10**
Oak Dri. Kimb —1B **22**
Oakenhall Av. Huck —4G **5**
Oakfield Clo. Nott —6C **34**
Oakfield Dri. Sand —2D **54**
Oakfield Dri. Huck —5F **5**
Oakfield Rd. Nott —6C **34**
Oakfield Rd. S'fd —4F **45**
Oakfields Rd. W Bri —2C **50**
Oak Flatt. Bees —5A **46**
Oakford Clo. Nott —5G **23**
Oak Gro. Huck —1H **13**
Oakham Clo. Nott —6D **14**
Oakham Rd. Rud —3H **59**
Oakham Way. Ilk —4H **19**
Oakington Clo. Nott —2F **25**
Oakland Av. Long E —2E **65**
Oakland Ct. Bees —2A **46**
Oakland Gro. Calv —3D **6**
Oaklands Av. Hean —3E **9**
Oakland St. Nott —2C **36**
Oakland Ter. Long E —2E **65**
Oakleigh Av. Nott —5E **27**
Oakleigh St. Nott —3B **24**
Oakley M. Nott —1F **23**
Oakley's Rd. Long E —6G **55**
Oakley's Rd. W. Long E
—1F **65**
Oak Lodge. Bing —5G **43**
Oak Lodge Dri. Kimb —6H **11**
Oakmead Av. Nott —1F **35**
Oakmere Clo. Edw —1E **61**

Oaks, The. Nott
—4A **38** (2H **3**)
Oak St. Nott —6F **25**
Oak Tree Av. Rad T —5F **41**
Oak Tree Clo. Huck —1D **12**
Oak Tree Clo. W Bri —3C **50**
Oak Tree Dri. Ged —5A **28**
Oakwell Cres. Ilk —1A **32**
Oakwell Dri. Ilk —1A **32**
Oakwood Dri. Nott —2A **36**
Oakwood Gdns. Nut —4D **22**
Oban Rd. Bees —5C **46**
Occupation Rd. Huck —6E **5**
Occupation Rd. Nott —2H **23**
Ockbrook Ct. Ilk —4B **20**
Ockerby St. Nott —1A **24**
Odesa Dri. Bulw —3H **23**
Ogdon Ct. Nott —3B **38**
Ogle Dri. Nott —6F **37** (6B **2**)
Ogle St. Huck —4E **5**
Okehampton Cres. Nott
—1E **27**
Old Acres. Wdbgh —6H **7**
Old Bank Ct. Nott —5B **24**
Old Brickyard. Nott —2C **38**
Oldbury Clo. Nott —6B **58**
Old Chu. St. Nott —1C **48**
Old Coach Rd. Nott —3E **35**
(in three parts)
Old Coppice Side. Hean
(in two parts) —6C **8**
Old Derby Rd. E'wd —2H **9**
Old Dri. Bees —3D **46**
Old Farm Ct. Bart —1E **67**
Old Farm Rd. Nott —5D **14**
Old Hall Clo. Calv —3C **6**
Old Hall Dri. Nott —6A **26**
Oldham Ct. Bees —1D **56**
Oldknow St. Nott —3D **36**
Old Lenton St. Nott
—4H **37** (3F **3**)
Old Main Rd. Bul —2G **29**
(in two parts)
Old Mnr. Clo. Wdbgh —6H **7**
Old Mkt. Sq. Nott
—5G **37** (4D **2**)
Old Melton Rd. Rud —6G **61**
Old Mill Clo. Bees —3A **56**
Old Mill Clo. B Vil —2B **14**
Old Mill Clo. Nott —4D **36**
Old Mill Ct. Bing —4E **43**
Old Oak Rd. Nott —3E **59**
Old Pk., The. Cotg —1F **63**
Old Rd. Rud —4H **59**
Old School Clo. Nott —5C **58**
Old St. Nott —4G **37** (2E **3**)
Old Tollerton Rd. Gam
—4E **51**
Olga Rd. Nott —3B **38**
Olive Av. Long E —4F **55**
Olive Gro. Bur J —2F **39**
Oliver Clo. Hean —3F **9**
Oliver Clo. Nott
—3E **37** (1A **2**)
Oliver Rd. Ilk —4G **31**
Oliver St. Nott —3E **37** (1A **2**)
Ollerton Rd. Arn —1A **16**
Olton Av. Bees —3F **47**
Olympus Ct. Huck —2D **12**
Onchan Av. Carl —3G **39**
Onchan Dri. Carl —3G **39**
Orange Gdns. Nott —1H **49**
Orby Clo. Nott —3B **38**
Orby Wlk. Nott —4B **38**
Orchard Av. Bing —5D **42**
Orchard Av. Carl —2G **39**
Orchard Bus. Pk. Ilk —6H **19**
Orchard Clo. Bur J —2F **29**
Orchard Clo. Huck —5E **5**
Orchard Clo. Nott —3A **58**
Orchard Clo. Rad T —6E **41**
Orchard Clo. Toll —5F **61**
Orchard Clo. W Hal —2C **30**
Orchard Ct. Carl —2G **39**
Orchard Ct. Ged —5F **27**
Orchard Ct. Lan M —2F **9**
Orchard Ct. Nott —1C **36**
Orchard Cres. Bees —6C **46**
Orchard Dri. Calv —3E **7**

Orchard Gro. Arn —1G **25**
Orchard Pk. Ind. Est. Sand
　　　　　—5E **45**
Orchard Rise. Hean —3D **8**
Orchards, The. Ged —6A **28**
Orchard St. Got —6H **67**
Orchard St. Huck —5E **5**
Orchard St. Ilk —2B **32**
Orchard St. Kimb —1H **21**
Orchard St. Lan M —2F **9**
Orchard St. Long E —6G **55**
Orchard St. Newt —4C **10**
Orchard, The. Ilk —3B **44**
Orchard Way. Sand —2C **54**
Orchid Clo. W Bri —1G **59**
Ordnance Ct. Bees —2C **56**
Orford Av. Nott —1D **58**
Orford Av. Rad T —1E **53**
Orion Clo. Nott —2E **35**
Orion Dri. Nott —2E **35**
Orlando Dri. Lan M —1H **39**
Orlock Wlk. Nott —2F **25**
Ormonde St. Lan M —1F **9**
Ormonde Ter. Lan M —1F **9**
Ormonde Ter. W Sta **25**
Ornsay Clo. Nott —4C **14**
Orpean Way. Bees —3G **55**
Orston Av. Arn —6C **16**
Orston Dri. Nott —5A **36**
Orston Grn. Nott —6B **36**
Orston Rd. E. W Bri —2B **50**
Orston Rd. W. W Bri —2A **50**
Orton Av. Bees —5C **46**
Ortzen Ct. Nott —3D **36**
Ortzen St. Nott —3D **36**
Orville Rd. Nott —2C **24**
Osborne Av. Nott —4G **25**
Osborne Clo. Sand —1D **54**
Osborne Gro. Nott —4G **25**
Osborne St. Nott —3C **36**
Osgood Rd. Arn —2E **27**
Osier Rd. Nott —2G **49**
Osman Clo. Nott —2F **49**
Osmaston Clo. Long E
　　　　　—2B **64**
Osmaston St. Nott —6D **36**
Osmaston St. Sand —6E **45**
Osprey Clo. Nott —4A **58**
Ossington Clo. Nott
　　　　　—3G **37** (1D **2**)
Ossington St. Nott —4D **22**
Osterley Gro. Nut —5D **22**
Oulton Clo. Arn —1B **26**
Oulton Lodge. Nott —4B **14**
Oundle Dri. Ilk —2C **32**
Oundle Dri. Nott —6A **36**
Ousebridge Cres. Carl
　　　　　—1A **40**
Ousebridge Dri. Carl —1A **40**
Oval Gdns. Nott —1B **36**
Overdale Clo. Long E —1B **64**
Overdale Rd. Nott —4A **24**
Overstrand Clo. Arn —1B **26**
Owen Av. Long E —1A **66**
Owers Av. Hean —6D **8**
Owlston Clo. E'wd —2B **10**
Owsthorpe Clo. Nott —5E **15**
Owthorpe Gro. Nott —5E **15**
Owthorpe Rd. Cotg —2F **63**
Oxborough Rd. Arn —6G **15**
Oxbow Clo. Nott —2G **49**
Oxburn Rd. Wat —5H **11**
Oxbury Rd. Wat —5H **11**
Oxclose La. Arn —1F **25**
Oxengate. Arn —1G **25**
Oxford Rd. W Bri —4C **50**
Oxford St. Carl —6G **27**
Oxford St. E'wd —3B **10**
Oxford St. Ilk —3B **32**
Oxford St. Long E —5F **55**
Oxford St. Nott
　　　　　—5F **37** (4B **2**)
Oxton Av. Nott —3G **25**
Oxton Rd. Colw —5G **39**
Ozier Holt. Colw —5G **39**
Ozier Holt. Long E —1E **65**

Packman Dri. Rud —5H **59**

Paddock Clo. Calv —3D **6**
Paddock Clo. Nott —2H **23**
Paddock Clo. Rad T —1E **53**
Paddocks, The. Edw —2D **60**
Paddocks, The. Nut —2B **22**
Paddocks, The. Sand —6C **44**
Paddocks View. Long E
　　　　　—5D **54**
Paddock, The. Att —4D **56**
Paddock, The. Bing —5E **43**
Padge Rd. Bees —5A **47**
Padgham Ct. Nott —5E **15**
Padley Ct. Nott —1G **23**
Padleys La. Bur J —2E **29**
Padstow Rd. Nott —1D **24**
Paget Cres. Rud —5G **59**
Paignton Clo. Nott —5H **23**
Paisley Gro. Chil —4C **56**
Palatine St. Nott
　　　　　—6F **37** (6B **2**)
Palin Ct. Nott —2D **36**
Palin Gdns. Rad T —6G **41**
Palin St. Nott —3D **36**
Palm Cotts. Nott —4H **25**
Palm Ct. Ind. Cen. Nott
　　　　　—6D **24**
Palmer Av. Huck —3E **5**
Palmer Cres. Carl —2F **39**
Palmer Dri. S'fd —6F **45**
Palmerston Gdns. Nott
　　　　　—3G **37** (1E **3**)
(in two parts)
Palm St. Nott —6D **24**
Palmwood Ct. Nott —2A **24**
Papplewick La. Huck —4F **5**
Park Av. Aws —2D **20**
Park Av. Bur J —3F **29**
Park Av. Carl —1H **39**
Park Av. E'wd —2A **10**
Park Av. Huck —4D **4**
Park Av. Ilk —1B **32**
Park Av. Keyw —4B **70**
Park Av. Kimb —3A **22**
Park Av. Nott —1G **37**
Park Av. Plum —3D **70**
Park Av. Stan —3A **30**
Park Av. W Bri —3B **50**
Park Av. Wdbgh —6F **7**
Park Av. Wd'p —2A **26**
Park Av. E. Keyw —4B **70**
Park Av. W. Keyw —4B **70**
Park Clo. Nott —5A **26**
Park Ct. Hean —4D **8**
Park Ct. Nott —2C **48**
Park Cres. E'wd —1B **10**
Park Cres. Ilk —1C **32**
Park Cres. Nott —5C **34**
Parkcroft Rd. W Bri —5B **50**
Parkdale Rd. Nott & Carl
　　　　　—3D **38**
Park Dri. Huck —6E **5**
Park Dri. Ilk —2B **32**
Park Dri. Nott —5E **37** (5A **2**)
Park Dri. Sand —2C **54**
Parker Clo. Arn —5D **16**
Parker St. Huck —4F **5**
Park Hall La. M'ley —5B **18**
Park Hall La. W Hal —1A **30**
Parkham Rd. Kimb —6H **11**
Park Heights. Nott —6E **37**
Park Hill. Aws —2D **20**
Park Hill. Nott —4E **37**
Park Ho. Gates. Nott —6H **25**
Parkland Clo. Nott —2A **58**
Park La. Nott —3C **24**
Park M. Nott —1G **37**
Park Ravine. Nott
　　　　　—6E **37** (6A **2**)
Park Rd. Bees —5E **47**
Park Rd. B Vil —1C **14**
Park Rd. Bram —3H **45**
Park Rd. Calv —3B **6**
Park Rd. Carl —2H **39**
Park Rd. Huck —4D **4**
Park Rd. Ilk —2B **32**
Park Rd. Nott —6B **36**
Park Rd. Plum —3D **70**
Park Rd. Rad T —5F **41**
Park Rd. Wd'p —2A **26**

Park Rd. E. Calv —2D **6**
Park Rd. N. Bees —5E **47**
Park Row. Nott
　　　　　—5F **37** (5C **2**)
Parkside. Nott —6E **35**
Parkside. Plum —3D **70**
Parkside Av. Long E —5D **54**
Parkside Dri. Long E —5D **54**
Parkside Gdns. N. Nott
　　　　　—6E **35**
Parkside Gdns. S. Nott
　　　　　—1E **47**
Parkside Rise. Nott —1E **47**
Parkstone Clo. W Bri —6G **49**
Park St. Bees —5E **47**
Park St. Hean —3B **8**
Park St. Long E —4E **55**
Park St. Nott —5D **36**
Park St. S'fd —5E **45**
Park Ter. Nott —5F **37** (4B **2**)
Park Ter. Plum —2D **70**
Park, The. Cotg —1F **63**
Park Valley. Nott
　　　　　—5F **37** (5B **2**)
Park View. Bees —5D **46**
Park View. Hean —4B **8**
Park View. Nott —5A **26**
Park View Ct. Nott
　　　　　—4H **37** (3G **3**)
Parkview Dri. Nott —6E **15**
Parkway Ct. Nott —4D **34**
Parkwood Ct. Nott —2C **24**
Parkwood Cres. Nott —4A **26**
Parkyn Rd. Day —1H **25**
Parkyns St. Rud —6G **59**
Parliament Ter. Nott
　　　　　—4F **37** (3C **2**)
Parr Ga. Bees —4A **46**
Parry Way. Arn —5D **16**
Parsons Meadow. Colw
　　　　　—5G **39**
Pasteur Ct. Nott —1C **48**
Pasture Clo. Nott —5G **39**
Pasture La. Long E —1A **66**
Pasture La. Rud —1D **68**
Pasture Rd. S'fd —2F **45**
Pastures Av. Nott —5B **58**
Pastures, The. Calv —3B **6**
Pastures, The. Gilt —5E **11**
Pateley Rd. Nott —3C **26**
Paton Rd. Nott —2C **24**
Patricia Dri. Arn —4C **16**
Patrick Rd. W Bri —3A **50**
Patterdale Clo. Gam —4E **51**
Patterdale Ct. Bees —1A **56**
Patterdale Rd. Wd'p —2B **26**
Patterson Rd. Nott —2D **36**
Pavilion Clo. Nott —2H **49**
Pavilion Rd. Arn —4F **15**
Pavilion Rd. Ilk —1A **20**
Pavilion Rd. W Bri —2A **50**
Paxton Gdns. Nott
　　　　　—4A **38** (2H **3**)
Payne Rd. Bees —2B **56**
Peache Way. Bees —5C **46**
Peachey St. Nott
　　　　　—4G **37** (2D **2**)
Peach St. Hean —4B **8**
Peacock Clo. Rud —1F **69**
Peacock Cres. Nott —3C **58**
Peacock Pl. Ilk —3H **19**
Peakdale Clo. Long E —1C **64**
Pearce Dri. Nott —2H **35**
Pearmain Dri. Nott —2B **38**
Pearson Av. Bees —6B **46**
Pearson Clo. Bees —6B **46**
Pearson Ct. Bees —3B **46**
Pearson St. N'fld —3A **40**
Pearson St. Nott —5D **24**
Pear Tree Clo. Nott —3C **24**
Pear Tree Orchard. Rud
　　　　　—6G **59**
Peary Clo. Nott —1D **24**
Peas Hill Rd. Nott —3H **37**
(in two parts)
Peatburn Av. Hean —4A **8**
Peatfield Clo. S'fd —2F **45**
Peatfield Rd. S'fd —2F **45**
Peck La. Nott —5G **37** (4E **3**)

Pedestrian Way. Nott —5D **14**
Pedley St. Ilk —2B **32**
Pedmore Valley. Nott —6E **15**
Peel St. Lan M —2F **9**
Peel St. Long E —5G **55**
Peel St. Nott —3F **37** (1C **2**)
Peel Vs. Nott —5A **26**
Pelham Av. Ilk —6A **20**
Pelham Av. Nott —1F **37**
Pelham Cres. Bees —4H **47**
Pelham Cres. Nott —5D **36**
Pelham Rd. Nott —1F **37**
Pelham St. Ilk —6A **20**
Pelham St. Nott
　　　　　—5G **37** (4E **3**)
Pemberton St. Nott
　　　　　—5H **37** (5G **3**)
Pembrey Clo. Trow —1F **45**
Pembridge Clo. Nott —5B **24**
Pembroke Dri. Nott —6G **25**
Pembury Rd. Nott —4E **35**
Penarth Gdns. Nott —4A **26**
Penarth Rise. Nott —4A **26**
Pendennis Clo. Ged —6B **28**
Pendine Clo. Red —4H **15**
Pendle Cres. Nott —6B **26**
Penhale Dri. Huck —6A **4**
Penhurst Clo. Nott —1E **59**
Penllech Clo. Nott —6E **15**
Penllech Wlk. Nott —6E **15**
Pen Moor Clo. Long E
　　　　　—1C **64**
Pennant Rd. Nott —5B **24**
Pennard Wlk. Nott —5B **58**
Penn Av. Nott —6C **36**
Pennhome Av. Nott —5G **25**
Pennie Clo. Long E —3F **65**
Pennine Clo. Arn —3B **16**
Pennine Clo. Long E —3F **65**
Pennyfields Boulevd. Long E
　　　　　—6D **54**
Pennyfoot St. Nott
　　　　　—5A **38** (5H **3**)
Penrhyn Clo. Nott
　　　　　—3H **37** (1F **3**)
Penrhyn Cres. Bees —1B **56**
Penrith Av. Rad T —5G **41**
Penrith Cres. Nott —5A **24**
Penshore Clo. Nott —4B **58**
Pentland Dri. Arn —3F **15**
Pentland Gdns. Long E
　　　　　—4C **54**
Pentridge Dri. Ilk —4G **19**
Pentwood Av. Arn —3B **16**
Peppercorn Gdns. Nott
　　　　　—3A **36**
Pepper Rd. Calv —2C **6**
Pepper St. Nott
　　　　　—5G **37** (5E **3**)
Percival St. Nott —5F **25**
Percy St. E'wd —3C **10**
Percy St. Ilk —2B **32**
Percy St. Nott —4B **26**
Peregrine Clo. Lent —5C **36**
Perivale Clo. Nott —4D **22**
Perlethorpe Av. Ged —5F **27**
Perlethorpe Av. Nott —5B **38**
Perlethorpe Clo. Ged —5G **27**
Perlethorpe Cres. Ged
　　　　　—5G **27**
Perlethorpe Dri. Ged —5F **27**
Perlethorpe Dri. Huck —4F **5**
Perry Gdns. Nott —4F **25**
Perry Gro. Bing —5F **43**
Perry Rd. Nott —5D **24**
Perth Dri. S'fd —2H **45**
Perth St. Nott —4G **37** (2E **3**)
Peters Clo. Arn —1E **27**
Peters Clo. Newt —3E **11**
Petersfield Clo. Nott —6D **14**
Petersgate. Long E —4C **54**
Petersgate Clo. Long E
　　　　　—3C **54**
Petersham M. Nott —6D **36**
Petersham Rd. Long E
　　　　　—3C **54**
Petworth Av. Bees —2H **55**
Petworth Dri. Nott —4D **24**
Peveril Ct. W Bri —4A **50**

Peveril Cres. Long E —2B **64**
Peveril Cres. W Hal —1C **30**
Peveril Dri. Ilk —5H **19**
Peveril Dri. Nott
　　　　　—6F **37** (6B **2**)
Peveril Dri. W Bri —2A **60**
*Peveril M. Nott —5E **37***
　　(off Alexander Rd.)
Peveril Rd. Bees —3F **47**
Peveril St. Huck —3E **5**
Peveril St. Nott —3F **37**
Philip Av. Newt —4C **10**
Philip Av. Nut —1C **22**
Philip Gro. Ged —5G **27**
Phoenix Av. Ged —5G **27**
Phoenix Cen. Nott —3G **23**
Phoenix Clo. Nott —1F **49**
Phoenix Ct. E'wd —4C **10**
Phoenix Ct. Nott —3D **48**
Phyllis Clo. Huck —2D **4**
Phyllis Gro. Long E —6H **55**
Piccadilly. Nott —1B **24**
Pickering Av. E'wd —3B **10**
Pieris Dri. Nott —4A **58**
Pierrepont Av. Ged —6G **27**
Pierrepont Rd. W Bri —3C **50**
Pilcher Ga. Nott
　　　　　—5H **37** (4F **3**)
Pilkington Rd. Nott —6C **26**
Pilkington St. Nott —6H **13**
Pimlico. Ilk —1A **32**
Pimlico Av. Bees —6B **34**
Pinder St. Nott
　　　　　—5H **37** (5G **3**)
Pine Av. Lan M —2E **9**
Pine Gro. Huck —1H **13**
Pine Hill Clo. Nott —4D **14**
Pinehurst Av. Huck —6A **4**
Pine Tree Wlk. E'wd —3A **10**
Pinewood Av. Arn —4D **16**
Pinewood Gdns. Nott —5B **58**
Pinfold. Bing —5F **43**
Pinfold Clo. Cotg —1F **63**
Pinfold Clo. Wdbgh —6G **7**
Pinfold Cres. Wdbgh —6G **7**
Pinfold La. Shelf —6H **29**
Pinfold La. S'fd —4F **45**
Pinfold Rd. Gilt —4E **11**
Pingle Cres. Nott —5D **14**
Pingle, The. Long E —5F **55**
Pintail Clo. Carl —4B **40**
Pippin Clo. Nott —2B **38**
Pitcairn Clo. Nott —2G **49**
Pit La. Ship —1F **19**
Plains Farm Clo. Nott —4C **26**
Plains Gro. Nott —4C **26**
Plains Rd. Nott —4C **26**
Plane Clo. Nott —6F **13**
Plantagenet Ct. Nott
　　　　　—4H **37** (2G **3**)
Plantagenet St. Nott
　　　　　—4H **37** (2G **3**)
Plantation Clo. Arn —4F **15**
Plantation Rd. Keyw —4B **70**
Plantation Rd. Nott —5C **34**
Plantation Side. Nott —2C **36**
Plantations, The. Long E
　　　　　—5C **54**
Plant La. Long E —3C **64**
Platt La. Keyw —3D **70**
Platts Av. Hean —4A **8**
Player St. Nott —3C **36**
Plaza Gdns. Nott —3C **24**
Pleasant Ct. Nott —2D **36**
Pleasant Row. Nott —2D **36**
Plough La. Nott
　　　　　—5A **38** (5H **3**)
Ploughman Av. Wdbgh
　　　　　—6H **7**
Plover Wharf. Nott —1E **49**
Plowman Ct. S'fd —5E **45**
Plowright Ct. Nott —2H **37**
Plowright St. Nott —2H **37**
Plumb Rd. Huck —4F **5**
Plumptre Almshouses. Nott
　　　　　—5G **3**
Plumptre Clo. E'wd —4B **10**
Plumptre Pl. Nott
　　　　　—5H **37** (5F **3**)

Plumptre Rd. Lan M —1F 9
Plumptre Sq. Nott
—5H 37 (5G 3)
Plumptre St. Nott
—5H 37 (5F 3)
Plumptre Way. E'wd —4B 10
Plumtree Gdns. Calv —3D 6
Plumtree Rd. Cotg —3D 62
Plungar Clo. Nott —3H 35
Podder La. Nott —1E 27
Pointers Ct. Nott —2C 38
Point, The. Nott —1H 37
Polperro Way. Huck —6A 4
Pond Hills La. Arn —5B 16
Pool Meadow. Colw —5H 39
Popham Ct. Nott
—5H 37 (5F 3)
Popham St. Nott
—5H 37 (5F 3)
Poplar Av. Nott —5E 25
Poplar Av. Sand —4C 44
Poplar Clo. Bing —5G 43
Poplar Clo. Carl —3F 8
Poplar Cres. Nut —1B 22
Poplar Rd. Breas —4B 54
Poplars Av. Bur J —2g 29
Poplars Clo. Plum —3D 70
Poplars Rd. Nott —1D 48
Poplars, The. Bees —4F 47
Poplars, The. W Bri —4B 50
Poplar St. Nott
—5H 37 (5G 3)
Poplar Way. Ilk —4H 31
Porchester Clo. Huck —4G 5
Porchester Rd. Bing —5D 42
Porchester Rd. Nott —5B 26
Porlock Clo. Long E —4C 54
Portage Clo. Rad T —1E 53
Port Arthur Rd. Nott —5C 38
Porter Clo. Nott —5A 58
Portinscale Clo. W Bri
—6E 51
Portland Ct. Nott —2F 25
Portland Cres. S'fd —5G 45
Portland Gdns. Huck —4D 4
Portland Grange. Huck —4C 4
Portland Pk. Clo. Huck —4D 4
Portland Rd. Bees —4H 55
Portland Rd. Carl —5E 27
Portland Rd. Gilt —5D 10
Portland Rd. Huck —4F 5
Portland Rd. Ilk —4B 20
Portland Rd. Long E —3C 64
Portland Rd. Nott
—4E 37 (2A 2)
Portland Rd. W Bri —5B 50
Portland St. Bees —4G 47
Portland St. Day —1A 26
Portree Dri. Nott —4D 14
Port Said Vs. Nott —6D 24
Postern St. Nott
—5F 37 (4C 2)
Potomac M. Nott
—5E 37 (5A 2)
Potters Ct. Bees —2D 46
Potters Way. Ilk —1C 32
Poulter Clo. Nott —2B 36
Poulton Dri. Nott —6B 38
Poultry. Nott —5G 37 (4E 3)
Poultry Arc. Nott —4E 3
Powers Rd. Nott —1B 38
Powis St. Nott —6H 13
Powtrell Clo. Ilk —3D 32
Poynton St. Nott
—4F 37 (3C 2)
Poyser Clo. New B —6E 25
Precinct, The. Cotg —2F 63
Premier Rd. Nott —1E 37
Prendwick Gdns. Nott
—5F 15
Prestwick Clo. Nott —5D 22
Prestwood Dri. Nott —2H 35
Pretoria Vs. Nott —5A 24
Previn Gdns. Nott —3H 37
Primrose Bank. Bing —5D 42
Primrose Clo. Nott —2H 37
Primrose Cres. Carl —2H 39
Primrose Hill. Ilk —4A 20
Primrose Rise. Newt —5D 10

Primrose St. Carl —2H 39
Primrose St. Ilk —4A 20
Primula Clo. Nott —3A 58
Prince Edward Cres. Rad T
—1E 53
Princess Av. Bees —5G 47
Princess Clo. Ged —5G 27
Princess Dri. Sand —1D 54
Princess St. Long E —5F 55
Princes St. E'wd —2B 10
Prince St. Ilk —3A 20
Prince St. Long E —5F 55
Prior Rd. Day —1H 25
Priors Clo. Bing —4G 43
Priory Av. Toll —4E 61
Priory Cir. Toll —4E 61
Priory Clo. Ilk —3G 31
Priory Ct. Ged —5H 27
Priory Ct. Nott —6A 26
Priory Cres. Ged —6H 27
Priory M. Nott —1C 48
Priory Rd. E'wd —4B 10
Priory Rd. Ged —6H 27
Priory Rd. Huck —4C 4
Priory Rd. W Bri —3B 50
Priory St. Nott —1C 48
Pritchard Dri. S'fd —5G 45
Private Rd. Sher & Mapp
—5G 25
Prize Clo. Nott —4A 58
Promenade. Nott
—4H 37 (2G 3)
Prospect Pl. Nott —6D 36
Prospect Rd. Carl —6C 26
Prospect Rd. Hean —5E 9
Prospect St. Nott —3C 36
Prospect Ter. Nott —3C 36
Providence Pl. Ilk —6A 20
Prudhoe Ct. Nott —2H 49
Pulborough Clo. Nott —3D 24
Pullman Rd. Nott —5B 38
Pumping Sta. Cotts. Nott
—6C 38
Purbeck Clo. Long E —6C 54
Purbeck Dri. W Bri —6G 49
Purchase Av. Los —3A 8
Purdy Meadow. Long E
—2B 64
Pyatt St. Nott —2H 49
Pygall Av. Got —6G 67
Pym Leys. Long E —2B 64
Pym St. Nott —3B 38
Pym Wlk. Nott —3A 38

Q

Quantock Clo. Arn —3F 15
Quantock Gro. Bing —5C 42
Quantock Rd. Long E —4C 54
Quarry Av. Nott —1H 23
Quarrydale. Huck —2D 4
Quarry Hill. Stan D —3B 44
Quarry Hill Ind. Est. Ilk
—4B 32
Quarry Hill Rd. Ilk —4B 32
Quayside Clo. Nott —2A 58
Queen Elizabeth Rd. Bees
—1A 56
Queen Elizabeth Way. Ilk
—4G 31
Queens Av. Ged —5G 27
Queens Av. Hean —3B 8
Queens Av. Ilk —4C 32
Queens Av. Stan —3A 30
Queensberry St. Nott —3C 24
Queen's Bower Rd. Nott
—5G 15
Queensbury Av. W Bri
—2G 59
Queen's Ct. Bing —4D 42
Queen's Dri. Bees —5G 47
Queen's Dri. Ilk —1A 32
Queens Dri. Kimb —1C 22
Queen's Dri. Nott —4E 49
Queens Dri. Sand —1D 54
Queen's Rd. Bees —6G 47
Queens Rd. Nott —6G 37
Queen's Rd. Rad T —5F 41
Queen's Rd. E. Bees —4H 47

Queens Rd. N. E'wd —3B 10
Queens Rd. S. E'wd —4B 10
Queen's Rd. W. Bees —1D 56
Queens Sq. E'wd —3B 10
Queen St. Arn —4B 16
Queen St. Huck —3D 4
Queen St. Ilk —1A 32
Queen St. Lan M —2G 9
Queen St. Long E —6G 55
Queen St. Nott
—4G 37 (3D 2)
Queens Wlk. Nott —2F 49
Queen Ter. Ilk —1A 32
Querneby Av. Nott —5A 26
Querneby Rd. Nott —5A 26
Quinton Clo. Nott —6E 49
Quorn Clo. Att —2E 57
Quorndon Cres. Long E
—2F 65
Quorn Gro. Nott —4E 25
Quorn Rd. Nott —4E 25

R

Racecourse Rd. Nott
—5D 38
Radbourne Rd. Nott —6B 38
Radburn Ct. S'fd —2G 45
Radcliffe Gdns. Carl —1F 39
Radcliffe Lodge. Rad T
—6E 41
Radcliffe Mt. W Bri —2B 50
Radcliffe Rd. Hol P & Rad T
—3F 51
Radcliffe Rd. Nott & Gam
—2A 50
Radcliffe St. Nott —2H 49
Radford Boulevd. Nott
—3C 36
Radford Bri. Rd. Nott —3A 36
Radford Ct. Nott —4D 36
Radford Ct. Ind. Est. Nott
—4D 36
Radford Cres. Ged —5G 27
Radford Gro. La. Nott
—3C 36
Radford Rd. Nott —5D 24
Radham Ct. Nott —5G 25
Radley Sq. Nott —2B 24
Radmarsh Rd. Nott —6G 36
Rad Meadows. Long E
—1E 65
Radnor Gro. Bing —5C 42
Radstock Rd. Nott —2C 38
Radway Dri. Nott —6E 49
Raeburn Dri. Bees —3G 55
Ragdale Rd. Nott —5H 13
(in two parts)
Raglan Clo. Nott —2H 37
Raglan Dri. Ged —6B 28
Raglan St. E'wd —4C 10
Raibank Gdns. Wd'p —2A 26
Railway Cotts. Kimb —1H 21
Rainham Gdns. Rud —1G 69
Raithby Clo. Nott —1E 25
Raleigh Clo. Nott —4A 58
Raleigh Ct. Nott —3E 37
Raleigh M. Nott
—4E 37 (2A 2)
Raleigh St. Nott
—4E 37 (2A 2)
Ralf Clo. W Bri —1A 60
Ramblers Clo. Colw —4G 39
Ramsdale Av. Calv —2B 6
Ramsdale Cres. Nott —4H 25
Ramsdale Rd. Carl —6G 27
Ramsey Clo. S'fd —1G 45
Ramsey Ct. Nott —2F 25
Ramsey Dri. Arn —1D 26
Ranby Wlk. Nott —3B 38
Rancliffe Av. Keyw —3B 70
Randal Gdns. Nott —2D 36
Randall St. Nott —2C 36
(in two parts)
Ranelagh Gro. Nott —4G 35
Ranmere Rd. Nott —2G 35
Ranmoor Rd. Ged —6H 27
Ranmore Clo. Bees —1B 46
Rannoch Rise. Arn —4B 16
Rannock Gdns. Keyw —4D 70

Ranskill Gdns. Nott —5E 15
Ransom Dri. Nott —6A 26
Ransom Rd. Nott —6A 26
Ranson Rd. Bees —3C 56
Ratcliffe St. E'wd —3B 10
Rathgar Clo. Nott —5D 34
Rathmines Clo. Nott —6C 36
Rathvale Ct. Bees —1A 56
Raven Av. Nott —3F 25
Ravenhill Clo. Bees —1B 56
Ravens Ct. Nott —2F 25
Ravensdale Av. Long E
—3D 54
Ravensdale Dri. Nott —6C 34
Ravensdene Ct. Nott —1H 37
Ravensmore Rd. Nott —6F 25
Ravenswood Rd. Arn —5B 16
Ravensworth Rd. Nott
—5H 13
Rawson St. Nott —6D 24
Rayleigh Clo. Ilk —4B 20
Raymede Clo. Nott —1D 24
Raymede Dri. Nott —1C 24
Raymond Dri. Bing —5G 43
Rayneham Rd. Ilk —4G 19
Rayner Ct. Nott —6A 36
Raynford Av. Bees —1D 56
Rays Av. Hean —4C 8
Ray St. Hean —4B 8
Read Av. Bees —5G 47
Read Lodge. Bees —5G 47
Readman Rd. Bees —2A 56
Rearsby Clo. Nott —4D 34
Recreation Rd. Sand —5D 44
Recreation St. Long E
—5H 55
Recreation Ter. S'fd —5F 45
Rectory Av. Nott —5F 35
Rectory Ct. Nott —5F 35
Rectory Ct. W Bri —4B 50
Rectory Dri., The. Ged
—5H 27
Rectory Gdns. Nott —5F 35
Rectory Pl. Bart —1E 67
Rectory Rd. Colw —4G 39
Rectory Rd. Cotg —2E 63
Rectory Rd. W Bri —4A 50
Redbourne Dri. Nott —3A 36
Redbridge Dri. Nott —4D 22
Redcar Clo. Ged —5G 27
Redcliffe Gdns. Nott —1G 37
Redcliffe Rd. Nott —1G 37
Redfield Rd. Lent —3C 48
Redfield Way. Nott —3C 48
Redgates Ct. Calv —3B 6
Redhill Lodge Dri. Red
—4H 15
Redhill Rd. Arn —4A 16
Redland Av. Carl —1H 39
Redland Clo. Bees —1C 56
Redland Clo. Ilk —4B 20
Redland Dri. Bees —2C 56
Redland Gro. Carl —1G 39
Red Lion Sq. Hean —3C 8
Redmays Dri. Bul —1H 29
Redmile Rd. Nott —5A 24
Redoubt St. Nott —4C 36
Redruth Clo. Nott —3C 34
Redwood. W Bri —5F 49
Redwood Av. Nott —6D 34
Redwood Ct. Huck —3D 4
Redwood Cres. Bees —6G 47
Reedham Wlk. Nott —5F 15
Reedman Rd. Long E
—3D 64
Rees Gdns. Nott —4E 15
Regatta Way. Nott —3E 51
Regency Ct. Bees —4G 47
Regents Pk. Clo. W Bri
—6G 49
Regent St. Bees —4G 47
Regent St. Ilk —2B 32
Regent St. Kimb —1H 21
Regent St. Long E —5F 55
Regent St. New B —6E 25
Regent St. Nott
—5F 37 (4B 2)
Regent St. Sand —6E 45
Regina Clo. Rad T —1E 53

Reigate Clo. Att —3E 57
Reigate Dri. Att —3E 57
Reigate Rd. Nott —5D 24
Rempstone Dri. Nott —2B 24
Renals Way. Calv —3D 6
Renfrew Dri. Nott —5E 35
Renne Hogg Rd. Nott —3E 49
Repton Dri. Ilk —2D 32
Repton Rd. Long E —3B 64
Repton Rd. Nott —1B 24
Repton Rd. W Bri —6A 50
Retford Rd. Nott —4E 25
Retlaw Ct. Bees —6D 46
Revelstoke Av. Nott —4B 14
Revelstoke Way. Nott —4B 14
Revesby Gdns. Nott —2A 36
Revesby Rd. Wd'p —2B 26
Revill Cres. S'fd —3H 45
Reydon Dri. Nott —6B 24
Reynolds Dri. Nott —4F 35
Rhoby Rise. Huck —4F 5
Rhyl Cres. Ged —5H 27
Ribblesdale Ct. Bees —1A 56
Ribblesdale Rd. Long E
—2C 64
Ribblesdale Rd. Nott —2G 25
Ribble St. Nott —4B 36
Riber Clo. Long E —2F 65
Riber Clo. W Hal —1C 30
Riber Cres. Nott —2D 24
Richardson Clo. Nott —4A 58
Richborough Pl. Nott —1E 47
Richey Clo. Arn —6D 16
Richmond Av. Breas —5C 54
Richmond Av. Calv —2E 7
Richmond Av. Ilk —3B 20
Richmond Av. Newt —3D 10
Richmond Av. Nott —2B 38
Richmond Av. Sand —1C 54
Richmond Clo. W Hal
—1B 30
Richmond Ct. Bees —6E 47
Richmond Dri. Bees —6E 47
Richmond Dri. Nott —5H 25
Richmond Dri. Rad T —5F 41
Richmond Gdns. Red —4A 16
Richmond Rd. W Bri —2B 50
Richmond Ter. Rad T —6F 41
Ricklow Ct. Nott —5E 15
Rick St. Nott —4H 37 (3F 3)
Ridding Ter. Nott
—3G 37 (1E 3)
Ridge La. Rad T —4G 41
Ridge Way. Nott —6C 14
Ridgeway Dri. Ilk —4F 31
Ridgeway Wlk. Nott —5E 15
Ridgewood Dri. Bees —1C 56
Ridgmont Wlk. Nott —5B 58
(in two parts)
Ridgway Clo. Nott —6E 51
Ridgway St. Nott —3A 38
Ridings, The. Bul —2G 29
Ridings, The. Keyw —4E 71
Ridsdale Rd. Nott —2G 25
Rifle St. Nott —4C 36
Rigg Hill Ct. Nott —2G 23
Rigley Av. Ilk —6B 20
Rigley Dri. Nott —6C 14
Ring Leas. Cotg —3F 63
Ringstead Clo. W Bri —6G 49
Ringstead Wlk. Nott —5F 15
Ringwood Cres. Nott —4A 36
Ringwood Rd. Bing —5C 42
Ripon Rd. Nott —4D 38
Riseborough Wlk. Nott
—4H 13
Rise Ct. Nott —6F 25
Risegate. Cotg —2F 63
Risegate Gdns. Cotg —2F 63
Riseholme Av. Nott —6C 34
Rise Pk. Rd. Nott —4B 14
Rise, The. Nott —4H 25
Risley Ct. Ilk —4B 20
Risley Dri. Nott —1F 49
Risley La. Breas —2A 54
Riste's Pl. Nott
—5H 37 (4F 3)

Ritson Clo. Nott —3H **37**
Riverdale Rd. Bees —3D **56**
Rivergreen. Nott —2C **58**
Rivergreen Clo. Bees —1C **46**
Rivergreen Cres. Bees
—1C **46**
Rivermead. Cotg —2F **63**
Rivermead. W Bri —4H **49**
River Rd. Colw —5G **39**
Riverside Clo. Bees —2H **57**
Riverside Ind. Pk. Nott
—3E **49**
Riverside Rd. Bees —2G **57**
Riverside Way. Nott —2F **49**
Riverview. Nott —2H **49**
Riverway Gdns. Nott —1H **49**
Rivington Rd. Tot —3G **55**
Road No.1. Carl —3H **39**
Road No.2. Carl —4B **40**
Road No.3. Carl —4B **40**
Road No.4. Carl —4B **40**
Road No.5. Carl —3H **39**
Road No.7. Carl —3H **39**
Road No.8. Carl —3H **39**
Robbie Burns Rd. Nott
—5F **15**
Robbinetts La. Coss —6F **21**
Roberts La. Huck —4D **4**
Roberts St. Ilk —3C **32**
Roberts St. Nott —5A **58**
Roberts Yd. Bees —4G **47**
Robey Dri. E'wd —2B **10**
Robey Ter. Nott —2D **36**
Robina Dri. Gilt —5E **11**
Robinet Rd. Bees —6F **47**
Robin Hood Chase. Nott
—2H **37**
Robin Hood Clo. E'wd —4B **10**
Robin Hood Dri. Huck
—1E **13**
Robin Hood Ind. Est. Nott
—4A **38** (3H **3**)
Robin Hood Rd. Arn —4G **15**
Robin Hood St. Nott
—4A **38** (3H **3**)
Robin Hood Ter. Nott
—4H **37** (2G **3**)
Robin Hood Way. Nott
—2F **49**
Robinia Ct. W Bri —6C **50**
Robinson Gdns. Nott —4A **58**
Robinson Rd. Nott —4B **26**
Robinswood Ho. Nott
—2H **35**
Robins Wood Rd. Nott
—3H **35**
Rob Roy Av. Nott —6D **36**
Roche Clo. Arn —6E **17**
Rochester Av. N'fld —2A **40**
Rochester Ct. Nott —1F **23**
Rochester Wlk. Nott —4D **58**
Rochford Ct. Edw —2E **61**
Rock Ct. Nott —4B **24**
Rock Dri. Nott —6E **37** (6A **2**)
Rockford Ct. S'fd —2G **45**
Rockford Rd. Nott —4D **24**
Rockingham Gro. Bing
—5C **42**
Rockley Av. Newt —4C **10**
Rockley Av. Rad T —5F **41**
Rockley Clo. Huck —5A **4**
Rock Side. Kimb —1H **21**
Rockside Gdns. Huck —4C **4**
Rock St. Nott —5G **13**
Rockwell St. S'fd —4G **45**
Rockwood Cres. Huck —5B **4**
Rockwood Wlk. Huck —5C **4**
Rodel Ct. Nott —3H **37** (1F **3**)
Roden St. Nott
—4A **38** (3H **3**)
Roderick St. Nott —3B **24**
Rodney Rd. W Bri —5C **50**
Rodney Way. Ilk —4B **20**
Rodwell Clo. Nott —5C **34**
Roecliffe. W Bri —1A **60**
Roehampton Dri. Trow
—1F **45**
Roe Hill. Wdbgh —4G **7**
(in two parts)

Roes La. Calv —3E **7**
Roker Clo. Nott —6G **23**
Roland Av. Nut —3E **23**
Roland Av. Wilf —4F **49**
Rolleston Clo. Huck —6B **4**
Rolleston Cres. Wat —4H **11**
Rolleston Dri. Arn —6E **15**
Rolleston Dri. Newt —5C **10**
Rolleston Dri. Nott —3C **24**
Roman Dri. Nott —3C **24**
Romans Ct. Nott —4C **24**
Romilay Clo. Bees —3G **47**
Romney Av. Nott —1D **46**
Romorantin Pl. Long E
—6G **55**
Rona Ct. Nott —2C **24**
Ronald St. Nott —4D **36**
Rookery Gdns. Arn —5B **16**
Rookwood Clo. Bees —5E **47**
Roosa Clo. Nott —2F **23**
Roosevelt Av. Long E —2E **65**
Roper Av. Hean —5C **8**
Ropewalk, The. Hean —5D **8**
Ropewalk, The. Ilk —6C **20**
Ropewalk, The. Nott
—4E **37** (3A **2**)
Ropewalk, The. Stan C
—6A **18**
Ropsley Cres. W Bri —2C **50**
Roscoe Av. Red —3A **16**
Roseacre. Bees —6G **47**
Rose Ash La. Nott —5F **15**
Rose Av. Ilk —5A **20**
Rosebank Dri. Arn —4D **16**
Roseberry Gdns. Huck
—5G **5**
Roseberry St. Nott —3C **24**
Rosebery Av. W Bri —2A **50**
Rose Clo. Nott —2H **37**
Rose Ct. Long E —4D **54**
Rosecroft Dri. Nott —1G **25**
Rosedale Clo. Long E
—1D **64**
Rosedale Dri. Nott —5B **34**
Rosedale Rd. Nott —3E **39**
Rosegarth Wlk. Nott —3B **24**
Rose Gro. Bees —6H **47**
Rose Gro. Keyw —3D **70**
Rosegrove Av. Arn —4B **16**
Rose Hill. Keyw —4C **70**
Roseland Clo. Keyw —5C **70**
Roseleigh Av. Nott —5D **26**
Rosemary Clo. Nott —6E **23**
Roseneath Av. Nott —3C **14**
(in two parts)
Rosewall Ct. Arn —6D **16**
Rosewood Cres. Hean —3F **9**
Rosewood Gdns. Nott
—6F **13**
Rosewood Gdns. W Bri
—2G **59**
Roslyn Av. Ged —5G **27**
Rossell Dri. S'fd —6G **45**
Rossendale. Ilk —3A **20**
Rossett Clo. Gam —5F **51**
Rossington Rd. Nott —4B **38**
Rosslyn Av. Huck —3G **5**
Rosslyn Dri. Nott —5G **23**
Rosthwaite Clo. W Bri
—6E **51**
Rothbury Av. Trow —1F **45**
Rothbury Gro. Bing —4C **42**
Rothesay Av. Nott —4D **36**
Rothley Av. Nott —4B **38**
Rothwell Clo. Nott —1E **59**
Rough Woods La. Huck
—1D **12**
Roundwood Rd. Arn —6G **15**
Rowan Av. S'fd —1G **45**
Rowan Clo. Bing —5G **43**
Rowan Clo. Calv —3B **6**
Rowan Clo. Ilk —4B **32**
Rowan Ct. Nut —1B **22**
Rowan Dri. Keyw —5E **71**
Rowan Dri. Nott —1B **58**
Rowan Gdns. Nott —6F **13**
Rowan Wlk. Nott —1C **38**
Rowe Gdns. Nott —1B **24**

Rowland Av. Map —5C **26**
Rowland M. Nott —2A **38**
Rowsley Av. Long E —2C **64**
Roxley Ct. Bees —4E **47**
Roxton Ct. Kimb —6H **11**
Royal Av. Long E —4F **55**
Royal M. Bees —2C **56**
Roy Av. Bees —1H **57**
Royce Av. Huck —1E **13**
Royston Clo. Nott —2F **49**
Ruby Paddocks. Kimb
—2H **21**
Ruddington Fields Bus. Pk.
Rud —2H **69**
Ruddington La. Nott —5F **49**
Rudge Clo. Nott —4F **35**
Ruffles Av. Arn —2D **26**
Rufford Av. Bees —3A **46**
Rufford Av. Ged —5F **27**
Rufford Clo. Huck —5G **5**
Rufford Gro. Bing —5D **42**
Rufford Rd. Long E —3D **64**
Rufford Rd. Nott —4G **25**
Rufford Rd. Rud —6H **59**
Rufford Wlk. Nott —6H **13**
Rufford Way. Nott —5D **50**
Ruffs Dri. Huck —6C **4**
Rugby Clo. Nott —6C **14**
Rugby Rd. W Bri —6G **49**
Rugby Ter. Nott —2D **36**
Rugeley Av. Long E —6H **55**
Ruislip Clo. Kimb —6G **11**
Runcie Clo. Cotg —3F **63**
Runnymede Ct. Bees —6G **47**
Runnymede Ct. Nott
—4E **37** (2A **2**)
Runswick Dri. Arn —5B **16**
Runswick Dri. Nott —4G **35**
Runton Dri. Nott —3D **24**
Rupert Rd. Bing —5D **42**
Rupert St. Ilk —6C **20**
Ruscombe Pl. Nott —3H **37**
Rushcliffe Av. Carl —1F **39**
Rushcliffe Av. Rad T —6F **41**
Rushcliffe Ct. Nott —1B **24**
Rushcliffe Rise. Nott —2H **25**
Rushcliffe Rd. Huck —6C **4**
Rushes, The. Got —6H **67**
Rushford Dri. Nott —5C **34**
Rush Leys. Long E —2F **65**
Rushmere Wlk. Arn —2B **26**
Rushton Gdns. Nott —2A **38**
Rushworth Av. W Bri —3A **50**
Rushworth Clo. Nott —2A **38**
Rushworth Ct. W Bri —3A **50**
Rushy Clo. Nott —4D **34**
Rushy La. Sand & Ris
—5B **44**
Ruskin Av. Bees —1D **56**
Ruskin Av. Long E —1C **64**
Ruskin Clo. Day —6H **15**
Ruskin St. Nott —4C **36**
Russell Av. Nott —4F **35**
Russell Ct. Long E —4F **55**
Russell Cres. Nott —4F **35**
Russell Dri. Nott —4E **35**
Russell Gdns. Bees —3C **56**
Russell Pl. Nott
—4F **37** (3C **2**)
Russell Rd. Nott —1D **36**
Russell St. Long E —4F **55**
Russell St. Nott
—3E **37** (1A **2**)
Russett Av. Carl —2G **39**
Russley Rd. Bees —4A **46**
Ruth Dri. Arn —4C **16**
Rutherford Ho. High S
—2B **48**
Ruthwell Gdns. Nott —3E **15**
Rutland Av. Bees —3A **56**
Rutland Gro. Sand —6E **45**
Rutland Rd. Bing —5F **43**
Rutland Rd. Ged —4F **27**
Rutland Rd. W Bri —2B **50**
Rutland St. Ilk —5B **20**
Rutland St. Nott
—5F **37** (5C **2**)
Rutland Ter. Ilk —5B **20**
Rutland Ter. Kimb —2A **22**

Rutland Vs. Nott —5B **38**
Rydal Av. Long E —3D **54**
Rydal Dri. Bees —3D **46**
Rydal Dri. Huck —3D **4**
Rydale Rd. Nott —2G **25**
Rydal Gdns. W Bri —6C **50**
Rydal Gro. Nott —4C **24**
Ryder St. Nott —3B **24**
Ryecroft St. S'fd —3H **45**
Ryehill Clo. Nott —1H **49**
Ryehill St. Nott —1H **49**
Ryeland Gdns. Nott —1G **49**
Ryemere Clo. E'wd —3A **10**
Rye St. Nott —6D **24**
Rylands Clo. Bees —1H **57**
Rylands Ct. Bees —6G **47**
Ryton Ct. Nott —2H **49**
Ryton Sq. Nott —5H **23**

Sabina St. Nott —4H **37**
Saddleworth Ct. Nott —3G **37**
Saffron Gdns. Nott —1F **49**
St Agnes Clo. Nott —1D **34**
St Aidans Ct. Nott —3C **24**
St Albans M. Nott —1C **24**
St Albans Rd. Arn —6H **15**
St Albans Rd. B Vil —1C **10**
St Albans Rd. Nott —5A **14**
St Albans St. Sher —4G **25**
St Andrew Clo. Got —6H **67**
St Andrews Clo. Nott —6A **14**
St Andrews Ct. Nott —6B **14**
St Andrew's Dri. Ilk —1A **32**
St Andrew's Rd. Nott —2F **37**
St Ann's Gdns. Nott —2A **38**
St Ann's Hill. Nott —2G **37**
St Ann's Hill Rd. Nott
—2G **37**
St Ann's St. Nott
—4G **37** (2E **3**)
St Ann's Valley. Nott —3A **38**
St Ann's Way. Nott —3G **37**
St Ann's Well Rd. Nott
—4H **37** (2F **3**)
St Anthony Ct. Nott —1C **48**
St Augustines Clo. Nott
—6E **25**
St Austell Dri. Nott —6F **49**
St Austins Ct. Carl —1H **39**
St Austins Dri. Carl —1H **39**
St Bartholomew's Rd. Nott
—2B **38**
St Catherines St. Rad T
—1E **53**
St Cecilia Gdns. Nott —3H **37**
St Chads. Carl —2H **39**
St Chad's Rd. Nott —4A **38**
St Christopher St. Nott
—5B **38**
St Cuthbert's Rd. Nott
—4A **38**
St Ervan Rd. Nott —5F **49**
St Georges Dri. Nott —1G **49**
St Helen's Cres. Bur J —3F **39**
St Helens Cres. Trow —5E **33**
St Helen's Gro. Bur J —4E **39**
St Helens Rd. W Bri —5B **50**
St Helen's St. Nott
—4E **37** (3A **2**)
St Helier. Nott —5E **37** (5A **2**)
St James Av. Ilk —2C **32**
St James Ct. Nott —5D **26**
St James's Ct. Sand —2D **54**
St James's St. Nott
—5F **37** (5C **2**)
(in two parts)
St James's Ter. Nott
—5F **37** (5C **2**)
St James St. S'fd —5E **45**
St James Ter. S'fd —5E **45**
St John's Ct. Carl —2F **39**
St John's Cres. Huck —6G **5**
St John's Rd. Ilk —2C **32**
St John's Rd. Rud —6G **59**
St Johns St. Long E —4F **55**
St Judes Av. Nott —5H **25**
St Laurence Ct. Long E
—1G **65**

St Lawrence Boulevd. Rad T
—1D **52**
St Lawrence Clo. Hean —3D **8**
St Leonards Dri. Nott —5F **35**
St Leven Clo. Nott —1D **34**
St Lukes Way. Stu B —1F **41**
St Margaret's Av. Nott
—1A **36**
St Mark's St. Nott
—4H **37** (2F **3**)
St Martins Clo. Nott —1E **35**
St Martin's Gdns. Nott
—6E **23**
St Martin's Rd. Nott —1E **35**
St Mary's Av. Ged —5G **27**
St Mary's Clo. Arn —4B **16**
St Mary's Clo. Att —4D **56**
St Mary's Cres. Rud —6G **59**
St Mary's Pl. Nott
—5H **37** (4F **3**)
St Marys Rd. Bing —4F **43**
St Marys Way. Huck —3D **4**
St Matthias Rd. Nott —3A **38**
St Mawes Av. Nott —5F **49**
St Michael's Av. Ged —5G **27**
St Michael's Av. Nott —1D **34**
St Michaels Sq. Bees —3B **46**
St Michaels View. Huck
—2F **5**
St Nicholas Clo. Arn —6A **16**
St Nicholas St. Nott
—5G **37** (5D **2**)
St Norbert Dri. Ilk —4G **31**
St Patrick's Rd. Huck —4D **4**
St Patrick's Rd. Nut —1B **22**
St Pauls Av. Nott —2D **36**
St Paul's St. Nott —4B **36**
St Pauls Ter. Nott —2D **36**
St Peter's Chambers. Nott
—4E **3**
St Peter's Chu. Wlk. Nott
—5G **37** (4E **3**)
St Peters Cres. Rud —6G **59**
St Peter's Ga. Nott
—5G **37** (4E **3**)
St Peter's Sq. Nott —4E **3**
St Peters St. Nott —4C **36**
St Saviours Gdns. Nott
—1H **49**
St Stephens Av. Nott —5B **38**
St Stephen's Rd. Nott
—5A **38**
St Vincent Clo. Long E
—1G **65**
St Wilfrid's Rd. W Hal
—2C **30**
Salamander Clo. Carl —5F **27**
Salcey Dri. Trow —1F **45**
Salcombe Cir. Red —4H **15**
Salcombe Cres. Rud —5H **59**
Salcombe Dri. Red —4H **15**
Salcombe Rd. Nott —4D **24**
Salford Gdns. Nott
—4H **37** (2G **3**)
Salisbury Ct. Nott —5A **26**
Salisbury Sq. Nott —5C **36**
Salisbury St. Bees —4G **47**
Salisbury St. Long E —6G **55**
Salisbury St. Nott —5C **36**
Salmon Clo. Nott —6F **13**
Salop St. Day —6H **15**
Saltburn Rd. Nott —2G **35**
Salterford Av. Calv —2D **6**
Salterford Rd. Huck —6C **4**
Salford Clo. Ged —5H **27**
Salthouse Ct. Bees —3G **47**
Salthouse La. Bees —3G **47**
Saltney Way. Nott —2E **59**
Samson Ct. Rud —5F **59**
Sandale Clo. Gam —5E **51**
Sandays Clo. Nott —2G **49**
Sandby Ct. Bees —6C **46**
(in two parts)

A-Z Nottingham 91

Sandfield Ct. Nott —1G **23**
Sandfield Rd. Arn —1B **26**
Sandfield Rd. Bees —3G **55**
Sandfield Rd. Nott —5D **36**
Sandford Av. Long E —6G **55**
Sandford Rd. Nott —5B **26**
Sandgate. Bees —2D **46**
Sandham Wlk. Nott —2C **58**
Sandhurst Dri. Bees —3C **56**
Sandhurst Dri. Rud —1F **69**
Sandhurst Rd. Nott —4H **13**
Sandiacre Rd. S'fd —5E **45**
Sandon St. Nott —6E **25**
Sandown Rd. Bees —2H **55**
Sandpiper Way. Lent —5C **36**
Sandringham Av. W Bri
　　　　　　　　　—3A **50**
Sandringham Cres. Nott
　　　　　　　　　—4C **34**
Sandringham Dri. Bees
　　　　　　　　　—2C **46**
Sandringham Pl. Huck —3F **5**
Sandringham Pl. Ilk —4H **31**
Sandringham Rd. Nott
　　　　　　　　　—5B **38**
Sandringham Rd. Sand
　　　　　　　　　—2D **54**
Sands Clo. Colw —4G **39**
Sandside. Cotg —3F **63**
Sandwell Clo. Long E —1C **64**
Sandyford Clo. Nott —4A **24**
Sandy La. Bees —2D **46**
Sandy La. Hol P —6B **40**
Sandy La. Huck —4E **5**
Sanger Clo. Nott —5A **58**
Sanger Gdns. Nott —5A **58**
Sankey Dri. Nott —6G **13**
Sapele Clo. Ged —5A **28**
Sargent Gdns. Nott —3B **38**
Saskatoon Clo. Rad T —1E **53**
Saunby Clo. Arn —6D **16**
Savages Rd. Rud —5G **59**
Savages Row. Rud —5G **59**
Saville Clo. S'fd —3G **45**
Saville Rd. Wd'p —2B **26**
Savina Ct. Bees —4H **47**
Savoy Workshops. Lent
　　　　　　　　　—6D **36**
Sawley Rd. Breas —6A **54**
Sawley Rd. Dray —2A **64**
Sawmand Clo. Long E —1E **65**
Saxelby Gdns. Nott —5H **13**
Saxondale Dri. Nott —2B **24**
Saxon Grn. Nott —6C **36**
Saxton Av. Hean —3D **8**
Saxton Clo. Bees —5H **47**
Scafell Clo. W Bri —6E **51**
Scafell Way. Nott —6B **58**
Scalby Clo. E'wd —3H **9**
Scalford Dri. Nott —5A **36**
Scarborough Av. Ilk —1A **32**
Scarborough St. Nott
　　　　　　　　　—4H **37** (2G **3**)
Scarf Wlk. Nott —4F **49**
Scargill Av. Newt —4D **10**
Scargill Rd. Newt —4D **10**
Scargill Rd. W Hal —1C **30**
Scargill Wlk. E'wd —2B **10**
Scarrington Rd. W Bri
　　　　　　　　　—2B **50**
Sceptre St. Nott —5G **25**
School Av. Huck —1D **12**
School Clo. Nott —2H **49**
School La. Bees —1C **56**
School La. Stan D —4B **44**
School Sq. W Hal —2C **30**
School Way. Nott —2H **49**
Scotholme Av. Nott —1D **36**
Scotland Bank. Cotg —2F **63**
Scotland Rd. Nott —4D **24**
Scott Av. Bees —6G **47**
Scott Clo. Nott —2F **23**
Scottsdale Wlk. Nott —6A **26**
Scrimshire La. Cotg —2E **63**
Script Dri. Nott —3C **24**
Scrivelsby Gdns. Bees
　　　　　　　　　—1D **56**

Scrooby Row. Nott —5E **15**
Seaburn Rd. Bees —2G **55**
Seaford Av. Nott —4H **35**
Seaford Way. Ilk —2B **20**
Seagrave Ct. Nott —6A **16**
Seagrave Rd. Nott —6D **22**
Seamer Rd. Kimb —6H **11**
Seatoller Clo. W Bri —6E **51**
Seaton Cres. Nott —6G **23**
Second Av. Bees —3E **47**
Second Av. Carl —2E **39**
Second Av. Ged —6H **27**
Second Av. Ilk —2B **32**
Second Av. Lent —5A **48**
Second Av. Nott —1F **37**
Second Av. Ris —1B **54**
Sedgebrook Clo. Nott
　　　　　　　　　—4A **24**
Sedgeley Rd. Toll —5F **61**
Sedgwick St. Lan M —2F **9**
Sedgewood Gro. Nott
　　　　　　　　　—2C **58**
Sedgley Av. Nott —4B **38**
Sedley Av. Nut —1C **22**
Seely Av. Calv —2B **6**
Seely Rd. Nott —4D **36**
Sefton Av. S'fd —3G **45**
Sefton Dri. Nott —6H **25**
Selby Clo. Bees —2G **55**
Selby La. Keyw —5C **70**
Selby Rd. W Bri —5B **50**
Selhurst Ct. Nott —2D **36**
Selhurst St. Nott —2D **36**
Selkirk Way. Nott —6F **25**
Sellars Av. Rud —1G **69**
Sellers Wood Dri. Bulw
　　　　　　　　　—6G **13**
Sellers Wood Dri. W. Bulw
　　　　　　　　　—6E **13**
Selside Ct. Bees —1A **56**
Selston Dri. Nott —6A **36**
Selwyn Clo. Nott —2C **24**
Serina Ct. W Bri —4A **50**
Serlby Rise. Nott —3B **38**
Serlby Rd. Newt —2C **10**
Seven Oaks Cres. Bees
　　　　　　　　　—2B **46**
Seven Oaks Rd. Ilk —2C **44**
Seventh Av. Lent —6A **48**
Severals. S'fd —4H **45**
Severn St. Nott —6H **13**
Seymour Rd. E'wd —4B **10**
Seymour Rd. Huck —6C **4**
Seymour Rd. W Bri —3D **50**
Seymour St. Nott —4A **38**
Shackleton Clo. Nott —5D **22**
Shacklock Clo. Arn —3E **15**
Shadwell Gro. Rad T —6E **41**
Shady La. Att —3D **56**
Shaftesbury Av. Bur J
　　　　　　　　　—2G **29**
Shaftesbury Av. Long E
　　　　　　　　　—3D **64**
Shaftesbury Av. Sand
　　　　　　　　　—6C **44**
Shaftesbury St. New B
　　　　　　　　　—6E **25**
Shakespeare Clo. Colw
　　　　　　　　　—4G **39**
Shakespeare St. Long E
　　　　　　　　　—4E **55**
Shakespeare St. Nott
　　　　　　—4F **37** (2C **2**)
Shakespeare Vs. Nott
　　　　　　—4G **37** (2D **2**)
Shaldon Clo. Nott —4D **14**
Shandwick Clo. Arn —3D **16**
Shanklin Dri. S'fd —4F **45**
Shanwell Clo. Nott —5D **22**
Shardale Gdns. Nott —3B **24**
Sharnford Way. Bees —5B **34**
Sharp Clo. Long E —1E **65**
Sharphill Rd. Edw —1D **60**
Shaw Cres. Huck —1E **13**
Shaw Gdns. Nott —5A **58**
Shaw St. Rud —6G **59**
Shaw St. E. Ilk —3C **32**
Shaw St. W. Ilk —3C **32**
Shearing Clo. Ged —6A **28**

Shearing Hill. Ged —6A **28**
Sheepfold La. Rud —1G **69**
Sheetstores Ind. Est. Long E
　　　　　　　　　—2F **65**
Shelby Clo. Lent —5C **36**
Sheldon Clo. Long E —2D **54**
Sheldon Rd. Los —1A **8**
Shelford Clo. Bees —1D **56**
Shelford Clo. Rad T —6G **41**
Shelford Cres. Bur J —2G **29**
Shelford Dri. Bing —5D **42**
Shelford Rise. Nott —3C **38**
Shelford Rd. Ged —4E **27**
Shelford Rd. Nwtn —1A **42**
Shelford Rd. Rad T —6F **41**
Shellburne Clo. Nott —5C **14**
Shelley Av. Nott —2C **58**
Shelley Clo. Huck —5B **4**
Shelley Clo. Nut —1B **22**
Shelley Rd. Day —6H **15**
Shelt Hill. Wdbgh —6H **7**
Shelton Av. Huck —1A **14**
Shelton Gdns. Rud —6F **59**
Shelton St. Nott
　　　　　　　　　—3G **37** (1E **3**)
Shenfield Gdns. Nott —4B **14**
Shepard Clo. Nott —1F **23**
Shepherd Ct. Huck —1D **12**
Shepherds Clo. Nott —2G **35**
Shepherds Wood Dri. Nott
　　　　　　　　　—2A **36**
Shepton Clo. Ilk —4H **19**
Shepton Cres. Nott —5H **23**
Sheraton Dri. Nott —6E **35**
Sherborne Rd. Nott —6G **23**
Sherborne Rd. W Bri —6B **50**
Sherbrook Av. Nott —1H **25**
Sherbrooke Clo. Calv —2C **6**
Sherbrooke Rd. Nott —6F **25**
Sherbrooke Ter. Nott —6F **25**
Sherbrook Rd. Nott —1G **25**
Sherbrook Ter. Day —1H **25**
Sheridan Ct. S'fd —1G **45**
Sheriffs Lea. Bees —3G **55**
Sheriffs Way. Nott —1G **49**
Sheringham Clo. Arn —1B **26**
Sherman Dri. Bees —3C **56**
Sherrington Clo. Nott —5A **58**
Sherwin Clo. Nott
　　　　　　　　　—3G **37** (1E **3**)
Sherwin Gro. Nott —6C **36**
Sherwin Rd. Nott —6C **36**
Sherwin Rd. S'fd —2H **45**
Sherwin Wlk. Nott —3G **37**
Sherwood Av. Calv —2B **6**
Sherwood Av. Nott —4H **25**
Sherwood Ct. Bees —2C **56**
Sherwood Gro. Bing —6D **42**
Sherwood Gro. Calv —2D **6**
Sherwood Rise. E'wd —4B **10**
Sherwood Rise. Nott —6E **25**
Sherwood St. Huck —5G **5**
Shilling Way. Long E —6C **54**
Shipley Comn. La. Ilk
　　　　　　　　　—3H **19**
Shipley Ct. Ilk —6H **19**
Shipley La. Hean —2D **18**
Shipley Rise. Carl —2G **39**
Shipley Rd. Nott —5F **23**
Shipstone St. Ilk —3D **32**
Shipstone St. Nott —1D **36**
Shirebrook Clo. Nott —4A **24**
Shirley Ct. Bees —3A **56**
Shirley Dri. Arn —6D **16**
Shirley Rd. Nott —1G **37**
Shirley St. Long E —3C **64**
Shores Wood Clo. Nott
　　　　　　　　　—5F **15**
Shortcross Av. Nott —3B **26**
Short Hill. Nott
　　　　　　　　　—5H **37** (5F **3**)
Short Stairs. Nott
　　　　　　　　　—5H **37** (5G **3**)
Shortwood Av. Huck —6D **4**
Shortwood Clo. Nott
　　　　　　　　　—5H **37** (5F **3**)
Shorwell Rd. Nott —2E **39**
Shotton Dri. Arn —3C **16**

Shrewsbury Rd. Nott —5C **38**
Shrimpton Ct. Rud —1H **69**
Sibson Wlk. Arn —3B **16**
Sidlaw Rise. Arn —3F **15**
Sidmouth Clo. Keyw —3C **70**
Sidney Rd. Bees —4E **47**
Sidney St. Kimb —1H **21**
Sidney St. Long E —1F **65**
Silbury Clo. Nott —6B **58**
Silver Birch Clo. Nott —3H **23**
Silverdale. S'fd —6G **45**
Silverdale Rd. Nott —5D **24**
Silverhill Clo. Strel —5D **22**
Silverwood Rd. Bees —5E **47**
Simkin Av. Nott —6C **26**
Simone Gdns. Nott —3D **58**
Simons Ct. Bees —2D **46**
Sinclair Clo. Hean —5B **8**
Sisley Av. S'fd —5G **45**
Sixth Av. Lent —6A **48**
Skeavington La. Ilk —2A **20**
Sketchley Ct. Nott —6G **13**
Sketchley St. Nott —3B **38**
Skiddaw Clo. W Bri —6E **51**
Skipton Cir. Nott —3C **38**
Skipton Clo. Ilk —4H **19**
Slack La. Hean —5C **8**
Slack Rd. Ilk —4D **18**
Slade Rd. Bees —6B **46**
Slaidburn Av. Nott —6E **49**
Sloan Dri. Bees —6B **34**
Sloane Ct. W Bri —2G **59**
Sloethorpe Gdns. Arn
　　　　　　　　　—5H **15**
Smalls Croft. Wdbgh —6G **7**
Smedley Av. Ilk —2C **32**
Smedley Clo. Nott —5H **23**
Smedley's Av. Sand —6D **44**
Smeeton St. Hean —4F **9**
Smite Ct. Nott —2B **36**
Smith Dri. Lan M —2E **9**
Smithfield Av. Trow —6F **33**
Smithurst Rd. Gilt —5C **10**
Smithy Clo. Nott —3B **58**
Smithy Cres. Arn —5B **16**
Smithy Row. Nott
　　　　　　　　　—5G **37** (4E **3**)
Smithy View. Calv —3C **6**
Smythson Dri. Nott —5C **35**
Snape Nook Ct. Nott —6F **13**
Snape Wood Rd. Nott
　　　　　　　　　—6F **13**
Snead Ct. Nott —4E **15**
Sneinton Boulevd. Nott
　　　　　　　　　—5B **38**
Sneinton Dale. Nott —5B **38**
Sneinton Hermitage. Nott
　　　　　　　　　—6A **38**
Sneinton Hollows. Nott
　　　　　　　　　—5B **38**
Sneinton Rd. Nott
　　　　　　　　　—5A **38** (4H **3**)
Soarbank Clo. Kimb —6G **11**
Sobers Gdns. Arn —1D **26**
Softwood Clo. Nott —6F **13**
Soloman Rd. Coss —5D **20**
Solway Clo. Bees —6E **47**
Somerby Ct. Bees —5B **34**
Somersby Rd. Nott & Mapp
　　　　　　　　　—2B **26**
Somerset Clo. Long E
　　　　　　　　　—5A **56**
Somerton Av. Nott —1E **59**
Sophie Rd. Nott —3D **36**
Soudan Dri. Nott —2F **49**
Southampton St. Nott
　　　　　　　　　—3A **38**
South Av. Rad T —5H **41**
Southchurch Ct. Nott —2D **58**
Southchurch Dri. Nott
　　　　　　　　　—4C **58**
Southcliffe Rd. Carl —2F **39**
　(in two parts)
South Ct. Bees —1H **57**
Southdale Dri. Carl —2F **39**
Southdale Rd. Carl —2F **39**
　(in two parts)
S. Devon Av. Nott —5D **26**
Southey St. Nott —3D **36**

Southfield Rd. Nott —3B **36**
Southfields. Long E —6G **55**
Southfields Ct. Bees —6B **46**
Southglade Rd. Nott —1C **24**
Southlea Rd. Carl —2F **39**
South Pde. Nott
　　　　　　　　　—5G **37** (4D **2**)
Southport Ter. Nott —2C **36**
South Rd. Bees —1G **57**
South Rd. Nott
　　　　　　　　　—6E **37** (6A **2**)
South Rd. W Bri —5A **50**
S. Sherwood St. Nott
　　　　　　　　　—4G **37** (2D **2**)
Southside. Arn —5E **17**
S. Snape Clo. Nott —6F **13**
South St. E'wd —3A **10**
South St. Gilt —5E **11**
South St. Huck —4E **5**
South St. Ilk —2B **32**
S. View Rd. Carl —5F **27**
Southwark St. Nott —4C **24**
Southwell Rd. Nott
　　　　　　　　　—5H **37** (4H **3**)
Southwold Dri. Nott —4A **36**
Sovereign Ct. Bees —6G **47**
Sovereign Gro. Long E
　　　　　　　　　—6D **54**
Sowbrook La. D Abb —5H **31**
Spalding Rd. Nott —4A **38**
Spaniel Row. Nott
　　　　　　　　　—5G **37** (5D **2**)
Spean Dri. Nott —1H **35**
Speedwell La. Kimb —1G **21**
Spencer Av. Map —2E **27**
Spencer Av. Sand —4D **44**
Spencer Clo. Rud —6F **59**
Spencer Cres. S'fd —3H **45**
Spencer Dri. Nut —1C **22**
Spey Clo. Huck —2D **12**
Spicer Clo. Bees —3C **56**
Spindle Gdns. Nott —6G **13**
Spindle La. Calv —5A **6**
Spindle View. Calv —4D **6**
Spinney Clo. Cotg —3F **63**
Spinney Clo. W Bri —1D **60**
Spinney Cres. Bees —2H **55**
Spinney Dri. Long E —3E **55**
Spinney Rise. Bees —2H **55**
Spinney Rd. Bing —5D **42**
Spinney Rd. Ilk —3A **32**
Spinney Rd. Keyw —4B **70**
Spinney Rd. Long E —3E **55**
Spinney, The. B Vil —1C **14**
Spinney, The. Bul —2H **29**
Spinney, The. Nut —4F **23**
　(Harcourt Cres.)
Spinney, The. Nut —1B **22**
　(Laurel Cres.)
Spinney, The. Wd'p —3A **26**
Spinney Way. Nott —1E **59**
Spinningdale. Arn —4D **16**
Spondon St. Nott —5G **25**
Spray Clo. Colw —4G **39**
Spridgeon Clo. Long E
　　　　　　　　　—3D **54**
Spring Clo. Wat —6A **12**
Springdale Gdns. Trow
　　　　　　　　　—1F **45**
Springfield Av. E'wd —3C **10**
Springfield Av. Sand —2C **54**
Springfield Ct. S'fd —2H **45**
Springfield Dri. Nott —1F **23**
Springfield Garden. Ilk
　　　　　　　　　—5B **32**
Springfield Rd. Huck —5B **4**
Springfield Rd. Red —4H **9**
Springfields. W Bri —5H **49**
Springfield St. Nott —6D **24**
Spring Grn. Nott —6C **58**
Springhead Ct. Bulw —1C **23**
Spring Hill. Kimb —2H **21**
Springhill Clo. Nott —6C **13**
Springland Farm Cotts. Nut
　(off Watnall Rd.) —1D **22**
Spring La. Hean —4C **8**
Spring La. Nott & Lamb
　　　　　　　　　—1E **27**

Spring Meadow. Cotg
—2G 63
Springmoor. Nott —4F 39
Spring Rd. Nott —6A 14
Spring St. Huck —3E 5
Spring Ter. Nut —2D 22
Spring, The. Long E —2F 65
Springwood Clo. Calv —3E 7
Springwood Gdns. Wd'p
—4B 26
Spruce Gdns. Nott —6G 13
Spruce Gro. Huck —4E 5
Sprydon Wlk. Nott —5D 58
Square, The. Bees —5F 47
Square, The. B Vil —1C 14
Square, The. Got —6H 67
Square, The. Woll —5E 35
Squires Av. Nott —4H 13
Squires Way. W Bri —5H 49
Stacey Av. Nott —6D 14
Stafford Av. Nott —1H 23
Stafford Ct. Carl —2A 40
Stafford Ct. Nott —2F 23
Stafford St. Long E —5H 55
Stagsden Cres. Nott —4C 34
Staindale Ct. Nott —6B 24
Staindale Dri. Nott —6B 24
Stainmore Gro. Bing —5C 42
Stainsborough Rd. Huck
—5A 4
Stainsby Av. Hean —4C 8
Stamford Clo. Long E
—3G 65
Stamford Ct. Nott —6F 15
(off Beckhampton Rd.)
Stamford Rd. W Bri —5B 50
Stamford St. Aws —3E 21
Stamford St. Hean —3C 26
Stamford St. Ilk —6B 20
Stamford St. Newt —4E 11
Stancliffe Av. Nott —6A 14
Standard Hill.
—5F 37 (5C 2)
Standhill Av. Carl —1D 38
Standhill Rd. Carl —6C 26
Stanesby Rise. Nott —3C 58
Stanford Gdns. Rad T —2F 41
Stanford St. Nott
—5G 37 (5D 2)
Stanhome Ct. W Bri —1H 59
Stanhome Dri. W Bri —1H 59
Stanhome Sq. W Bri —1H 59
Stanhope Cres. Arn —5A 16
Stanhope Cres. Sto B —2F 41
Stanhope Rd. Arn —5A 16
Stanhope Rd. Ged —3F 27
Stanhope St. Ilk —3C 32
Stanhope St. Long E —5F 55
Stanhope St. Nott
—5A 38 (4H 3)
Stanhope Stan D —3B 44
Stanhope Way. Bing —5E 43
Staniland Clo. Bees —3C 56
Stanley Av. Nott —1E 37
Stanley Clo. Nott —2A 42
Stanley Dri. Nott —2A 46
Stanley Pl. Nott
—4F 37 (3C 2)
Stanley Rd. For F —1E 37
Stanley Rd. Map —5C 26
Stanley Rd. W Bri —5B 50
Stanley St. Ilk —2B 32
Stanley St. Long E —6G 55
Stanmore Clo. Nut —4D 22
Stanmore Gdns. Arn —1A 26
(in two parts)
Stansfield St. Nott —4C 36
Stanstead Av. Nott —5B 14
Stanstead Av. Toll —5F 61
Stanthorne Clo. Nott —1E 59
Stanton Clo. Stan W —5G 71
Stanton Ga. Stan D —2E 45
Stanton La. Stan W —5H 71
Stanton Rd. Ilk —3B 32
Stanton Rd. Sand —4B 44
Stanway Clo. Nott —6A 36
Stanwick Clo. Nott —1E 35
Stapleford By-Pass. Sand &
S'fd —1C 54

Stapleford La. Bees —1H 55
Stapleford Rd. Trow —5E 33
Staplehurst Dri. Nott —3E 25
Staples St. Nott —5A 26
Stapleton Rd. Ilk —3A 20
Starch La. Sand —4D 44
Starthe Bank. Hean —3D 8
Starthwood Rd. Huck
—1D 12
Stathern Wlk. Nott —6F 15
Station Av. Ged —6A 28
Station Rd. Aws —2E 21
Station Rd. Bees —5F 47
Station Rd. Bulw —1A 24
Station Rd. Bur J —4F 29
Station Rd. Carl —2G 39
Station Rd. Huck —4F 5
Station Rd. Ilk —6B 20
(in three parts)
Station Rd. Kimb —1H 21
Station Rd. Lan M —3E 9
Station Rd. Long E —5H 55
Station Rd. Nott —1H 25
Station Rd. Plum —1C 70
Station Rd. Sand —6E 45
Station Rd. Stan —4A 30
Station St. Bing —4F 43
Station St. Ilk —5C 20
Station St. Long E —6G 55
Station St. Nott
—6G 37 (6E 3)
Station Ter. Huck —4F 5
Station Ter. Rad T —6E 41
Staunton Dri. Nott —3G 25
Staverton Rd. Nott —3D 34
Steadfold Clo. Nott —1H 23
Steads Clo. Carl —2H 39
Steedman Av. Nott —3C 26
Steinbeck Rd. Carl —2E 39
Stella Av. Toll —5F 61
Stepney Ct. Nott —6F 23
Sterndale Rd. Long E
—1D 64
Steven Clo. Bees —1H 55
Stevenholme Cres. Nott
—1E 25
Steven's La. Breas —5A 54
Stevenson Gdns. Rud
—1H 69
Stevens Rd. Sand —6C 44
Stewarton Clo. Arn —4D 16
Stiles Rd. Arn —1E 27
Stinsford Clo. Nott —5G 15
Stirling Gdns. Bees —3C 56
Stirling Gro. Kimb —6G 11
Stirling Gro. Nott —5D 58
Stockdale Clo. Arn —3E 15
Stockgill Clo. W Bri —5E 51
Stockhill Cir. Nott —4A 24
Stockhill La. Nott —4A 24
Stocks Rd. Kimb —6G 11
Stockton St. Nott —6H 13
Stockwell. Nott —6H 13
Stoddard Dri. Hean —3D 8
Stoke Ferry La. Shelf —6F 29
Stoke La. Bur J —4F 29
Stoke La. Ged & Sto B
—6B 28
Stolle Clo. Arn —1E 27
Stoneacre. Nott —5F 15
Stonebridge Ct. Ind. Est. Nott
—2H 3
Stonebridge Rd. Nott
—4A 38 (2H 3)
Stonehaven Clo. Arn —4D 16
Stoneleigh Clo. Bees —6A 46
Stoneleigh St. Nott
—4E 37 (2A 2)
Stone Meadows. Long E
—2G 65
Stonepit Clo. Nott —6B 26
Stoneycroft Rd. Nott —2C 24
Stoney Houghton Gdns. Nott
—5F 13
Stoney La. Trow —3D 32
Stoney St. Bees —4F 47
Stoney St. Nott
—5H 37 (4F 3)

Stoppard Clo. Ilk —5H 19
Storey Av. Ged —5G 27
Stornoway Ct. Bees —6G 47
Storth Av. Huck —5E 5
Story Gdns. Huck —4G 5
Stotfield Rd. Nott —4B 34
Stourdale Clo. Long E
—1C 64
Stowe Av. W Bri —6H 49
Stragglethorpe La. Rad T
—2C 52
Strand, The. Att —4D 56
Stratford Clo. Colw —4G 39
Stratford Rd. W Bri —4B 50
Stratford St. Ilk —3B 20
Strathglen Clo. Kimb —6G 11
Strathmore Clo. Huck —6C 4
Stratmore Rd. Arn —4D 16
Strelley La. Nott —2B 34
Strelley Rd. Nott —1C 34
Strelley St. Nott —6H 13
Striding Edge Clo. Long E
—3D 54
Stripes View. Calv —3D 6
Strome Clo. Nott —1G 49
Strome Ct. Nott —1G 49
Stuart Clo. Arn —5D 16
Studland Way. W Bri —6G 49
Sturgeon Av. Nott —1D 58
Sturton St. Nott —1E 37
Styring St. Bees —5F 47
Sudbury Av. Ilk —2C 32
Sudbury Av. Sand —4C 44
Sudbury Ct. Long E —3B 64
Sudbury M. E'wd —4A 10
Suez St. Nott —6D 24
Suffolk Av. Bees —1A 58
Suffolk Av. Huck —4G 5
Sullivan Clo. Nott —2B 38
Sumburgh Rd. Nott —4E 59
Summerfields Way. Ilk
—3G 19
Summerfields Way S. Ilk
—5H 19
Summer Leys Rd. Nott
—1H 37
Summer Way. Rad T —5E 41
Summerwood La. Nott
—5B 58
Sunbourne Ct. Nott —3E 37
(off Waterloo Promenade)
Sunbury Gdns. Arn —4C 16
Sunderland Gro. Nott
—5D 22
Sunlea Cres. S'fd —6H 45
Sunningdale Dri. Toll —4F 61
Sunningdale Av. Hean —5D 8
Sunningdale Dri. Ilk —4F 31
Sunningdale Rd. Wdbgh
—5G 7
Sunningdale Rd. Nott —1C 24
Sunninghill Clo. W Hal
—1B 30
Sunninghill Dri. Nott —2C 58
Sunninghill Rise. Arn —4C 16
Sunnydale Rd. Nott —3D 38
Sunnyside Rd. Bees —5C 46
Sunrise Pk. Clo. W Bri
—6G 49
Sunrise Av. Nott —2D 24
Surbiton Ct. Nott —6A 26
Surbiton Clo. W Hal —1B 30
Surbiton Sq. Nott —4H 23
Surfleet Clo. Nott —6C 34
Surgey's La. Arn —4B 16
Surrey Ct. Nott —6A 26
Susan Clo. Huck —2F 5
Susan Dri. Nott —3B 24
Sussex St. Nott
—5G 37 (5E 3)
Sussex Way. Sand —4D 44
Sutherland Dri. W Bri
—1C 60
Sutherland Rd. Nott —2D 38
Sutton Ct. E'wd —3B 10
Sutton Gdns. Rud —1G 69
Sutton Passeys Cres. Nott
—6A 36

Sutton Rd. Arn —3B 16
Swains Av. Nott —3C 38
Swaledale Clo. Nott —6B 24
Swallow Gdns. Carl —6D 26
Swan Meadow. Colw —5G 39
Swansdowne Dri. Nott
—3D 58
Sweeney Ct. Nott —5E 15
Sweet Leys Rd. Nott —2G 49
Swenson Av. Nott —6C 36
Swift Ct. E'wd —3B 10
Swigert Clo. Nott —2F 23
Swildon Wlk. Nott —5D 14
Swinburne St. Nott —4B 38
Swinburne Way. Day —6G 15
Swindon Clo. Gilt —6E 11
Swiney Way. Bees —3A 56
Swingate. Kimb —2A 22
Swinscoe Gdns. Nott —5D 14
Swinstead Clo. Nott —3F 35
Swithland Dri. W Bri —1A 60
Sycamore Clo. Bing —5G 43
Sycamore Clo. Huck —6C 4
Sycamore Clo. M'ley —4D 18
Sycamore Clo. Rad T —1F 53
Sycamore Ct. Bees —4G 47
Sycamore Cres. Kimb
—3A 22
Sycamore Cres. Sand —4C 44
Sycamore Dri. Ilk —2C 32
Sycamore Gro. Nott —6B 26
Sycamore Rise. Nott —3A 24
Sycamore Rd. Aws —2D 20
Sycamore Rd. Long E
—2E 65
Sycamores, The. E'wd
—5A 10
Sydenham Ct. Nott —1C 48
Syderstone Wlk. Arn —2B 26
Sydney Gro. Rad T —6E 41
Sydney Rd. Nott —4H 35
Syke Rd. Nott —5D 14
Synge Clo. Nott —5A 58

Taft Av. Sand —5D 44
Talbot Ct. Rad T —6E 41
Talbot Dri. S'fd —1F 45
Talbot St. Nott —4F 37 (3B 2)
Tamarix Clo. Ged —5A 28
Tambling Clo. Arn —1D 26
Tame Clo. Nott —1C 58
Tamworth Gro. Nott —3D 58
Tamworth Rd. Long E
—3D 64
Tamworth Rd. Shard —6A 64
Tangmere Cres. Nott —6E 23
Tanners Wlk. Nott
—5G 37 (5E 3)
Tantum Av. Los —1A 8
Tanwood Rd. Bees —4B 56
Tarbert Clo. Nott —1F 49
Target St. Nott —4C 36
Tatham's La. Ilk —5A 20
(in two parts)
Tattershall Dri. Bees —4H 47
Tattershall Dri. Nott
—5E 37 (4A 2)
Taunton Rd. W Bri —5B 50
Taupo Dri. Huck —6B 4
Tavern Av. Nott —5A 24
Tavistock Av. Nott —6G 25
Tavistock Clo. Huck —6B 4
Tavistock Ct. Nott —6G 25
Tavistock Dri. Nott —6G 25
Tavistock Rd. W Bri —5B 50
Taylor Clo. Nott —5C 38
Taylor Cres. S'fd —3H 45
Taylor La. Los —1B 8
Taylor St. Ilk —6B 20
Teak Clo. Nott —2H 37
Tealby Clo. Nott —6F 13
Teal Clo. Carl —3B 40
Teal Wharf. Nott —1E 49
Teasels, The. Bing —6D 42
Technology Dri. Bees
—6G 47
Teesbrook Dri. Nott —5B 34
Teesdale Ct. Bees —1A 56

Teesdale Rd. Long E —2C 64
Teesdale Rd. Nott —5E 25
Telford Dri. Newt —2D 10
Templar Lodge. Bees —5H 47
Templar Rd. Bees —5H 47
Temple Cres. Nott —3D 22
Temple Dri. Nut —3E 23
Templeman Clo. Rud —5F 59
Templeoak Dri. Nott —6C 34
Tenbury Cres. Nott —6H 23
Tene Clo. Arn —3B 16
Tennis Ct. Ind. Est. Nott
—6C 38
Tennis Dri. Nott
—5E 37 (4A 2)
Tennis M. Nott
—5E 37 (4A 2)
Tennis View. Nott
—5E 37 (4A 2)
Tennyson Av. Ged —6H 27
Tennyson Ct. Huck —5B 4
Tennyson Ct. Nott —4F 25
Tennyson Dri. Att —3D 56
Tennyson Rd. Wd'p —3A 26
Tennyson St. Ilk —4A 20
Tennyson St. Nott
—3E 37 (1A 2)
(in two parts)
Tenter Clo. Long E —2F 65
Tenter Clo. Nott —5D 14
Terrace St. Nott —2D 36
Terrian Cres. W Bri —4B 50
Terton Rd. Nott —5D 14
Tetney Wlk. Nott —2G 35
Tettenbury Rd. Nott —4D 24
Teversal Av. Nott —5D 36
Tevery Clo. S'fd —3G 45
Teviot Rd. Nott —2D 24
Tewkesbury Clo. W Bri
—5C 50
Tewkesbury Dri. Kimb
—6G 11
Tewkesbury Dri. Nott —3C 24
Tewkesbury Rd. Long E
—2G 65
Thackerays La. Wd'p —2H 25
Thackeray Rd. Nott —4D 36
Thames St. Nott —6H 13
Thane Rd. Lent —5B 48
Thaxted Clo. Nott —3D 34
Theatre Sq. Nott —3D 2
Thelda Rd. Keyw —4C 70
Thetford Clo. Arn —1C 26
Third Av. Carl —1D 38
Third Av. Ged —6H 27
Third Av. Ilk —2B 32
Third Av. Lent —5A 48
Third Av. Nott —1F 37
Thirlbeck. Cotg —4G 63
Thirlmere. W Bri —6E 51
Thirlmere Clo. Long E
—3D 54
Thirlmere Clo. Nott —2B 38
Thirlmere Rd. Long E
—3D 54
Thirston Clo. Nott —6F 13
Thistle Clo. Newt —5D 10
Thistledown Rd. Nott —6C 58
Thistle Grn. Hean —4F 9
Thomas Av. Rad T —6H 41
Thomas Clo. Nott —3H 37
Thompson Clo. Bees —2C 56
Thompson St. Lan M —2F 9
Thomson Gdns. Nott —4E 15
Thoresby Av. Ged —5C 27
Thoresby Av. Nott —6B 38
Thoresby Clo. Rad T —5G 41
Thoresby Ct. Nott —1H 37
Thoresby Dale. Huck —4F 5
Thoresby Rd. Bees —2C 46
Thoresby Rd. Bing —5C 42
Thoresby Rd. Long E —1D 64
Thoresby St. Nott
—5A 38 (5H 3)
Thor Gdns. Nott —4D 14
Thornbury Way. Nott —6D 14
Thorncliffe Rise. Nott
—1G 37
Thorncliffe Rd. Nott —1G 37

Thorndale Rd. Calv —3D **6**
Thorndale Rd. Nott —5A **24**
Thorn Dri. Newt —5D **10**
Thorndyke Clo. Bees —1H **57**
Thorner Clo. Nott —2C **24**
Thorney Hill. Nott —2B **38**
Thorneywood Mt. Nott
—2B **38**
Thorneywood Rise. Nott
—2B **38**
Thorneywood Rd. Long E
—5H **55**
Thornfield Ind. Est. Nott
—4B **38**
Thorn Gro. Huck —1H **13**
Thornhill Clo. Bees —1C **46**
Thornley St. Nott —2C **36**
Thornthwaite Clo. W Bri
—5E **51**
Thornton Av. Red —4H **15**
Thornton Clo. Nott —5E **55**
Thorntons Clo. Cotg —2G **63**
Thornton Ter. Nott —2D **36**
Thorntree Clo. Breas —4B **54**
Thorn Tree Gdns. E'wd
—1B **10**
Thorold Clo. Nott —3C **58**
Thoroton Rd. W Bri —2B **50**
Thoroton St. Nott —4E **37**
Thorpe Clo. Nott —5D **14**
Thorpe Clo. S'fd —4E **45**
Thorpe Cres. Nott —5D **26**
Thorpe Hill Dri. Hean —6C **8**
Thorpe Leys. Long E —2G **65**
Thorpe Rd. E'wd —1B **10**
Thorpe's Rd. Hean —4B **8**
Thorpe St. Ilk —4A **20**
Thrapston Av. Arn —3B **16**
Thraves Yd. Rad T —6E **41**
Three Tuns Rd. E'wd —3C **10**
Thrumpton Av. Long E
—6H **55**
Thrumpton Dri. Nott —2F **49**
Thurgarton Av. Nott —5B **38**
Thurgarton St. Nott —5B **38**
Thurland St. Nott
—5G **37** (4E **3**)
Thurlby La. Stan W —6F **71**
Thurlestone Dri. Nott —1E **27**
Thurloe Ct. W Bri —2G **59**
Thurman Dri. Cotg —2F **63**
Thurman St. Ilk —3C **32**
Thurman St. Nott —3D **36**
Thurmans Yd. Nott —3D **36**
Thursby Rd. Nott —2C **58**
Thymus Wlk. Nott —4A **58**
Thyra Ct. Nott —6A **26**
Thyra Gro. Bees —5G **47**
Thyra Gro. Nott —6A **26**
Tidworth Clo. Nott —3G **35**
Tilberthwaite Clo. Gam
—5E **51**
Tilbury Rise. Nott —4G **23**
Tilford Gdns. S'fd —5G **45**
Tilstock Ct. Wat —5A **12**
Tilton Gro. Ilk —4G **31**
Tim La. Bur J —3F **29**
Tinsley Rd. E'wd —4A **10**
Tintagel Grn. Nott —4C **58**
Tintern Dri. Nott —5B **24**
Tippett Ct. Nott —3B **38**
Tip Tree Clo. Kimb —6H **11**
Tiree Clo. Trow —6F **33**
Tishbite St. Nott —6H **13**
Tissington Clo. Nott —1E **37**
Tissington Rd. Nott —1E **37**
Titchfield St. Huck —4E **5**
Titchfield Ter. Huck —4F **5**
Tithby Dri. Nott —3F **35**
Tithby Rd. Bing —6E **43**
Tithe Gdns. Nott —4E **15**
Tithe La. Calv —3D **6**
Tiverton Clo. Huck —6B **4**
Tiverton Clo. Nott —5H **23**
Tobias Clo. Nott —5D **14**
Todd Clo. Nott —5A **58**
Todd Ct. Nott —5A **58**
Toft Clo. Cotg —3E **63**
Toft Rd. Bees —2A **56**

Token Ho. Yd. Nott
—5G **37** (4E **3**)
Tollerton Grn. Nott —2B **24**
Tollerton La. Toll —5F **61**
Tollerton Rd. Rad T —5F **51**
Tollhouse Hill. Nott
—4F **37** (3C **2**)
Tomlinson Av. Got —6G **67**
Tonbridge Mt. Nott —1D **46**
Tonnelier Rd. Nott —2C **48**
Top Rd. Rud —1G **69**
Top Valley Dri. Nott —5C **14**
Top Valley Way. Nott —6C **14**
Torbay Cres. Nott —2F **25**
Torkard Dri. Nott —5D **14**
Torrington Ct. Nott —5H **25**
Torvill Dri. Nott —4E **35**
Toston Dri. Nott —5A **36**
Totland Dri. Nott —5B **24**
Totland Rd. Bees —1C **46**
Totley Clo. Nott —3A **14**
Totnes Clo. Huck —5B **4**
Totnes Rd. Nott —4D **38**
Toton La. S'fd —4F **45**
Tottle Gdns. Nott —3B **36**
Tottle Rd. Nott —3E **49**
Tower Cres. Kimb —3A **22**
Towe's Mt. Carl —2G **39**
Towle St. Long E —3C **64**
Towlson Ct. Bees —2D **56**
Towlsons Croft. Nott —4B **24**
Townsend Ct. Nott —4E **15**
Townside Clo. Long E
—3D **64**
Town St. Bees —3B **46**
Town St. Sand —6D **44**
Town View. Kimb —6H **11**
Towson Av. Lan M —3G **9**
Towyn Ct. Nott —6E **15**
Tracy Clo. Bees —2E **47**
Trafalgar Clo. Nott —3D **36**
Trafalgar Rd. Bees —1G **57**
Trafalgar Rd. Long E —1F **65**
Trafalgar Sq. Long E —6H **55**
Trafalgar Ter. Long E —6G **55**
Traffic Ter. Nott —6G **37**
Trafford Gdns. Nott —2B **36**
Tranby Gdns. Nott —5F **35**
Travers Rd. Sand —5C **44**
Treegarth Sq. Nott —4F **15**
Tree View Clo. Arn —4G **15**
Trefan Gdns. Nott —6E **15**
Trelawn Clo. Nott —5B **24**
Tremadoc Ct. Nott —1F **37**
Tremayne Rd. Nott —5C **34**
Trenchard Clo. Nwtn —2B **42**
Trent Av. Rud —5G **69**
Trent Boulevd. W Bri —2B **50**
Trent Bri. Nott —2A **50**
Trent Bri. Bldgs. W Bri
—2A **50**
Trent Clo. Nott —6B **38**
Trent Cotts. Long E —3E **65**
Trent Ct. W Bri —2C **50**
Trent Cres. Att —2E **57**
Trentdale Rd. Carl —3F **39**
Trent Dri. Huck —2D **12**
Trent Gdns. Bur J —3G **29**
Trentham Dri. Nott —2A **36**
Trentham Gdns. Bur J
—4D **28**
Trentham Gdns. Nott —2A **36**
Trent Ho. Long E —3C **64**
Trent La. Bur J —3G **29**
Trent La. Long E —4G **65**
Trenton Clo. Bees —2A **46**
Trenton Dri. Long E —5A **56**
Trent Rd. Bees —1G **57**
Trent Rd. Ilk —5H **31**
Trent Rd. Nott —5B **38**
Trentside. Bees —2G **57**
Trentside. W Bri —3A **50**
Trentside N. W Bri —2A **50**
Trent S. Ind. Pk. Nott —6C **38**
Trent St. Long E —5G **55**
Trent St. Nott —6H **37** (6F **3**)
Trent Vale Rd. Bees —1G **57**

Trentview Ct. Nott —1B **50**
Trent View Gdns. Rad T
—4G **41**
Tressall Clo. Ilk —1C **32**
Trevelyan Rd. W Bri —3B **50**
Trevino Gdns. Nott —5E **15**
Trevone Av. S'fd —5G **45**
Trevor Rd. Bees —6F **47**
Trevor Rd. W Bri —5C **50**
Trevose Gdns. Nott —4H **25**
Treyford Clo. Nott —1E **59**
Triangle, The. Ilk —3C **32**
Tricornia Dri. Nott —3H **23**
Tring Vale. Nott —3E **25**
Trinity Av. Nott —6C **36**
Trinity Row. Nott
—4G **37** (3D **2**)
Trinity Sq. Nott
—4G **37** (3D **2**)
Trinity Wlk. Nott
—4G **37** (3E **3**)
Trinstead Way. Nott —6G **15**
Triumph Rd. Nott —5B **36**
Trivett Sq. Nott
—5H **37** (5G **3**)
Troon Clo. Kimb —6G **11**
Trough La. Wat —5H **11**
Trough Rd. Wat —5A **12**
Troutbeck. Cotg —2G **63**
Troutbeck Cres. Bees —3C **46**
Trowell Av. Ilk —4C **32**
Trowell Av. Nott —4B **34**
Trowell Gdns. Nott —4C **34**
Trowell Gro. Long E —3D **54**
Trowell Gro. Trow —6F **33**
Trowell Pk. Dri. Trow —1F **45**
Trowell Rd. Nott —4B **34**
Trowell Rd. S'fd —1G **45**
Trueman Gdns. Arn —1D **26**
Trueman St. Ilk —3B **20**
Truman Clo. Nott
—3H **37** (1F **3**)
Trumans Rd. Nott —2H **49**
Truman St. Huck —5E **5**
Truman St. Kimb —6F **11**
Truro Cres. Nott —2C **36**
Tudor Clo. Colw —4G **39**
Tudor Clo. Long E —4F **55**
Tudor Ct. S'fd —6F **45**
Tudor Falls. Hean —2C **8**
Tudor Gro. Nott —2F **37**
Tudor Pl. Ilk —4G **31**
Tudor Rd. W Bri —4B **50**
Tudor Sq. W Bri —4B **50**
Tudwal Clo. Nott —6E **15**
Tudwal Wlk. Nott —6E **15**
Tulip Av. Nott —1H **37**
Tulip Rd. Aws —2D **20**
Tunnel Rd. Nott
—5E **37** (4A **2**)
Tunstall Cres. Nott —6G **23**
Tunstall Dri. Nott —3D **24**
Tunstall Rd. Wd'p —3B **26**
Turnberry Clo. Bees —5C **46**
Turnberry Ct. Edw —2E **61**
Turnberry Rd. Nott —1B **24**
Turner Av. Lan M —2E **9**
Turner Clo. S'fd —5G **45**
Turner Dri. Gilt —6D **10**
Turner Rd. Long E —3E **65**
Turner St. Huck —4E **5**
Turneys Ct. Nott —1A **50**
Turney St. Nott —2H **49**
Turnpike La. Bees —3G **47**
Turpin Av. Ged —4F **27**
Turrell Ct. Bram —2D **46**
Turton Clo. Lan M —2E **9**
Tuxford Wlk. Nott —3B **38**
Twells Clo. Nott —2B **38**
Twitchell, The. Bees —1E **57**
Twycross Rd. Nott —6F **15**
Twyford Clo. Hean —1A **8**
Twyford Clo. W Hal —1B **30**
Twyford Gdns. Nott —1C **58**
Twyford Rd. Long E —3B **64**
Tyburn Clo. Arn —4E **15**
Tynedale Clo. Long E —1C **64**

Tynedale Clo. Nott —6B **24**
Tyne Gdns. Huck —2D **12**

Ulldale Ct. Bees —1B **56**
Ullscarf Clo. W Bri —6E **51**
Ullswater Clo. Gam —5E **51**
Ullswater Clo. Ged —5H **27**
Ullswater Cres. Bees —2C **46**
Ullswater Dri. Huck —4D **4**
Union Rd. Ilk —2A **32**
Union Rd. Nott
—4G **37** (2E **3**)
Union St. Bees —5F **47**
Union St. Bing —5E **43**
Union St. Long E —5G **55**
Unity Cres. Nott —5E **27**
University Boulevd. Bees &
Nott —3H **47**
Uplands Ct. Nott —3F **35**
Upminster Dri. Arn —4B **16**
Up. Barn Clo. Hean —3D **8**
Up. Canaan. Rud —5H **59**
Up. College St. Nott
—4F **37** (3B **2**)
Up. Dunstead Rd. Lan M
—2F **9**
Up. Eldon St. Nott —5A **38**
Up. Nelson St. Hean —4B **8**
Up. Orchard St. S'fd —4G **45**
Up. Parliament St. Nott
—4F **37** (3C **2**)
Up. Wellington St. Long E
—4E **55**
Uppingham Cres. W Bri
—6H **49**
Uppingham Gdns. Nott
—1H **49**
Upton Clo. Hean —4E **9**
Upton Dri. Nott —2H **25**
Upton M. Nott —1D **38**
Utile Gdns. Nott —6G **13**

Vale Clo. E'wd —3D **10**
Vale Cres. N. Nott —3B **36**
Vale Cres. S. Nott —3B **36**
Vale Gdns. Colw —4F **39**
Vale Rd. Colw —4F **39**
Valeside Gdns. Colw —4G **39**
Vale, The. Ilk —4A **20**
Valetta Rd. Arn —6D **16**
Valley Dri. Newt —4D **10**
Valley Farm Ct. Nott —5E **15**
Valley Gdns. W Bri —6E **51**
Valley Rd. Bees —6A **46**
Valley Rd. Carl —6D **26**
(in two parts)
Valley Rd. Ilk —4A **32**
Valley Rd. Kimb —6F **11**
Valley Rd. Nott —5C **24**
Valley Rd. Rad T —4G **41**
Valley Rd. W Bri —6C **50**
Valley View. Ilk —4A **32**
Valmont Rd. Bees —3A **46**
Valmont Rd. Nott —4E **25**
Vancouver Av. Rad T —1E **53**
Vanguard Rd. Long E
—2G **65**
Varden Av. Bees —2G **47**
Varney Rd. Nott —2D **58**
Vaughan Av. Huck —2G **5**
Vaughan Rd. Bees —1A **56**
Venn Ct. Bees —5F **47**
Ventnor Rise. Nott —3D **24**
Venus Clo. Nott —2C **24**
Verbena Clo. Nott —2H **37**
Verder Gro. Nott —5C **14**
Verne Clo. Carl —2E **39**
Vernon Av. Bees —5F **47**
Vernon Av. Carl —1H **39**
Vernon Av. Old B —4C **24**
Vernon Av. Wilf —3F **49**
Vernon Ct. Nut —4F **23**
Vernon Dri. Nut —4F **23**
Vernon Pk. Dri. Nott —4C **24**
Vernon Pl. Nott —3B **24**
Vernon Rd. Nott —3B **24**

Vernon St. Ilk —3B **20**
Vernon St. Nott
—4F **37** (3B **2**)
Veronica Dri. Carl —6F **27**
Veronica Dri. Gilt —5E **11**
Veronica Wlk. Nott —4A **58**
Vicarage Av. Ilk —3H **19**
Vicarage Clo. Nott —4D **24**
(Perry Rd.)
Vicarage Clo. Nott —3G **37**
(St Ann's Way.)
Vicarage Dri. Bur J —3E **29**
Vicarage Gdns. Hean —4D **8**
Vicarage Grn. Edw —2D **60**
Vicarage La. Rad T —6E **41**
Vicarage La. Rud —6G **59**
Vicarage St. Bees —5E **47**
Vicarage St. Ilk —3H **19**
Vickers St. Nott —1H **37**
Victor Cres. Sand —1E **55**
Victoria Av. Nott —5B **38**
Victoria Bus. Pk. N'fld
—3B **40**
Victoria Cen. S. Nott
—4G **37** (3E **3**)
(off Lincoln St.)
Victoria Clo. Arn —3B **16**
Victoria Ct. Long E —5G **55**
Victoria Cres. Nott —5H **25**
Victoria Embkmt. Nott
—2G **49**
Victoria Gdns. Wat —4A **12**
Victoria Parkway. N'fld
—3B **40**
Victoria Rd. Bing —4G **43**
Victoria Rd. N'fld —2H **39**
Victoria Rd. Nott —4F **25**
Victoria Rd. Sand —6D **44**
Victoria Rd. W Bri —4A **50**
Victoria Shopping Cen. Nott
—4G **37** (3E **3**)
Victoria St. E'wd —2B **10**
Victoria St. Ged —6H **27**
Victoria St. Huck —3D **4**
Victoria St. Ilk —4B **20**
Victoria St. Kimb —1A **22**
Victoria St. Long E —2D **64**
Victoria St. Nott
—5G **37** (4E **3**)
Victoria St. Rad T —6F **41**
Victoria St. S'fd —4F **45**
Victoria Ter. Nott —5A **38**
Victor Ter. Nott —5G **25**
Victory Clo. Long E —1G **65**
Victory Rd. Bees —1G **57**
Village Clo. Edw —2D **60**
Village Rd. Clif —3A **58**
Village St. Edw —2C **60**
Village, The. D Abb —6D **30**
Village, The. W Hal —2C **30**
Villa Rd. Keyw —3D **70**
Villa Rd. Nott —2G **37**
Villa St. Bees —4F **47**
Villiers Rd. W Bri —5C **50**
Villiers Rd. Wd'p —3H **25**
Vincent Av. Bees —6F **47**
Vincent Av. Ilk —1B **32**
Vincent Gdns. Nott —2C **36**
Vine Cres. Sand —5D **44**
Vine Farm Clo. Cotg —2E **63**
Vine Farm Clo. Ilk —3H **31**
Vines Cross. Nott —1E **47**
Vine Ter. Huck —4E **5**
Violet Av. Newt —5D **10**
Violet Clo. Nott —4B **24**
Violet Rd. Carl —5F **27**
Violet Rd. W Bri —3C **50**
Vista, The. S'fd —6G **45**
Vivian Av. Nott —1F **37**
Vulcan Clo. Nott —3C **24**
Vyse Dri. Long E —1D **64**

Waddington Dri. W Bri
—1H **59**
Wade Av. Ilk —2C **32**
Wadham Rd. Wd'p —2A **26**
Wadhurst Gdns. Nott —3A **38**
Wadhurst Gro. Nott —1D **46**

Wadsworth Rd. S'fd —3H **45**
Wainfleet Clo. Ilk —4G **19**
Waingrove. Nott —2E **59**
Wakefield Av. Rad T —5G **41**
Walbrook Clo. Nott —4B **58**
Walcote Dri. W Bri —1G **59**
Walcott Grn. Nott —4B **58**
Waldemar Gro. Bees —5G **47**
Waldron Clo. Nott —1H **49**
Walesby Cres. Nott —3A **36**
Walgrave Wlk. Nott —6E **15**
Walker Gro. S'fd —5G **45**
Walkers Clo. Bing —5E **43**
Walker St. E'wd —3C **10**
Walker St. Nott
—5A **38** (3H **3**)
Walker's Yd. Rad T —6F **41**
Walk Mill Dri. Huck —2F **5**
Wallace Av. Carl —2H **39**
Wallace St. Got —5H **67**
Wallan St. Nott —3C **36**
Wallet St. N'fld —2A **40**
Wallet St. Nott —1H **49**
Wallett Av. Bees —3F **47**
Wallis St. Nott —3C **24**
Walnut Clo. Ilk —2C **32**
Walnut Dri. Bees —3B **46**
Walnut Gro. Calv —2D **6**
Walnut Gro. Rad T —6F **41**
Walnut Tree Gdns. Nott
—6F **13**
Walsham Clo. Bees —3C **56**
Walsingham Rd. Wd'p
—2C **26**
Walter St. Nott
—3E **37** (1A **2**)
Waltham Clo. W Bri —5D **50**
Walton Av. Nott —4B **38**
Walton Ct. Carl —2G **39**
(in two parts)
Walton Ct. W Hal —1B **30**
Walton Cres. Carl —2G **39**
Walton Dri. Keyw —4D **70**
Walton M. Nott —2C **38**
Walton Rd. Arn —4C **16**
Walton St. Long E —5F **55**
Wansbeck Clo. Nott —4E **37**
Wansford Av. Arn —3B **16**
Wanstead Way. Nott —4C **14**
Ward Av. Huck —2D **4**
Ward Av. Nott —4D **26**
Wardle Gro. Arn —5C **16**
Wardlow Rd. Ilk —4A **20**
Ward's La. Breas —5A **54**
Ward St. Nott —1C **36**
Wareham Clo. Nott —4G **23**
Wareham Clo. W Bri —5C **50**
Warkton Clo. Bees —6C **46**
Warner St. Nott —3C **36**
Warren Av. Nott —5E **25**
Warren Av. S'fd —4F **45**
Warren Ct. S'fd —4F **45**
Warrender Gro. Bees —2C **46**
Warrener Gro. Nott —5C **14**
Warrenhill Clo. Arn —6G **15**
Warren La. Lock —5C **84**
Warren Rd. Huck —6B **4**
Warrington Rd. Nott —6A **14**
Warser Ga. Nott
—5H **37** (4F **3**)
Warsop Clo. Strel —5D **22**
Warton Av. Nott —1B **38**
Warwick Av. Bees —4F **47**
Warwick Av. Wd'p —2A **26**
Warwick Dri. Ilk —4G **19**
Warwick Gdns. Cotg —4F **63**
Warwick Rd. Long E —6H **55**
Warwick Rd. Nott —5H **25**
Warwick St. Nott —1C **48**
Wasdale Clo. W Bri —6E **51**
Washdyke La. Huck —2C **4**
Washington Ct. Arn —6B **16**
Washington Dri. S'fd —1H **45**
Wasnidge Clo. Nott
—4H **37** (2G **3**)
Wasnidge Wlk. Nott —4H **37**
Watchwood Gro. Calv —2D **6**
Watcombe Cir. Nott —5F **25**

Watcombe Rd. Nott —6G **25**
Watendlath Clo. W Bri
—6E **51**
Waterdown Rd. Nott —4B **58**
Waterford St. Nott —4C **24**
Waterhouse La. Ged —5A **28**
Water La. Rad T —6F **41**
Waterloo Cres. Nott —3E **37**
Waterloo La. Trow —3H **33**
Waterloo Promenade. Nott
(in two parts) —3E **37**
Waterloo Rd. Bees —6G **47**
Waterloo Rd. Lin —1E **5**
Waterloo Rd. Nott —3E **37**
Watermeadows, The. Long E
—5D **54**
Water Orton Clo. Bees
—2G **55**
Waterside Clo. Gam —5E **51**
Waterside Clo. Sand —2D **54**
Waterside Gdns. Nott —1D **49**
Waterway Rd. Nott —1H **49**
Waterway St. W. Nott
—1G **49**
Waterway, The. Sand —1E **55**
Watford Rd. Nott —5H **23**
Watkinson St. Hean —3B **8**
Watkin St. Nott
—3G **37** (1E **3**)
Watnall Rd. Huck —3D **12**
Watnall Rd. Nut —1C **22**
Watson Av. Hean —3D **8**
Watson Av. Nott —3D **38**
Waveney Clo. Arn —1C **26**
Waverley Av. Bees —5G **47**
Waverley Av. Ged —6A **28**
Waverley Mt. Nott —3E **37**
Waverley St. Long E —5G **55**
Waverley St. Nott
—3E **37** (1A **2**)
Waverley Ter. Nott
—4F **37** (2C **2**)
Wayford Wlk. Nott —5H **13**
Wayne Clo. Nott —4C **58**
Weardale Rd. Nott —5E **25**
Wearmouth Gdns. Nott
—4E **15**
Weaver Row. Ilk —1B **32**
Weaverthorpe Rd. Wd'p
—2C **26**
Webb Rd. Nott —2H **35**
Webster Av. E'wd —4B **10**
Weedon Clo. Nott —3C **38**
Weekday Cross. Nott
—5G **37** (5E **3**)
Weetman Gdns. Nott —6E **15**
Weightman Dri. Gilt —6D **10**
Welbeck Av. Ged —5F **27**
Welbeck Av. Ilk —4H **31**
Welbeck Clo. Nott —3G **37**
Welbeck Gdns. Bees —2H **55**
Welbeck Gdns. Wd'p —3C **26**
Welbeck Gro. Bing —5C **42**
Welbeck Rd. Long E —2D **54**
Welbeck Rd. Rad T —5G **41**
Welbeck Rd. W Bri —3A **50**
Welbeck Wlk. Nott —3G **37**
Welby Av. Nott —5D **36**
Welch Av. S'fd —3H **45**
Weldbank Clo. Bees —1B **56**
Welham Cres. Arn —6C **16**
Welland Ct. Nott —3B **38**
Wellesley Cres. Nott —5D **22**
Wellin Clo. Edw —2D **60**
Wellin Ct. Edw —2D **60**
Wellington Cir. Nott
—5F **37** (4B **2**)
Wellington Cres. W Bri
—4B **50**
Wellington Pl. E'wd —3B **10**
Wellington Rd. Bur J —2G **29**
Wellington Sq. Nott —4E **37**
Wellington St. E'wd —2B **10**
Wellington St. Hean —3B **8**
Wellington St. Long E
—2E **55**
Wellington St. Nott
—3G **37** (1E **3**)
Wellington St. S'fd —5E **45**

Wellington Ter. Nott —4E **37**
Wellington Vs. Nott —4E **37**
Wellin La. Edw —2D **60**
Wells Gdns. Nott —1B **38**
Wellspring Dale. S'fd —6G **45**
Wells Rd., The. Nott —2B **38**
Welstead Av. Nott —5G **23**
Welton Gdns. Nott —5G **13**
Welwyn Rd. Nott —4E **35**
Wembley Gdns. Bees —1B **46**
Wembley Rd. Arn —2D **26**
Wemyss Gdns. Nott —6B **36**
Wendling Gdns. Nott —5F **15**
Wendover Dri. Nott —5H **23**
Wenlock Clo. Gilt —5E **11**
Wensleydale Clo. Nott
—6B **24**
Wensleydale Rd. Long E
—1D **64**
Wensley Rd. Wd'p —2A **26**
Wensor Av. Bees —3F **47**
Wentworth Ct. Kimb —1G **21**
Wentworth Croft. Hean
—2E **9**
Wentworth Rd. Bees —5C **46**
Wentworth Rd. Nott —5F **25**
Wentworth Way. Edw —2D **60**
Wesleyan Chapel Wlk. S'fd
—4F **45**
*Wesley Ct. Nott —5G **25***
(off Drayton St.)
Wesley Gro. Nott —6F **25**
Wesley Pl. S'fd —3G **45**
Wesley St. Ilk —3A **20**
Wesley St. Lan M —2G **9**
Wesley St. Nott —6F **25**
Wesley Way. Rud —1H **69**
West Av. Sand —5C **44**
West Av. S'fd —3G **45**
West Av. W Bri —4A **50**
Westbourne Ct. Bees —2H **45**
Westbury Clo. Bees —1C **56**
Westbury Rd. Nott —5D **24**
Westby La. Aws —3E **21**
Westcliffe Av. Ged —4F **27**
Westcliffe Av. Rad T —5G **41**
West Clo. Keyw —5C **70**
West Cres. Bees —1H **57**
Westcross Av. S'fd —3G **45**
Westdale Clo. Long E —2C **64**
Westdale Ct. Carl —5F **27**
Westdale Cres. Carl —6G **27**
Westdale La. E. Carl —5E **27**
Westdale La. W. Map —4C **26**
West Dri. Nott —3H **47**
West End. Bees —6F **47**
West End. Calv —2A **6**
W. End Arc. Nott
—5F **37** (4C **2**)
W. End Cres. Ilk —1H **31**
W. End Dri. Ilk —1H **31**
W. End St. S'fd —5E **45**
W. End Vs. Rad T —6E **41**
Westerfield Way. Nott
—1E **59**
Westerham Clo. Nott —2D **34**
Westerham Rd. Rud —1F **69**
Westerhope Clo. Edw —1E **61**
Westerlands. S'fd —4H **45**
Western Av. Bing —4D **42**
Western Boulevd. Nott
—1B **36**
Western Dri. Hean —5D **8**
Western Fields. Rud —1F **69**
Western Gdns. Nott —1B **36**
Western St. Nott
—4H **37** (3F **3**)
Western Ter. Nott —5E **37**
Westfield Av. Hean —5D **8**
Westfield Clo. Ilk —3G **31**
Westfield Dri. Ilk —5H **19**
Westfield Gro. Bing —5D **42**
Westfield La. Wdbgh —6E **7**
W. Furlong. Cotg —3G **63**
West Ga. Long E —6G **55**
Westgate Ct. Bees —6E **47**
Westgate St. Nott —3A **38**
W. Glaisdale Dri. Nott —3D **34**

Westhay Ct. Nott —4A **36**
Westholme Gdns. Nott
—3A **36**
Westhorpe Av. Nott —4B **38**
Westhorpe Dri. Long E
—5E **55**
Westland Av. Huck —5D **12**
W. Leake La. Thrum —6C **66**
Westleigh Rd. Nott —5E **23**
West Mnr. Ct. Bees —6D **46**
W. Midland Ct. Nott —6F **25**
Westminster Av. Sand
—6E **45**
Westminster Clo. Nott
—2A **38**
West Moor. Nott —5F **39**
Westmoore Clo. Nott —4D **26**
Westmoore Ct. Nott —4D **26**
Westmoreland Ct. Nott
—6F **25**
Weston Av. Nott —3E **37**
Weston Clo. Wd'p —3A **26**
Weston Cotts. Nott —3C **36**
Weston Cres. Long E —3B **64**
Weston St. Hean —5E **9**
Weston Ter. Nott —4G **25**
West Pk. Ct. Long E —6F **55**
Westray Clo. Bees —6B **34**
West St. Arn —6A **16**
West St. Hean —3B **8**
West St. Huck —4E **5**
West St. Ilk —2A **32**
West St. Kimb —3A **22**
West St. Lan M —2F **9**
West St. Nott —5A **38** (4H **3**)
West St. Shelf —6H **29**
West Ter. Huck —4E **5**
West Ter. Ilk —6B **20**
West View. W Bri —6H **49**
Westview St. Carl —1H **39**
Westview Rd. Carl —1H **39**
Westville Dri. Huck —2E **13**
Westville Gdns. Nott —2H **37**
West Wlk. Nott
—5A **38** (4H **3**)
Westward Av. Bees —6G **47**
Westway. Cotg —3F **63**
Westwick Rd. Nott —3C **34**
Westwick St. Ilk —3C **32**
Westwood Rd. Nott —5B **38**
Wetherby Clo. Kimb —1G **21**
Wetherby Clo. Nott —6H **23**
Wetherlam Clo. Nott —1G **49**
Weybridge Clo. W Hal
—1B **30**
Wharfedale. Nott —6B **34**
Wharfedale Rd. Long E
—2G **55**
Wharf La. Rad T —6E **41**
Wharf Rd. Nott
—6F **37** (6C **2**)
Wharncliffe Rd. Ilk —1A **32**
Whatton Rise. Nott —3F **25**
Wheatacre Rd. Nott —4D **58**
Wheat Clo. Nott —4D **34**
Wheatcroft View. W Bri
—2G **59**
Wheatfields Rd. Nott —2C **38**
Wheatgrass Rd. Bees —6B **46**
Wheatley Dri. Carl —2F **39**
Wheatley Gro. Bees —1F **57**
Wheatsheaf Ct. Bur J —3F **29**
Wheeldale Clo. Nott —5B **34**
Wheeldon Ct. Nott —6D **24**
Wheeler Av. E'wd —4D **10**
Wheeler Ga. Nott
—5G **37** (4D **2**)
Wheldon Av. Carl —5E **27**
Whernside Rd. Wd'p —2A **26**
Whetstone Clo. Nott —4D **22**
Whickham Ct. Nott —2H **49**
Whilton Cres. W Hal —1B **30**
Whimsey Pk. Carl —3H **39**
Whinfell Clo. Nott —3D **58**
Whiston Clo. Nott —1E **25**
Whitbread St. Nott —2A **36**
Whitburn Rd. Bees —2G **55**
Whitby Clo. Nott —5B **34**
Whitby Cres. Wd'p —2C **26**

Whitby Rd. Newt —2C **10**
Whitchurch Clo. Nott —5E **15**
Whitcombe Gdns. Nott
—5E **15**
Whiteacre. Bur J —2E **29**
Whitebeam Gdns. Nott
—6F **13**
Whitechapel St. Nott —5B **24**
White City Trading Est. Nott
—6C **38**
White Furrows. Cotg —3E **63**
Whitegate Vale. Nott —4B **58**
Whitehead Clo. Ilk —5H **19**
Whitelands. Cotg —3G **63**
Whiteley Clo. S'fd —3G **45**
White Lodge Gdns. Nott
—2D **34**
Whitemoor Av. Nott —6B **24**
Whitemoor Ct. Nott —1B **36**
Whitemoor Ct. Ind. Est. Nott
—1B **36**
Whitemoor Rd. Nott —5B **24**
Whitemoss Clo. Nott —6E **35**
White Rd. Nott —4C **24**
White's Av. Nott —3D **38**
Whites Croft. Wdbgh —6F **7**
Whitestone Av. S'fd —5G **45**
Whiteways Ct. Nott —4C **58**
Whitfield Clo. Nott —5F **49**
Whiting Av. Bees —3H **55**
Whittaker Rd. Bees —2A **56**
Whittier Rd. Nott —6C **38**
Whittingham Rd. Nott
—4C **26**
Whitton Clo. Bees —3C **56**
Whitton Clo. Nott —4F **15**
Whitwell Clo. Nott —5F **23**
Whitwell Rd. Nott —5E **23**
Whitworth Dri. Ged —5C **28**
Whitworth Dri. Rad T —1E **53**
Whitworth Rise. Nott —5D **14**
Whitworth Rd. Ilk —3B **32**
Whyburn La. Huck —4A **4**
Whyburn St. Huck —5G **5**
Whysall St. Hean —3C **8**
Whyston Ct. Huck —6A **4**
Wichnor Clo. Nott —1C **58**
Wickens Wlk. Nott —3A **38**
Wicket Gro. Lent —5C **36**
Wickstead Clo. Wd'p —4B **26**
Widdowson Clo. Bulw
—5F **13**
Widdowson's Row. Rud
—6G **59**
Widecombe La. Nott —5B **58**
Wighay Rd. Huck —2D **4**
Wigley Clo. Nott —3A **38**
Wigman Rd. Nott —1D **34**
Wigwam Gro. Huck —4G **5**
Wigwam La. Huck —4G **5**
Wilden Cres. Nott —3C **58**
Wildman St. Nott —3E **37**
Wilford Cres. Rud —6G **59**
Wilford Cres. E. Nott —2G **49**
Wilford Cres. W. Nott —2G **49**
Wilford Gro. Nott —1G **49**
Wilford Ind. Est. Nott —1F **59**
Wilford La. Wilf & W Bri
—5F **49**
Wilford Rd. Nott —1F **49**
(in two parts)
Wilford Rd. Rud —2F **59**
Wilford St. Nott
—6G **37** (6D **2**)
Wilfrid Gro. W Bri —2A **60**
Wilkins Gdns. Nott —4A **58**
Wilkinson Av. Bees —5F **47**
Wilkinson St. Nott —6B **24**
Willaston Clo. Nott —3A **24**
Willbert Rd. Arn —5C **16**
Willerby Rd. Wd'p —2C **26**
Willersley Dri. Nott —1G **49**
Willesden Grn. Nut —4D **22**
William Av. E'wd —3B **10**
William Booth Rd. Nott
—5C **38**
William Clo. Ged —1B **40**
William Lee Bldgs. High S
—3B **48**

William Olds Ct. Nott —4G **35**
William Rd. S'fd —4F **45**
William Rd. W Bri —3A **50**
Williams Rd. Bees —2A **56**
William St. Huck —4E **5**
William St. Long E —3E **55**
Willoughby Av. Long E
—3E **55**
Willoughby Av. Nott —5D **36**
Willoughby Clo. Nott —3H **47**
Willoughby Ct. Nott —6D **36**
Willoughby Rd. W Bri
—5B **50**
Willoughby St. Bees —5G **47**
Willoughby St. Nott —6D **36**
Willow Av. Carl —1A **40**
Willow Av. Huck —1D **12**
Willow Av. Long E —4F **55**
Willow Av. S'fd —5F **45**
Willow Brook. Keyw —5E **71**
Willowbrook Ct. Nott —2G **49**
Willow Clo. Bur J —2F **29**
Willow Clo. Rad T —1F **53**
Willow Cotts. Nott —2G **35**
Willow Ct. W Bri —6H **49**
Willow Cres. Ged —5A **28**
Willowdene. Cotg —2G **63**
Willow Hill Clo. Bulw —1G **23**
Willow Ind. Est. Nott —5A **14**
Willow La. Ged —5H **27**
Willow Rise. Sand —6D **44**
Willow Rd. Bing —5G **43**
Willow Rd. Carl —1A **40**
Willow Rd. Nott —2C **48**
Willow Rd. W Bri —1A **60**
Willows, The. Bees —6F **47**
Willows, The. Nott —2D **36**
Willow Wong. Bur J —2F **29**
Willwell Dri. W Bri —2G **59**
Wilmington Gdns. Nott
—1H **25**
Wilmot Ho. Long E —2C **64**
Wilmot La. Bees —6F **47**
Wilmot St. Hean —4C **8**
Wilmot St. Ilk —6A **20**
Wilmot St. Long E —2C **64**
Wilne Av. Long E —3C **64**
Wilne Clo. Long E —3B **64**
Wilne La. Dray & Long E
—3A **64**
Wilne Rd. Long E —3B **64**
Wilson Av. Los —1A **8**
Wilson Clo. Arn —1D **26**
Wilson Rd. E'wd —4B **10**
Wilsons Ct. Rud —6G **59**
Wilsthorpe Rd. Breas —5B **54**
Wilsthorpe Rd. Long E
—5D **54**
Wilton Pl. Ilk —6B **20**
Wilton Rd. Nott —3C **36**
Wilton St. Ilk —6B **20**
Wilton St. Nott —3C **24**
Wilton Ter. Nott —3C **24**
Wimbledon Rd. Nott —4E **25**
Wimborne Clo. W Bri —6G **49**
Wimbourne Rd. Nott —3D **36**
Wimpole Rd. Bees —2D **46**
Winchester Av. Bees —3E **47**
Winchester Ct. Nott —4A **26**
Winchester Cres. Ilk —1C **32**
Winchester St. Nott —4H **25**

Winchester Ter. Nott —4G **25**
Windermere Av. Ilk —4G **31**
Windermere Clo. Gam
—4E **51**
Windermere Clo. Ged —5H **27**
Windermere Gdns. Long E
—3D **54**
Windermere Rd. Bees
—2D **46**
Windermere Rd. Huck —4D **4**
Windermere Rd. Long E
—3C **54**
Windermere Rd. Nott —1E **37**
Windles Sq. Calv —3E **7**
Windley Dri. Ilk —4H **19**
Windmill Av. Huck —5E **5**
Windmill Clo. Nott —4B **38**
Windmill Ct. Keyw —5D **70**
Windmill Gro. Huck —4E **5**
Windmill La. Nott —5A **38**
Windmill View. Nott —5A **38**
Windrush Dri. Bees —2D **46**
Windsor Clo. Hean —2C **8**
Windsor Clo. Huck —3F **5**
Windsor Clo. Trow —4D **32**
Windsor Ct. Bing —5C **42**
Windsor Ct. Sand —1D **54**
Windsor Ct. W Hal —1B **30**
Windsor Cres. Ilk —4H **31**
Windsor Cres. S'fd —4G **45**
Windsor Cres. W'p —1C **26**
Windsor St. Bees —5G **47**
Windsor St. S'fd —4G **45**
Wing All. Nott —5H **37** (4F **3**)
Wingate Clo. Nott —3F **35**
Wingbourne Wlk. Nott
—4A **14**
Wingfield Dri. Bees —2G **47**
Wingfield Dri. Ilk —4H **19**
Wings Dri. Huck —1D **12**
Winifred Cres. Bur J —3F **29**
Winifred St. Huck —5F **5**
Winrow Gdns. Nott —4A **24**
Winscale Av. Nott —5E **15**
Winscale Gdns. Nott —5E **15**
Winscombe Mt. Nott —6B **58**
Winsford Clo. Nott —5H **23**
Winster Av. Carl —6F **27**
Winster Clo. Bees —2F **47**
Winster Way. Long E —2B **64**
Winston Clo. Map —2E **37**
Winston Clo. S'fd —3G **45**
Winterbourne Dri. S'fd
—2G **45**
Winterton Clo. Arn —1B **26**
Winterton Rise. Nott —6F **15**
Winthorpe Rd. Arn —6C **16**
Wintringham Cres. W'p
—2C **26**
Wirksworth Rd. Ilk —4F **31**
Wisa Ter. Nott —4H **25**
Wishford Av. Nott —6C **36**
Wisley Clo. W Bri —2G **59**
Wistow Clo. Nott —1C **36**
Withern Rd. Nott —6F **23**
Witney Clo. Nott —5C **14**
Wittering Clo. Long E
—2G **65**
Wiverton Rd. Bing —5E **43**
Wiverton Rd. Nott —1E **37**
Woburn Clo. Edw —1E **61**

Woburn Croft. Sand —1C **54**
Woburn Rise. W'p —2D **26**
Wodehouse Av. Got —5H **67**
Wolds La. Clip —5D **62**
Wolds La. Nor W —6B **62**
Wolds Rise. Keyw —4D **70**
Wollaton Av. Ged —4F **27**
Wollaton Ct. Nott —1C **24**
Wollaton Cres. Bees —3E **47**
Wollaton Hall Dri. Nott
—6B **36**
Wollaton Paddocks. Nott
—4D **34**
Wollaton Rise. Nott —1E **47**
Wollaton Rd. Bees —2E **47**
Wollaton Rd. Nott —5E **35**
Wollaton St. Nott
—4F **37** (3B **2**)
Wollaton Vale. Nott —5B **34**
Wolsey Av. Nott —4D **36**
Wood Av. Sand —5C **44**
Woodbank Dri. Nott —1D **46**
Woodborough La. Arn &
Wdbgh —2D **16**
Woodborough Rd. Nott
—3G **37** (1E **3**)
Woodbridge Av. Nott —4B **48**
Woodchurch Rd. Arn —4F **15**
Wood End Rd. Hean —3C **8**
Woodfield Rd. Nott —6E **23**
Woodford Clo. Nott —4C **14**
Woodford Rd. Huck —5F **5**
Woodford Rd. Wd'p —2C **26**
Woodgate Clo. Cotg —2E **63**
Woodgate Ct. Nott —4E **37**
Woodgate La. Cotg —1D **62**
Wood Gro. Calv —2D **6**
Woodhall Rd. Nott —4E **35**
Woodhedge Dri. Nott —1C **38**
Woodhouse St. Nott —4B **38**
Woodhouse Way. Nott
—1D **34**
Woodkirk Rd. Nott —3D **58**
Woodland Av. Breas —5B **54**
Woodland Av. Ilk —3H **19**
Woodland Av. Nott —2A **24**
Woodland Clo. Cotg —3F **63**
Woodland Clo. Rad T —6H **41**
Woodland Dri. Nott —6H **25**
Woodland Dri. Nott —3F **23**
Woodland Farm Clo. Huck
—1D **12**
Woodland Gro. Bees —6D **46**
Woodland Gro. Colw —3H **39**
Woodland Gro. W'p —2H **25**
Woodland Rd. W Bri —2B **50**
Woodlands. Wat —6A **12**
Woodlands Gro. Huck
—1D **12**
Woodland Way. E'wd —3A **10**
Wood La. Ged —6A **28**
Wood La. Huck —4C **4**
Woodlane Gdns. Nott —2B **38**
Woodlark Ho. Nott —2B **38**
Woodleys. Nott —3C **38**
Woodley Sq. Nott —3C **14**
Woodley St. Rud —6G **59**
Wood Link. Nott —6E **13**
Woodsend Clo. Bur J —3F **29**
Woodsford Gro. Nott —3C **58**

Woodside. E'wd —3A **10**
Woodside Av. Nut —1B **22**
Woodside Clo. Rad T —6H **41**
Woodside Cres. Long E
—5D **54**
Woodside Dri. Arn —5H **15**
Woodside Rd. Bees —2F **47**
Woodside Rd. Bur J —4D **28**
Woodside Rd. Chil —1A **56**
Woodside Rd. Rad T —6H **41**
Woodside Rd. Sand —6C **44**
Woods La. Calv —3C **6**
Woodstock Av. Nott —3C **36**
Woodstock Cres. Ilk —2H **19**
Woodstock Rd. Bees —2G **55**
Woodstock St. Huck —5F **5**
Woodstock St. W. Huck
—5F **5**
Woodston Wlk. Arn —3C **16**
Wood St. Arn —5B **16**
Wood St. E'wd —2B **10**
Wood St. Ilk —6B **20**
Wood St. Nott —4E **37** (3A **2**)
Woodthorpe Av. Wd'p
—3A **26**
Woodthorpe Ct. Nott —4A **26**
Woodthorpe Dri. Wd'p &
Mapp —3H **25**
Woodthorpe Gdns. Nott
—4B **26**
Woodthorpe Rd. Nott
—4B **26**
Woodvale. Nott —5C **34**
Woodview. Cotg —2G **63**
Wood View. Edw —2D **60**
Woodview Ct. Nott —4E **39**
Woodville Clo. Bees —5C **46**
Woodville Dri. Nott —4G **25**
Woodville Rd. Nott —5G **25**
Woodward St. Nott —2H **49**
Woodyard La. Nott —4G **35**
Woolacombe Clo. Nott
—2F **27**
Woolaton St. Huck —4F **5**
Woolmer Rd. Nott —2G **49**
Woolpack La. Nott
—5H **37** (4F **3**)
(in two parts)
Woolsington Clo. Nott
—5D **22**
Woolsthorpe Clo. Nott
—3F **35**
Woolsthorpe Cres. Ilk
—5H **31**
Wootton Clo. Nott —2D **34**
Worcester Gdns. W'p
—1A **26**
Worcester Rd. Wd'p —2A **26**
Wordsworth Av. Huck —5B **4**
Wordsworth Rd. Aws —2E **21**
Wordsworth Rd. Day —6H **15**
Wordsworth Rd. Nott
—3C **36**
Wordsworth Rd. W Bri
—5A **50**
Worksop Rd. Nott —4B **38**
Worrall Av. Arn —6B **16**
Worrall Av. Long E —4G **55**
Worth St. Carl —1G **39**
Wortley Av. Trow —6F **33**
Wortley Clo. Ilk —1C **32**

Wortley Hall Clo. Nott
—1A **48**
Worwood Dri. W Bri —1G **59**
Woulds Field. Cotg —4F **63**
Wray Clo. Nott —4A **38**
Wrenthorpe Vale. Nott
—4C **58**
Wrights Orchard. Keyw
—5C **70**
Wright St. N'fld —2H **39**
Wroughton Ct. E'wd —3C **10**
Wroxham Dri. Nott —6D **34**
Wychwood Dri. Trow —1F **45**
Wychwood Rd. Bing —5C **42**
Wycliffe Gro. Nott —5A **26**
Wycliffe St. Nott —6D **24**
Wycombe Clo. Nott —5B **58**
Wye Gdns. Nott —3B **36**
Wykes Av. Ged —5H **27**
Wymondham Clo. Arn
—1C **26**
Wynbreck Dri. Keyw —4D **70**
Wyndale Dri. Ilk —3G **31**
Wyndham Ct. Bees —1B **56**
Wyndham M. Nott —2F **37**
Wyndings, The. Wd'p —3B **26**
Wynhill Ct. Bing —4C **42**
Wynndale Dri. Nott —4E **25**
Wynwood Clo. Bees —3B **56**
Wynwood Rd. Bees —4B **56**
Wynyard Clo. Ilk —4H **19**
Wyrale Dri. Nott —6E **23**
Wysall La. Keyw —6C **70**
Wyton Clo. Nott —2E **25**
Wyvern Av. Long E —1F **65**
Wyvern Clo. Newt —5C **10**
Wyville Clo. Nott —4C **36**

Yalding Dri. Nott —5C **34**
Yalding Gdns. Nott —5C **34**
Yarwell Clo. Nott —2E **39**
Yatesbury Cres. Nott —1E **35**
Yates Gdns. Nott —5E **15**
Yeoman Av. B Vil —1D **14**
Yewbarrow Clo. W Bri
—6E **51**
Yew Clo. Nott —5H **25**
Yewdale Clo. Nott —5B **58**
Yew Tree Av. Nott —6G **25**
Yew Tree Clo. Rad T —6D **40**
Yew Tree Ct. Bees —5G **47**
Yew Tree La. Ged —5A **28**
Yew Tree La. Nott —3A **58**
Yew Tree Rd. Huck —6F **5**
Yonge Clo. Rad T —1E **53**
York Av. Bees —1F **57**
York Av. Sand —6C **44**
York Clo. Ged —5H **27**
York Dri. Nott —5D **22**
Yorke St. Huck —4E **5**
York Ho. Nott —4G **37** (2E **3**)
York Rd. Long E —4E **55**
York St. N'fld —2A **40**
York St. Nott —3G **37** (1E **3**)
Young Clo. Nott —2F **23**
Yvonne Cres. Carl —2H **39**

Zulla Rd. Nott —1G **37**
Zulu Rd. Nott —6D **24**

Every possible care has been taken to ensure that the information given in this publication is accurate and whilst the publishers would be grateful to learn of any errors, they regret they cannot accept any responsibility for loss thereby caused.

The representation on the maps of a road, track or footpath is no evidence of the existence of a right of way.

The Grid on this map is the National Grid taken from the Ordnance Survey map with the permission of the Controller of Her Majesty's Stationery Office.

Copyright of Geographers' A-Z Map Co. Ltd.

No reproduction by any method whatsoever of any part of this publication is permitted without the prior consent of the copyright owners.